Neil Jordan

INTERVIEWS

Edited by Carole Zucker

University Press of Mississippi / Jackson

www.upress.state.ms.us

The University Press of Mississippi is a member
of the Association of American University Presses.

First printing 2013
∞
"Many Happy Returns" by W. H. Auden
Copyright © 1942 by W. H. Auden, renewed
Reprinted by permission of Curtis Brown, Ltd.

Library of Congress Cataloging-in-Publication Data

Neil Jordan: interviews / edited by Carole Zucker.
    pages cm — (Conversations with filmmakers series.)
  Includes index.
    ISBN 978-1-61703-745-0 (hardback) — ISBN 978-1-61703-746-7 (ebook) 1. Jordan,
Neil, 1950-—Interviews. 2. Motion picture producers and directors—Great Britain—
Interviews. I. Zucker, Carole.
  PN1998.3.J67A5 2013
  791.4302'33092—dc23   2012044793

British Library Cataloging-in-Publication Data available

"Many Happy Returns" by W. H. Auden
(written for the poet's seven-year-old godson)

So I wish you first a
Sense of theatre; only
Those who love illusion
And know it will go far:
Otherwise we spend our
Lives in a confusion
Of what we say and do with
Who we really are.

Contents

Introduction

With each successive outing, Neil Jordan—without doubt the most interesting filmmaker to emerge thus far from Ireland—astonishes the viewer with the eclectic, catholic range of his interests. From *Angel* (1982) to *The Borgias* (2011), Jordan's peregrinations through genre often expand or efface the boundaries between categories. Jordan is deeply idiosyncratic, always experimenting with form, unapologetically changing styles from film to film. He is a master at creating moods and situations that can be sensed, but that are too complex to be grasped immediately. Jordan is a filmmaker who loves both the image, and the use of language that expresses and transforms meaning. He has no trepidations about making bold, outré gestures in his work. Jordan is one of the most poetic, intelligent, and gifted of contemporary filmmakers.

As much as Jordan experiments with form and generic convention, his work tends to circulate around repeated themes. Among them are a fascination with storytelling, and how the stories are enacted through various modes of performance; the quest for identity and wholeness; meditations on innocence; permutations of the family unit; violence and its attendant psychic and physical damage; impossible love and erotic tension; the dark and irrational aspects of the human soul; and characters who are, in some way, haunted by loss. His films continually embrace the most profound question one can ask: What does it mean to be human?

A prominent attribute of Jordan's work is his approach to character. He does not have a strong investment in probing his characters' psychology in the traditional sense; he is most interested in their immediate feelings, moments of revelation, and sensations so beloved by the Romantics. One knows very little about Jordan's characters, their backstories are minimal, at best; we enter their lives in medias res. And yet, one cannot call these films apsychological (in the way one might consider the work of Antonioni), because there is access to the emotional sensibilities of the characters. Characters have definition and amplitude; feelings are experienced and enacted; emotional journeys occur that result in major alterations of a character's life. Jordan's main concern is something I would call "sensual meaning," something that is provisional and fleeting, and made up of the melding of image, sound, performance, narrative, and dialogue. One intuits not only from character traits, but from sensory materials.

It is impossible to consider Jordan's work without contextualizing him as a filmmaker who came into adulthood just as the troubles resurfaced in Ireland in the late 1960s. The interviews beginning with *Angel* (1982) (both by Mario Falsetto and Michael Open) are a way of comprehending the violence and sectarian hostilities of The Troubles.[1] The director utilizes the political turmoil to interrogate the journey of a lone individual who gradually loses his connection not only with the external world, but with his identity. He becomes a self-appointed executioner, who avenges the death of a girl he barely knew. The central question is: What happens to a human being once he becomes enmeshed in violence? The interviews also focus our attention on Jordan as a first-time director, as he learns the process of filmmaking, as well as the attendant contretemps that accompany this newfound responsibility. Jordan's move from literature to film also elicited disapproval and disappointment for his (temporary) abandonment of the grand Irish literary tradition.

Angel marks Jordan's initial partnership with Stephen Rea, who would become a fixture in the director's films. Jordan manifests a strong personal vision in his freshman film, and also his great indebtedness to European Art Cinema, particularly of the French New Wave, New German Cinema, and Italian films. There is a good deal of experimentation with off-screen sound, color, and genre. The manipulation of genre is something Jordan will deploy throughout his career, most often finessing several genres simultaneously.

Unlike the sacred and national origins treated in myth and legend, another form of storytelling—fairy tales—are a narrative form that engages with personal and social origins, providing a rich body of cultural imagery and history for a filmmaker concerned with the negotiation of identity. Moreover, the instability of fairy tales, historically contingent, forever reworked by the new teller, allows for the kind of creative maneuvers that subtend the director's interrogation of the power of narrative and myth. Rather than following the paths of archetypal and structural absolutes or overlaying moral and social codes in his use of fairy tales, Jordan builds upon the disruptive elements of this durable narrative form.

Marina Warner writes of how "all the wonders that create the atmosphere of fairy tales disrupt the apprehensible world in order to open spaces for dreaming alternatives. . . . The dimension of wonder creates a huge theater of possibility in the stories: anything can happen" (Warner 1994, xvi). While the sense of enchantment that often accompanies ruptures in identity and narrative allows for rearrangements of the real, for Jordan, it frequently entails a fundamental loss and the impossibility of healing what really hurts. Jordan captures the threat of change and the uncertainty of desire implicit in fairy tales, as well as the often catastrophic effects of growing up.

Jordan's use of the fairy tale is not a correction or parody of their supposedly outdated values; rather, he investigates what it means to listen to fairy tales, to trust narratives, and follow their paths. His films often show the messy results of fairy tales, the awkward ways in which we interact with our shared store of narratives, and the complex interrelation of past and future that make fairy tales such vivid material for impassioned pastiche.

Neil Jordan wrote a piece that I have included, in which he interpolates passages from Angela Carter's short story "The Company of Wolves," with his 1984 film of the same title. His admiration for Carter is tangible, as is his pleasure in their collaboration. In "Wolf at the Door," the interviewers, Steven Taylor and Paul Jenkins, discuss the technical aspects of the film, made with animatronic figures well before the advent of computer-generated effects. Jordan's enchantment with the work of the great set designer, the late Anton Furst who worked on *Aliens* (1986) and *Batman* (1989), is substantial.

In Jordan's next film, *Mona Lisa* (1986), we enter a dark world characterized by duplicity, corruption, perversity, and violence. We witness the horror of pedophilia, young girls lured into sex trafficking and used with impunity to satisfy the depraved appetites of the rich. The lost girls are first tormented by their pimps and then, drugged and helpless, utterly devoured in the insatiable maws of the sex trade.

Yet, faced with this sordidness, somehow the main character, George (Bob Hoskins, for whom the role was written), is never defiled by the venality of the inhumane world into which he ventures, an underworld milieu in which his position is, at best, marginal. It is mid-1980s London and George has just been released from a seven-year prison sentence—a sacrifice he made for his boss, the real perpetrator of the crime, Dinny Mortwell (Michael Caine). Mortwell not only remained free but has in the interim become the kingpin of the underworld, trading in pornography, sexual slavery, and drugs.

George's reemergence into London is portrayed primarily through the character's literal point-of-view, and/or from the perspective of his consciousness. From the opening scene we see George as a solitary, rather naïve outsider in a bleak, working-class environment. As Jordan remarks in Falsetto's interview: "I had to model the city to make it part of George's brain. I created a version of London that people hadn't seen, because it probably isn't there." The streets and buildings of London become increasingly unrecognizable and foreign to George and to the viewer, satisfying Jordan's absorption with the process of defamiliarization.

The postmodern hybridity of genre is invoked and appropriated in *Mona Lisa*. The film has been called a neo-noir, and it does indeed contain a variety of stylistic and thematic gestures that are textbook cases of film noir. While Jordan engages with the broad outlines of the film-noir genre in *Mona Lisa*, the viewer fathoms that the film is not located in a specific generic niche. In fact, George's character, in his mortifying lack of refinement, is almost a parody of the typical noir hero. George's existence is riddled by a sense of loss, unclear priorities, and self-doubt. A hallmark of Jordan's work is the fragmentation of his characters' understanding of themselves, which in turn leads to a rupture in the narrative configuration—including a jumble of disparate genres. A sense of displacement is fundamental among many of Jordan's characters, and George in *Mona Lisa* must confront the confusing debris of his once-familiar universe.

Jordan is far too eclectic a filmmaker to adhere to generic codes, the super-text as proscribed by Aristotle. Nor is Jordan involved consciously in the process of tracing the history of culture, although his films may very well perform this function. The director uses generic style and themes as it suits a particular work.

Jordan's first foray into the vortex of Hollywood studio filmmaking is examined in Falsetto's interview with the director. His infelicitous first endeavor, *High Spirits* (1988), culminated with the film being taken out of the director's hands by the studio. They wanted a juvenile comedy, while Jordan was interested in a light-hearted rendering of some of the more clichéd and antediluvian, but charming versions of Auld Ireland. He next worked as a director for hire, with David Mamet taking over the scriptwriting function for *We're No Angels* (1989). In Jonathan Romney's interview with Jordan, the director says, "It's important to me to work with comparative freedom. I wouldn't want to become a Hollywood director. I wouldn't want to be stuck there." The experience was mixed, and Jordan refers to Sean Penn, who costarred with Robert de Niro, as "a . . . brooding personality," although he is more forthcoming about his relationship with Penn in the Falsetto interview. "Brooding" is obviously a coded designation for "difficult" and perhaps insecure and attention-seeking.

Following these unsettling experiences, Jordan returned to Dublin. As Jordan explains, "I made *The Miracle* (1991) to my own satisfaction. . . . When you make films, I think you should tell an audience what you feel" (Thomson 1990/91, 8). The film is touched upon briefly in the Falsetto interview—Jordan has not spoken in great detail about this film.

The narrative follows two teenagers around a seaside summer resort as they fabricate stories about the people they see walking on the promenade. Their language is playful and imaginative and outstrips their experience of life. The teenagers are played by two fifteen-year-old first-time actors, Niall Byrne as Jimmy and Lorraine Pilkington as Rose. They were chosen from among three hundred school children in the Dublin area. The cast was rounded out by the ever-brilliant Donal McCann who plays Sam, Jimmy's alcoholic/musician father, and Beverly D'Angelo as Renée, an American actor starring in a third-rate musical production of *Destry Rides Again* in Dublin. Jimmy and Rose are intrigued by Renée, and begin following her about, making up stories about her past. Jimmy, beset by the agony of his raging adolescent hormones, becomes obsessed by Renée.

Jordan is returning to very familiar territory in *The Miracle*. In many ways, the film represents a variation on the director's award-winning collection of short stories, *Night in Tunisia*, published in 1976. The title story in the compilation corresponds wholly to the sensibility of *The Miracle*. A musician father is at odds with his son, who rejects any intimate, familial overtures his father might extend. As in *The Miracle*, the father would like his son to play in his band, which the boy reluctantly does for an evening. Jordan's fascination with the family romance and jazz are both found in *Night in Tunisia*, as is his preoccupation with budding adolescent love and most especially, concupiscence.

Jordan's own father may have provided at least some of the substance and inspiration for this film. He was an "educationist," a teacher and mathematician who seems to have been fairly strict with his son. He limited the film-going of the cinema-struck Jordan *fils*, and forbade the reading of comic books. (Although perversely, but probably not unusually, Jordan's father had his own private stockpile of comics.) Another convergence between Jordan's life and the story is that he and his father played music together, Jordan on classical guitar with his father on the violin. Jordan is characteristically reticent when discussing his father, although he admits that he "naturally" went against his father's wishes by refusing a career in teaching.

Jordan also seizes upon issues of masculinity, as he does in many of his films. "What is particularly Irish about *The Miracle* is that it deals with a specifically Irish kind of failure to understand women on the part of men. It grapples with the inarticulacy that the male character needs in order to keep going" (*The Miracle* press kit). The characters have great difficulty communicating with one another over the issues of friendship, carnality, love, parental concern, and tensions arising within the family unit. While the characters attempt to come to grips with these problems, they seem doomed to be eternally misunderstood.

Renée is confused about what role to play with Jimmy; there is a strong push-pull element to their relationship. The meaning of the words "mother" and "lover" seem to confound Renée. She enjoys male attentions and has difficulty refraining from flirtatious, come-hither conduct. Beneath this superficial behavior, however, is a maelstrom of conflicted feelings. Is she attracted to Jimmy because of her maternal feelings for him? Or as she nears the slippery slope of her forties, is she flattered by the attentions of a young boy? Is she displacing her love for Sam onto their son? These anxieties remain unsettled in the film, but they undoubtedly intensify the film's erotic tensions.

Jordan is dealing with the contemporary family as fragmented, a place where things are in a state of deterioration. He says: "I had the idea of using incest as an expression of rupture within a family, a prism where different aspects of what that implies are explored: mother-love, jealousy, sexual attraction" (*The Miracle* press kit). Incestuous love is the old, old song too exotic to be told. In recasting taboos from father-daughter desire to mother-son desire, Jordan is exploring untrammelled territory in fairy lore. In discussing taboos in the tales, Tatar points out that "there are virtually no male counterparts to 'Donkeyskin' (mother/son incest seems to resist representation in folklore)" (Tatar 1992, 106). Jordan probes a dark recess of the mind that has not been substantially addressed in thousands of years of folklore and fairy tales (although Oedipus is an obvious exception). Much of the film's discomfort factor can thus be understood as a sort of visceral reaction to this taboo representation. Similarly, Jordan not only adopts fairy tale rhetoric that looks closely at human taboos regarding incest, but he compounds the discomfort of it all by substituting an even more un-representable taboo—mother/son coupling, and offers us very little magic or wonder to sweeten the situation. Instead, we get a painful story of recognition, which climaxes in Jimmy's faux rape, in his attempt to extort the truth from Renée. Jordan constantly crosses boundaries, and has always been drawn to imaginative extremes in human experience.

The child-like capacity of Jordan to enjoy films for their own sake, rather than as great works of art or masterworks, shines through his article "Neil Jordan's Guilty Pleasures." In his essay for *Film Comment*, Jordan muses about films that have, in some way, captured his imagination—from the kitsch of *Darby O'Gill and the Little People* (1959) to the adolescent pleasures of *Pretty in Pink* (1986) and *Dirty Dancing* (1987), and the joys of Vincente Minelli's *Barefoot Contessa* (1954) to what he calls a "truly shameful pleasure . . . the dreadful" *El Topo* (1970). The list illuminates Jordan's sense of humor as well as his cinephilia.

Jordan's next effort was *The Crying Game* (1992)—a surprising commercial success in large measure because of Miramax's campaign that urged reviewers and audience members not to spoil the film's big reveal, a gambit which paid off handsomely at the box office. The film had a generally excellent critical reception, and enjoyed large-scale public support. Critics of a certain persuasion targeted the filmmaker's perceived lack of "correctness" in his treatment of gender, race, and postcolonial politics. Because the film is occupied, at least on a certain level, with a veritable hornet's nest of loaded issues such as homosociality, homosexuality, transvestism, interracial romance, and sectarian violence in Ireland, it would have been odd for critics to overlook the representation of these matters. As much of the criticism of *The Crying Game* is rooted in the film's ideology, I included Marina Burke's interview with Jordan in which the predominant ideological conflict is given a good rehearsal. It is, at best, a prickly affair, in which you can virtually see Jordan's hackles rise. Falsetto's interview operates in a completely different, far more empathetic register. The lack of sympathy amongst some critics for Jordan's film stems from a fundamental misapprehension of the director's artistic project. Jordan, even while using identity politics as an arena in which the narrative is played out, is much more intrigued by the fundamental humanity of his characters. As Jack Boozer writes, "Jordan can hardly be accused of unawareness of the crises and conditions that exist. His focus simply emphasizes the microcosm of individual character development, of any possibility of finding a path through the circulating signifiers that pass for contemporary meaning and truth" (Boozer 1995, 179). Jordan's ideas are most clearly expressed in this statement: "I just wanted to displace the concept of national identity, the concept of belonging to your tribe, the idea of tradition and so on. I wanted to wreck that and replace it with something that's plural and infinite, something that's moving all the time" (Hughes 1998, 125).

Stephen Rea began working with Jordan on *Angel*, and has now made ten films with the director. He is often referred to as Jordan's doppelgänger or alter ego. Rea speaks with clarity about working on *The Crying Game*, and particularly about working with Jaye Davidson, a nonactor. I have extracted a section of an interview I did with Rea, an actor I found to be exceedingly knowledgeable and articulate. This interview was originally in the traditional question and answer format. All of the interviews in the book (*In the Company of Actors*) were edited to enable the reader to experience them as seamless narratives told from the actors' perspective, with headings substituting for my original questions.

After the tremendous critical and commercial success of *The Crying Game*, Jordan was offered the opportunity to direct a screen adaptation of Anne Rice's hugely popular novel, *Interview with the Vampire* (1994). One can see why Jordan was drawn to the book's sense of loss, inner anguish, and pain, an aggregate of sentiments that can also be used to describe *The Crying Game*. As well, the filmmaker consistently uses dramatic situations played out *in extremis*. Lestat (Tom Cruise) can be seen as Louis's (Brad Pitt's) antagonist, but it is essentially Louis's internal discord that provides the film's most powerful dramatic material.[2] The Falsetto interview provides a great measure of insight into the origin of the film, and the difficulties in the filming process.

The thematics found in *Vampire* are Romantic: man lost in a fallen world, exiled from love; the source of evil and suffering in this fallen world; questions of origins and identity; and finally, the anxiety about God's very existence. Unquestionably, Jordan's work draws sustenance from these notions. Armand (Antonio Banderas), the world's oldest vampire, says to Louis: "Your fall from grace has been the fall for centuries." The time before the fall in literature is prelapsarian, the time after the fall of the angels is postlapsarian. (Some would say this terminology applies to the fall of Adam and Eve into knowledge, shame, and identity.)

Neil Jordan—a director who has a deep investment in the mysterious, shadow-filled heart of humankind, has created a virtuoso rendering of a soul in torment. The music of the night sings to us of pain, betrayal, and madness. Jordan has claimed that John Milton's *Paradise Lost* was the most significant influence in his adaptation of the book. The story of the angels expelled by God after they participate in a rebellion tantamount to a palace revolt is well-known. Because of their abortive mutiny, the fallen angels cascade from heaven down into the dust of hell. With *Paradise Lost*, Satan assumes the stature of fallen beauty: "splendour shadowed by sadness and death"; he is "majestic though in ruin" (Praz, 56). This description is perfectly embodied by Pitt's incarnation of Louis. Louis is far more sensitive than Lestat and appreciates the beauty of the mortal world. He is capable of being both tender and understanding, particularly with Claudia (Kirsten Dunst), and still hopes to find some measure of goodness in the world.

The Romantics obsessed over having to choose between God's bountiful presence and his complete absence, the latter signifying a world in which transcendence and enlightenment are absent. Probably the most important distinction between Louis and Lestat is that Lestat no longer believes in God. Lestat is beguiled by the here and now and does not care to seek redemption. Louis is consumed by guilt and the knowledge that he can never in all of eternity attain redemption. In essence, it is a vision of the unending pain of existence, a portrait of despair, suffering, and annihilation.

Jordan's next film developed from a project he had worked on since the early 1980s and about which he says in his diary of the shooting of *Michael Collins* (1996): "[It was] a story waiting to burst. Maybe because it has remained unmade for so long. Or maybe because this particular part of Irish history was an embarrassed secret for so long. The main opposition to the film will be from within this country. There's a series of resentments, sectarian and class differentiation that disguise themselves here as politics. And maybe the main objection is that the story is being told at all, in any form" (Jordan 1996, 55).

Neil Jordan's remarks on the reception of *Michael Collins* proved to be extraordinarily prescient, if somewhat understated. As a filmmaker and screenwriter he undertook the task of chronicling one of the most iconic figures in Irish history: a man who still arouses fervent responses of reverence or antipathy ninety years after his assassination at the age of thirty-one. Jordan's film covers six of the most turbulent and complicated years in Irish history, recounting events that continue to call forth passionate, dissonant, and conflicting perspectives.

In a long interview with Séamas McSwiney, who probes the subject with acuity and an impressive factual acquaintance with the subject, Jordan remarks on the great difficulty of creating a "dispassionate work of history," and says that he was aiming for a sort of "elegiac realism," combining scenes of discussion with "quite operatic" scenes.

After the large studio films, *Interview with the Vampire* and *Michael*

Collins, as is his pattern, Jordan returned to a small film. As Jordan says in his 1998 interview with Ted Sheehy, "[Warner Bros.] said to me, 'What are you doing next?'—and I had it set up independently . . . 'I'm doing a small Irish movie and it really is not for you,' and I meant it. But the more I said that the more they were interested in it." There is a potent interface between the work of filmmaker Neil Jordan and novelist Patrick McCabe. *The Butcher Boy* (1997) would represent a particular attraction for Jordan, because it is conceptualized in the Ireland of the 1950s and early '60s in which Jordan grew up, a time governed by the paranoiac and somewhat mad A-Bomb and anti-Communist hysteria, the mysticism and paralysis of a country still dominated by archaic religious beliefs and superstitions, and the repressive, largely rural, small-town milieux that characterized the era. And as Jordan has said of his films, they are "all basically about the clash between the real world and the world of imagination and unreality. The constant concern is to do with realistic and surrealistic explanations of human behavior and whether human beings answer to rational modes of thought or are inspired by things quite irrational and unknown to themselves" (McIlroy, 108). McCabe's creation of Francie Brady—in all his extravagant aberrance—harmonizes perfectly with Jordan's continual interrogation of the limits and necessity of human reason. McCabe, who has been dubbed the "high priest of rural Irish dementia" (Lacey, 50), shares Jordan's Weltanschauung in his concern for the liminal states between rationality and unbalance, and what might be called the social fantastic. In the Falsetto interview, Jordan calls Francie the "unaccommodated man." Childhood as an idyllic time was a crucial subject for the Romantics as it is for Jordan. But it is an idyll that is short-lived and tinged with a sense of what is lost over the course of a human life. The paradisal child often assumes a perverse and ironic dimension for Jordan, a rendition of childhood that bespeaks the Romantic agony and despair at the fallen world. Childhood and imagination lie on one side of the divide, and reason on the other.

Jordan's next outing, *In Dreams* (1999), was almost universally vilified by critics. Perhaps it is a law of nature that following upon the art-house success of *The Butcher Boy*, a film so completely unlike *Butcher Boy* would be deemed a failure. Jordan says in Douglas Eby's interview that he "wanted to make a psychological horror film . . . but of a kind that hasn't been done for quite a while, because it's not *Scream*, and not a slasher movie. It's one that takes the subject quite seriously, and is deeply disturbing, quite scary." The film was made with the support of Dreamworks, partially owned by Jordan's long-time champion, David Geffen.

I discussed the film at some length in my long mid-career overview with Jordan, which was conducted in 2011. I was somewhat apprehensive about reconnecting with Jordan. I had written a book published in 2008 about his work called *The Cinema of Neil Jordan: Dark Carnival*. In the research stage of the book I spent about two weeks poking around Jordan's home outside of Dublin perusing his files (for which I am eternally grateful). However, Jordan barely spoke to me during the entire period of time. He mumbled inaudibly on occasion when we bumped into each other in the labyrinthine corridors of the house. I realized later that it was not due to any personal animus, but rather, as John Boorman, Jordan's long-time friend confided to me on one occasion, that Jordan was not "a people person." Upon publication, Jordan sent me a note of congenial appreciation, although he felt he could not possibly intellectualize his work as I had done. When we spoke in 2011, he was in the midst of producing, directing, and writing *The Borgias*, which was scheduled for broadcast several weeks later on Showtime. I felt I talked to at least two Jordans—one who was witty, humorous, and intelligent and sometimes indulgent, and another who was equally sullen and ill-humored, and not amenable to cerebral queries on my part. As a veteran of many, many interviews with actors and directors, I had witnessed this sort of Jekyll and Hyde syndrome before, and found it not entirely uncommon among sensitive, creative people. When speaking of *In Dreams*, Jordan talked about one of the major pitfalls of working on a Hollywood studio film: "[They say] but that's why we want you, you're going to make it your own, you're going to make it this thing. And then you start working on the film . . . you're trying to make it your own, they say 'Hang on, this is not what we want, we want a nuts and bolts horror movie here.'"

The Gothic pervades Jordan's entire oeuvre, and *In Dreams* clearly embraces the traditional Gothic values. In contradistinction to Romanticism, in the Gothic, there is no sense of possible redemption, and the imagination is granted no power over events. Whereas the Romantics were troubled with issues of origins and identity, in the Gothic, identity is broken down entirely. The world is seen as a place of fragmentation and chaos, disorder and defenselessness, especially for women.

The Gothic is a menace to the human soul through an overabundance of imagination, transgressive behaviors, and the lurking power of evil and spiritual corruption that undermines the moral authority of the individual. This may occur either through supernatural or natural forces. The mind itself may be denied wholeness or the ability to communicate pain to others. Once we reach the twentieth century, the site of horror is located in the institutions such as psychiatric hospitals and the criminal underworld. This description could very well act as a précis for Neil Jordan's filmography. Jordan is the interrogator par excellence of the boundaries of a desacralized world. The limits of rationality, individual freedom, sexual identity are, among other constructs, subject to Jordan's scrutiny. The abrogation of convention is tied to the disintegration of social adhesion that characterizes the millennial era.

As Ted Sheehy's interview with Jordan on *The End of the Affair* (2000) emphasizes, the main attraction for the director was the adaptation of Graham Greene's novel, and the problematic of the story being told from two different points-of-view, as well as the intensity of the sexuality in the film. Gerry McCarthy, in the same year, gets to the heart of one of the primary underpinnings of the director's work as it manifests itself in *Affair* (as well as in his other films): Where does human rationality end and the irrational and mystical begin?

In our interview, Jordan and I went on at some length about the notion of impossible love that permeates his films. We also talked about the fact that *Affair* was the first time in his career that Jordan had filmed love-making scenes. Jordan asserts that it is "embarrassing for everyone," and goes on to say that violence is much easier to film than sex because of the intimacy involved.

Jordan then directed *Not I* (2000), as part of the project of re-staging all of Samuel Beckett's work for "Beckett on Film Project"—a collaboration between Teleflís Éireann and Channel 4. Other participating directors were Anthony Minghella, Richard Eyre, David Mamet, Katie Mitchell, Karel Reisz, and Atom Egoyan. Ted Sheehy conducts a roundtable interview with Jordan, Minghella, and Irish director Damien O'Donnell. Jordan says, "It was an opportunity to do something you'd never get the opportunity to do." Jordan's production of *Not I* stars Julianne Moore in a role initially played by Beckett's muse, Billie Whitelaw.

Jordan used three cameras to film Mouth, the main character, in huge close-up. As he says, quite poetically: "It looks like a cave, it looks like a vagina, it looks like Marilyn Monroe's lips . . . it creates its own associations. But it definitely looks like a birth canal . . . it looks like somewhere where you'd be born out of, somewhere where you might die." The director was more interested in the visceral experience than an intellectual discussion of Beckett.

Jordan's next venture was a remake of a sort of Jean-Pierre Melville's *Bob le Flambeur* (1956). I use this tentative phrase because it adheres so loosely to Melville's original. The Melville film focuses on the heist, whereas Jordan, as usual, in *The Good Thief* (2002) is more interested in the human dimensions. He declares in both the Tara Brady and Paddy Kehoe interviews that the film became about fakes—including his "fake" remake of the Melville original. We talked extensively about his work with Nick Nolte and the film as an examination of masculinity. We also discussed the soundtrack by long-time collaborator Elliot Goldenthal, and the inventiveness of cinematographer Chris Menges, with whom he first worked on *Angel*. *The Good Thief* contains all of the director's trademark themes, albeit couched in an exploratory, jazzy style. There are the usual suspects: storytelling, permutations of the family unit, impossible love, homoeroticism, oedipal subtexts, hybrid genre, the mythopoeic, the spiritual, and exile. The film is situated in a very particular location—Nice, and filmed in spaces that are unfamiliar or defamiliarized. There is also an emphasis on the fairy tale quality of the narrative when the newly wealthy Anne (newcomer, Nutsa Kukhiandze, a seventeen-year-old Georgian actor) and Bob (Nick Nolte) walk into the light of the rising sun—all of their difficulties have been effaced, and their world is now one of glamor and paradisal glory. This is preceded by one of the opening incidents in the film in which a disheveled Nolte is found shooting up heroin on the floor of a bathroom.

After a hiatus of three years, during which Jordan wrote the novel *Shade* (2004), he reteamed with Patrick McCabe to film the latter's book *Breakfast on Pluto* (2005). In the film's opening sequence, Kitten Braden, given a charismatic embodiment by Cillian Murphy, begins to weave an extraordinary tale with himself as its central performer and star. On the soundtrack we hear the Rubettes singing "Sugar Baby Love." The film's opening song presages the central importance of the extensive, carefully selected songs which supply the viewer with the giddy delights that popular music always seems to communicate in movies. (This is the first film in which Jordan has not used an orchestrated soundtrack as well as popular tunes.) The music selection incorporates many of the era's popular (though not necessarily best) songs by such performers as Bobby Goldsboro ("Honey"), Harry Nilsson ("You're Breakin' My Heart"), T-Rex ("Children of the Revolution"), and Dusty Springfield ("The Windmills of Your Mind"), among many others. Music will play an important role in setting the film's whimsical, sometimes deliberately saccharine and almost always ironic tone. But these modest delights act as another escape for Kitten from the harsh realities and emotional chaos of his life. They are one means of coping with being queer in small-town Ireland in the late 1960s through the early '70s. The character's writing, and his inclination to retreat from unpleasant realities in the safety of the women's magazines he devours, provides a pathetic fortification against the brutality of the world in which he lives.

In his interview with Lir Mac Cárthaigh, Jordan talks about the departures he made from McCabe's novel. One of the divergences was transforming the character of Bertie into a magician, played by Stephen Rea. Rea has another new accent, one of those "failed middle-class English gents," as Jordan puts it. The director adds a Grand Guignol aspect to Bertie's magic show, "a bit more like a horror movie version of a magician." The film also features Roxy Music's Bryan Ferry as a crazed homophobe and Gavin Friday, a Dublin singer, composer, and painter, as an IRA-connected musician who falls for Kitten.

Jordan went on to another large-scale, Hollywood-financed film, *The Brave One* (2007), because, as he says in our interview, "Jodie Foster sent me the script, and I read it, and there was something very vulgar and compelling about the basic drive of the script. And, I just liked the unholy dynamic of it." The film rekindles the idea of impossible love, as the main character, Erica (Foster), a vigilante murderer, is attracted to the police officer (Terrence Howard) pursuing her. Jordan says: "I do love that about it, and that's one of the things that drew me to the project. These two characters who know each other so well, there's so much distance between them, and there has to be so much distance between them. So I thought that was fascinating."

The Brave One opens with a sweet romantic scene between Erica and her fiancé, David (Naveen Andrews). They are then brutally attacked in Central Park—David dies and Erica, though comatose, lives, but barely. Erica's lack of affect is contrasted by her outbursts of violence, thus accommodating Jordan's penchant for probing the effects of trauma on identity, most often coupled with a sense of loss. The film grants the teller of the tale a wide berth for the creative deployment of fairy tales. The director chooses to focus on the more troubled constituents of this particular narrative form. Jordan's fairy tales often mine the territory of crushing social events as found in all of his films from *Angel* onward. There is a feeling that his characters are often unable to return to normality in order to heal the source of their wounds. Jordan's storytelling arises from popular culture, and the vigilante film, like the horror film, expresses the social anxieties of the times, and can be seen as a contemporaneous articulation of the fairy tale—but one that is registered in the key of apocalypticism.

In *The Brave One* the misrule of the fairy tale becomes millenarian thought, so prevalent in the post-9/11 world. The agents and events in the Book of Revelation, the notion of the "last days" have always had a strong pull on Western intellect and imagination. One of the most important components and influences of eschatological thinking is polarity—the Manichean forces of light and dark with no middle ground. Creative energies are generated by the tension between Good and Evil. Millenarianism is generally preoccupied with violence as something that will destroy historical evil. It is swift and absolute like Erica's transgressive vengeance-fueled exterminations. Visionary poets such as Blake, Wordsworth, Coleridge, Southey in England, and Hölderlin in Germany embraced the French Revolution as a crisis that inspired new hope, but also darkened the imagination (Abrams 1984, 225-57). The dark Romanticism at the heart of *The Brave One* is another manifestation of the director's links to that cultural and historical movement.

The city is filmed almost always at night. There is an atmosphere that is strongly reminiscent of the way in which London is filmed in *Mona Lisa*. One might consider this film as the progeny of the vigilante film, e.g., *Death Wish* (1974), but the oneiric quality of the photography by Philippe Rousselot, with whom Jordan has collaborated four times, aligns itself more with the stylized surreal than with the sort of realistic drama of the iconic Michael Winner–Charles Bronson film. It is, like *Mona Lisa*, a rendering of a nightmarish, mythopoeic reimagining of a city.

Erica's violence becomes a mission to rid the city of pestilential, nocturnal creatures, and certainly, *Taxi Driver* (1976) can be seen as an übertext for *The Brave One*. (It is of course, ironic, intentionally or not, that Jodie Foster played a lost waif to Harvey Keitel's pimp in the Scorsese film.) The narrative patterning of *The Brave One* reflects its mythic origin, and certainly Erica is a mythological heroine of a sort. She is bound and determined to endure the horror of her emotional voyage of discovery, even while her quest mobilizes the most monstrous side of her being. In some ways, *The Brave* One is a deeply tragic film. Not tragic in the Aristotelian sense, but a more contemporary form of tragedy. It is not about the fall of a great, flawed individual, but about the loss of human feeling. There is no sense of redemption at the end of *The Brave One*, perhaps Jordan's most grim work.

Once again, after filming a Hollywood feature, Jordan moved back to a more intimate arena. The film *Ondine* (2009) was made virtually in his backyard, near his country home in County Cork. I was struck by the obvious connection to Celtic myth and folklore, as well as the connection with W. B. Yeats, another native of Jordan's Sligo birthplace. Jordan said: ". . . the reason I talked about Yeats with regard to *Ondine* is because Yeats collected fairy tales. Early on in his career he had a book called *The Irish Fairy and Folk Tales of Ireland*. And, I thought, it is an endemic part of the Irish imagination, that seems to have fallen into disarray or disuse recently. He published that collection when he was about nineteen or twenty. One of these fairy tales he collected was called the *Lady of Gollerus*, and it was about a fisherman who pulls a woman from the sea, he marries her, and she goes back to the sea, eventually." When I probed him about the fairy tale connection, Jordan talked about the nonrational aspect as well as the universality that appealed to him. This specific story of a woman pulled out of the sea by a recovering alcoholic fisherman, played beautifully by Colin Farrell, exerted a pull for the director. He said: "When I began to look at *Ondine*, I said okay, the Irish version of that is the selkie, and the one that everybody knows is the Hans Christian Anderson fairy tale, *The Little Mermaid*. There is a French version of it, which is actually called *Ondine*. And, I believe there's a Filipino version of it too. So it's one of these universal connections, and I began to write this little fantasy that I thought would be lovely, and charming, and it would turn into this movie script, and I made it." (N.B. There is a medieval version of the story in France called Mélusine by Jean d'Arras in the thirteenth century.)

Although *Ondine* received lukewarm reviews, it was a personal, small project that Jordan seeks after his forays into Hollywood.

For Jordan's next venture, he turned to a story he had been trying to film for years. When I had initially spoken to him in 2007, he was in the midst of scouting for locations in Italy for the film, which would be the story of the Borgias, the Renaissance family reminiscent of the dynasty portrayed in *The Godfather* films. Numerous actors were scheduled to sign on for the film, but at some point, financing fell through. Jordan then struck a deal with Showtime, and *The Borgias* became a series in 2011. Jordan is responsible for writing the scripts, and he directed the first two episodes before turning this task over to Simon Cellan Jones, John Maybury, and Jeremy Podewsa. It was a first for Jordan, to have his work filmed by another director, and it discomfited him somewhat. But with a project on such a large scale, it may have been a necessity.

I asked Jordan about the attraction of the subject. He said: "To me the whole series is about power. And the interplay of power and religion, that's what I wanted to examine, that's what attracted me to it, the reason I made it. Machiavelli's *The Prince* really hooked me into it. The point of view I want to take in my whole series is, what people do to get power, what it does to them once they have gotten it, and how they have to disguise their efforts to get it." I was struck by one line in particular about "the silence of God as your witness," which addresses the loneliness of Jeremy Irons, the historical figure of Rodrigo Borgia who becomes the Pope. There is a distinct look of discomfort on Irons's face as the crown is placed on his head. When I mentioned this to Jordan he replied that it is indeed a key line in the series: "I wanted him to be overawed suddenly by the thing he had grasped, I wanted him to face this, to have this terrible sense of aloneness, which is painful, because there's nobody else he can talk to except this imagined God who doesn't talk to him really."

As one might expect in a Showtime series, *The Borgias* has a large quota of sex and violence. Jordan made an interesting comment about the sexual content: ". . . sex must have been much more fun in those days, because it was so forbidden, and so bound up with spiritual yearning. Those Catholics had the great thing of confession didn't they, the great institution. They could confess, they can sin as much as they want and confess the next day and be washed clean. I mean . . . that's one of the reasons the subject interested me so much is because of the Catholic Church. When I grew up in Ireland as a Catholic, that specific mindset I find absolutely fascinating. And, the way one can have a world full of such guilt, and then such possibility of redemption at the same time."

Jordan's next project was another novel, *Mistaken*, released in 2011 to very good reviews, particularly (but not unexpectedly) in the *Irish Times*. During this time he was working on *Byzantium* (2012), which features a mother/daughter team of vampires. Both the novel and the film mark a return to vampire lore.

Although Jordan's films may be read through the filter of theoretical, historical, and cultural perspectives, it is really the experiential component that most interests the filmmaker. He has repeatedly said that abstract thought holds no interest for him. I think of Jordan as a postmodern romantic, postmodern in that he destabilizes boundaries, appropriates a variety of artistic referents, and transfuses genres, romantic in his embrace of perception, intuition, and sensation. Most importantly, Jordan's work is embedded within the mythopoeic tradition of William Blake and W. B. Yeats.

My gratitude to the following:

Concordia University, Faculty of Fine Arts, for their financial support of this project.

Leila Salisbury, University Press of Mississippi, whose patience and responsiveness has been generous. And Valerie Jones who answered all my many questions promptly.

This book is dedicated to my husband, Mario Falsetto:

"I carry your heart, I carry it in my heart."—e.e. cummings

CZ

Notes

1. The reader should note that although the interview with Mario Falsetto was conducted in 1997 and published in 2000, this deviation in chronology (as well as a similar course of action in the placement of an extract of the interview I did with Stephen Rea), was motivated by my concern for a sense of the coherence of the collection as a whole.

2. Jordan petitioned the Writers Guild of America for a 50 percent credit for the screenplay of *Interview with the Vampire*. Although lines of dialogue from the source book are used in the film, after reading a number of drafts in Jordan's personal files that were inscribed "Written by Neil Jordan," it is clear that Jordan wrote the final script. There is no draft in which both the names of Anne Rice and Jordan appear together. Jordan lost his grievance and Rice was give sole credit for the script.

Works Cited

Abrams, M. H. "Apocalypse: Theme and Romantic Variations." In *The Correspondent Breeze: Essays on English Romanticism*. New York and London: W. W. Norton and Company, 1984.

Boozer, J. "Bending Phallic Patriarchy in *The Crying Game*." *Journal of Popular Film and Television* 22, no. 4 (Winter 1995): 172–79.

Hughes, E., and T. Paulin, in *Writing Irish: Selected Interviews with Irish Writers from the Irish Literary Supplement*, edited by J. P. Myers, Jr. Syracuse: Syracuse University Press, 1998, 115–27.

Jordan, N. *Michael Collins: Screenplay and Film Diary*. New York: Plume Books, 1996.

Lacey, C. in *Publishers Weekly*, November 16, 1998, 50.

McIlroy, B. "Interview with Neil Jordan." *World Cinema 4*. Ireland and London: Flicks, 1984, 108–18.

Praz, M. *The Romantic Agony*. Translated by Angus Davidson. New York: Meridian Books, 1956.

Tatar, M. *Off with Their Heads! Fairy Tales and the Culture of Childhood*. Princeton, N.J.: Princeton University Press, 1992.

Thompson, S. "Miracle Man." *Irish Stage and Screen* 3 (1990/91): 7–8.

Warner, M. *From the Beast to the Blonde: On Fairy Tales and Their Tellers*. London: Chatto and Windus, 1994.

Chronology

1950   Born February 25, 1950, County Sligo, of mother, Angela (a painter), and father, Michael (a teacher).

1956   Family moves to Dublin. Jordan attends St. Paul's College, Clontarf, and the University College of Dublin, where he studies Irish History and English Literature.

1974   Starts Irish Writers Cooperative in 1974.

1976   Wins the Guardian Prize for Fiction for his collection of short stories, *Night in Tunisia*. Unspecified Date: Marries Vivienne Shields; they have two children, Anna and Sarah.

1979   Publishes first novel, *The Past*.

1981   Creative Associate on John Boorman's *Excalibur*. Shoots documentary, "making of" film.

1982   Directs first film, *Angel*, and begins association with actor, Stephen Rea. Wins London Evening Standard Most Promising Newcomer Award.

1983   Publishes *Dream of the Beast* a.k.a. *Nightlines* (in North America).

1984   Directs *The Company of Wolves*. Wins London Critics Circle Award for Best Film and Best Director.

1986   Directs *Mona Lisa*. Bob Hoskins wins Best Actor Award at Cannes and Academy Award nomination for Best Actor.

1988–89   Travels to United States to direct *High Spirits* and *We're No Angels*.

1991   Returns to Dublin to film *The Miracle* with paramour Beverly D'Angelo. During this time a child, Ben, is conceived with a Dublin architect.

1992   Jordan writes and directs *The Crying Game*. The film is nominated for six Academy Awards, and Jordan wins for Best Screenplay. The film wins Best Film at the BAFTAs.

1994   Directs *Interview with the Vampire* and publishes novel *Sunrise with Sea Monster*.

1996   Directs *Michael Collins*. Wins Best Film at Venice Film Festival. Jordan is made an officer of the order in France as part of L'imaginaire Irlandais, for his contribution to cinema.

1997   Directs *The Butcher Boy*, adapted from Patrick McCabe's novel. Wins Best Director Award at Berlin Film Festival.

1999   Directs *In Dreams* with Annette Bening and Robert Downey, Jr., and *The End of the Affair*, which receives Best Screenplay at the BAFTA awards.

2000   Directs short *Not I* which premieres at Cannes Film Festival.

2001   Honorary Doctorate conferred by Queens University of Belfast.

2002   Directs *The Good Thief*, which premiered at the Toronto Film Festival.

2003   Sets up production company, Company of Wolves, with long-time collaborator Stephen Wooley. The company produces *The Actors* and *Intermission* the same year.

2004   Marries long-time companion, Brenda Rawn, with whom he has two children, Dashiel and Daniel.

2005   Publishes novel *Shade*.

2009   Directs *Ondine* with Colin Farrell.

2011   Produces, writes, and directs two episodes of Showtime network series *The Borgias*. Publishes novel *Mistaken*.

2012   The second season of *The Borgias* commences. Directs *Byzantium*.

Filmography

ANGEL (1982)
Ireland
Production Company: A Motion Picture Company of Ireland Production. In association with Bord Scannán na hÉireann/Irish Film Board/Channel 4 Films
Producer: Barry Blackmore
Executive Producer: John Boorman
Director: **Neil Jordan**
Screenplay: **Neil Jordan**
Cinematography: Chris Menges
Editor: J. Patrick Duffner
Music: Keith Donald
Cast: Veronica Quilligan (Annie), Stephen Rea (Danny), Honor Heffernan (Deirdre), Donal McCann (Bonner), Ray McAnally (Bloom)
Color, 92 minutes

THE COMPANY OF WOLVES (1984)
UK
Production Company: ITC Entertainment, Cannon Films, Palace Productions, The Cannon Group Inc.
Producer: Chris Brown, Stephen Woolley
Executive Producer: Stephen Woolley, Nik Powell
Director: **Neil Jordan**
Screenplay: **Neil Jordan**
Cinematography: Bryan Loftus
Editor: Rodney Holland
Music: George Fenton
Cast: Sarah Patterson (Rosaleen), Angela Lansbury (Granny), David Warner (Father), Tusse Silberg (Mother), Micha Bergese (Huntsman),

Kathryn Pogson (Young Bride), Stephen Rea (Young Groom), Graham
Crowden (Old Priest)
Color, 95 minutes

MONA LISA (1986)
UK
Production Company: Handmade Films
Producer: Patrick Cassavetti, Stephen Woolley
Executive Producer: George Harrison, Denis O'Brien
Director: **Neil Jordan**
Screenplay: **Neil Jordan**
Cinematography: Roger Pratt
Editor: Lesley Walker
Music: Michael Kamen
Cast: Bob Hoskins (George), Cathy Tyson (Simone), Michael Caine
(Mortwell), Robbie Coltrane (Thomas), Clarke Peters (Anderson),
Sammi Davis (May)
BAFTA Awards, 1986: nominated for Best Film, Best Direction, and Best
Screenplay—Original; Cannes Film Festival, 1986: nominated for Palme
d'Or; Golden Globes, 1986: nominated for Best Screenplay—Motion
Picture
Color, 94 minutes

HIGH SPIRITS (1988)
USA
Production Company: Palace Pictures, Vision P.D.G
Producer: David Saunders, Stephen Woolley
Executive Producer: Mark Damon, Moshe Diamant, Eduard Sarlui
Director: **Neil Jordan**
Screenplay: **Neil Jordan**
Cinematography: Alex Thomson
Editor: Michael Bradshell
Music: George Fenton
Cast: Peter O'Toole (Peter Plunkett), Donal McCann (Eamon), Steve
Guttenberg (Jack Crawford), Beverly D'Angelo (Sharon Brogan Craw-
ford), Jennifer Tilly (Miranda), Liam Neeson (Martin Brogan), Daryl
Hannah (Mary Plunkett Brogan)
Color, 96 minutes

WE'RE NO ANGELS (1989)
USA
Production Company: Paramount
Producer: Art Linson
Executive Producer: Robert De Niro
Director: **Neil Jordan**
Screenplay: David Mamet
Cinematography: Philippe Rousselot
Editor: Mick Audsley, Joke van Wijk
Music: George Fenton
Cast: Robert De Niro (Ned), Sean Penn (Jim), Demi Moore (Molly), Hoyt
Axton (Father Levesque), Bruno Kirby (Deputy), Ray McAnally (Warden), James Russo (Bobby), John C. Reilly (Young Monk)
Color, 106 minutes

THE MIRACLE (1991)
UK
Production Company: Promenade Film Productions
Producer: Redmond Morris, Stephen Woolley
Executive Producer: Nik Powell, Bob Weinstein, Harvey Weinstein
Director: **Neil Jordan**
Screenplay: **Neil Jordan**
Cinematography: Philippe Rousselot
Editor: Joke van Wijk
Music: Anne Dudley
Cast: Beverly D'Angelo (Renee Baker), Donal McCann (Sam), Niall
Byrne (Jimmy), Lorraine Pilkington (Rose)
Berlin International Film Festival, 1991: nominated for Golden Berlin
Bear; Evening Standard British Film Awards, 2001: Evening Standard
British Film Award for Best Screenplay
Color, 97 minutes

THE CRYING GAME (1992)
UK
Production Company: Palace Pictures/Channel 4 Films
Producer: Stephen Woolley
Executive Producer: Nik Powell
Director: **Neil Jordan**
Screenplay: **Neil Jordan**
Cinematography: Ian Wilson

Editor: Kant Pan
Music: Anne Dudley
Cast: Forest Whitaker (Jody), Miranda Richardson (Jude), Stephen Rea (Fergus), Adrian Dunbar (Maguire), Jaye Davidson (Dil), Jim Broadbent (Col)
Academy Awards, US, 1993: Best Writing, Screenplay Written Directly for the Screen, and nominated for Best Director; BAFTA Awards, 1993: Alexander Korda Award for Best British Film, nominated for Best Direction, Best Film, and Best Screenplay—Original; Independent Spirit Awards, 1993: Best Foreign Film
Color, 111 minutes

INTERVIEW WITH THE VAMPIRE (1994)
USA
Production Company: Geffen Pictures
Producer: David Geffen, Stephen Woolley
Director: **Neil Jordan**
Screenplay: Anne Rice
Based on the novel *Interview with the Vampire* by Anne Rice (1976)
Cinematography: Philippe Rousselot
Editor: Mick Audsley, Joke van Wijk
Music: Elliot Goldenthal
Cast: Tom Cruise (Lestat de Lioncourt), Brad Pitt (Louis de Pointe du Lac), Kirsten Dunst (Claudia), Stephen Rea (Santiago), Antonio Banderas (Armand), Christian Slater (Daniel Malloy)
Color, 122 minutes

MICHAEL COLLINS (1996)
USA
Production Company: Warner Bros. Pictures
Producer: Stephen Woolley
Co-Producer: Redmond Morris
Director: **Neil Jordan**
Screenplay: **Neil Jordan**
Cinematography: Chris Menges
Editor: J. Patrick Duffner, Tony Lawson
Music: Elliot Goldenthal
Cast: Ian Hart (Joe O'Reilly), Julia Roberts (Kitty Kiernan), Liam Neeson (Michael Collins), Aidan Quinn (Harry Boland), Stephen Rea (Ned Broy), Alan Rickman (Eamon de Valera), Brendan Gleeson (Liam

Tobin), Gerard McSorley (Cathal Brigha), Charles Dance (Soames),
Jonathan Rhys-Meyers (Collins's assassin)
Venice Film Festival, 1996: Golden Lion
Color, 132 minutes

THE BUTCHER BOY (1997)
USA
Production Company: Geffen Pictures, Warner Bros. Pictures, Butcher
Boy Film
Producer: Redmond Morris, Stephen Woolley
Executive Producer: **Neil Jordan**
Director: **Neil Jordan**
Screenplay: **Neil Jordan**, Pat McCabe
Based on the novel *The Butcher Boy* by Pat McCabe (1992)
Cinematography: Adrian Biddle
Editor: Tony Lawson
Music: Elliot Goldenthal
Cast: Eamonn Owens (Francie Brady), Sean McGinley (Sergeant), Peter
Gowen (Leddy), Alan Boyle (Joe Purcell), Andrew Fullerton (Phillip
Nugent), Fiona Shaw (Mrs. Nugent), Aisling O'Sullivan (Ma Brady),
Stephen Rea (Da Brady), John Kavanagh (Dr. Boyd)
Berlin International Film Festival, 1998: Silver Berlin Bear for Best Direc-
tor and nominated for Golden Berlin Bear
Color, 110 minutes

IN DREAMS (1999)
USA
Production Company: DreamWorks Pictures
Producer: Charles Burke, Stephen Woolley
Director: **Neil Jordan**
Screenplay: **Neil Jordan**, Bruce Robinson
Based on the novel *Doll's Eyes* by Bari Wood (1992)
Music: Elliot Goldenthal
Cinematography: Darius Khondji
Editor: Tony Lawson
Cast: Annette Bening (Claire Cooper), Katie Sagona (Rebecca Cooper),
Aidan Quinn (Paul Cooper), Robert Downey Jr. (Vivian Thompson),
Paul Guilfoyle (Det. Jack Kay), Stephen Rea (Dr. Silverman)
Color, 98 minutes

THE END OF THE AFFAIR (1999)
USA/Germany
Production Company: Columbia Pictures
Producer: **Neil Jordan**, Stephen Woolley
Co-Producer: Kathy Sykes
Director: **Neil Jordan**
Screenplay: **Neil Jordan**
Based on the novel *The End of the Affair* by Graham Greene (1951)
Cinematography: Roger Pratt
Editor: Tony Lawson
Music: Michael Nyman
Cast: Ralph Fiennes (Maurice Bendrix), Stephen Rea (Henry Miles), Julianne Moore (Sarah Miles), Ian Hart (Mr. Parkis), Samuel Bould (Lance Parkis)
BAFTA Awards, 2000: BAFTA Film Award Best Screenplay—Adapted, nominated for BAFTA Film Award for Best Film and for David Lean Award for Direction; Golden Globes, 2000: nominated for Best Director—Motion Picture; Evening Standard British Film Awards, 2001: Evening Standard British Film Award for Best Screenplay
Color, 102 minutes

THE GOOD THIEF (2002)
Canada
Production Company: Alliance Atlantis Communications, Double Down Films, Metropolitan Films, TNVO
Producer: Seaton McLean, John Wells, Stephen Woolley
Executive Producer: Kristin Harms, **Neil Jordan**, Thierry Seaward
Director: **Neil Jordan**
Screenplay: **Neil Jordan**
Cinematography: Chris Menges
Editor: Tony Lawson
Music: Elliot Goldenthal
Cast: Nutsa Kukhianidze (Anne), Ouassini Embarek (Said), Marc Lavoine (Remi), Nick Nolte (Bob Montagnet), Tchéky Karyo (Roger), Gérard Darmon (Raol), Saïd Taghmaoui (Paolo), Emir Kusturica (Vladimir)
Color, 108 minutes

BREAKFAST ON PLUTO (2005)
Ireland/UK
Production Company: Pathé Pictures International, Northern Ireland
Film and Television Commission
Producer: **Neil Jordan**, Alan Moloney, Stephen Woolley
Executive Producer: François Ivernel, Brendan McCarthy, Cameron
McCracken, Mark Woods
Director: **Neil Jordan**
Screenplay: **Neil Jordan**
Based on the novel *Breakfast on Pluto* by Pat McCabe (1999)
Cinematography: Declan Quinn
Editor: Tony Lawson
Music: Anna Jordan
Cast: Cillian Murphy (Patrick "Kitten" Braden), Eva Birthistle (Eily
Bergin), Liam Neeson (Father Liam), Mary Coughlan (Housekeeper),
Conor McEvoy (Young Patrick Braden), Ruth McCabe (Ma Braden),
Liam Cunningham (1st Biker), Gavin Friday (Billy Hatchett), Brendan
Gleeson (John Joe Kenny), Ian Hart (PC Wallis), Patrick McCabe (Peep-
ers Egan/Schoolmaster), Eamonn Owens (Jackie Timlin)
Irish Film and Television Awards, 2007: IFTA Award for Best Director
and Best Script for Film, and nominated for IFTA Award for Best Film
Color, 135 minutes

THE BRAVE ONE (2007)
USA/Australia
Production Company: Redemption Pictures, Silver Pictures, Village
Roadshow Productions
Producer: Susan Downey, Joel Silver
Executive Producer: Bruce Berman, Herb Gains
Director: **Neil Jordan**
Screenplay: Roderick Taylor and Bruce A. Taylor; revised by Cynthia
Mort and Michael Seitzman; current revisions by **Neil Jordan**
Cinematography: Philippe Rousselot
Editor: Tony Lawson
Cast: Jodie Foster (Erica), Terrence Howard (Dectective Mercer), Mary
Steenburgen (Carol), Jane Adams (Nicole), Douglas J. Aguirre (CSU
Detective), Naveen Andrews (David), James Biberi (Det. Pitney), Angelo
Bonsignore (Cameraman)
Color, 119 minutes

ONDINE (2009)
Ireland
Production Company: Wayfare Entertainment, Little Wave, Octagon Films
Producer: Ben Browning, James Flynn, **Neil Jordan**
Director: **Neil Jordan**
Screenplay: **Neil Jordan**
Cinematography: Christopher Doyle
Editor: Tony Lawson
Cast: Colin Farrell (Syracuse), Alicja Bachleda (Ondine), Stephen Rea (Priest), Dervla Kirwan (Maura), Don Wycherley (Kettle), Alison Barry (Annie)
Irish Film and Television Awards, 2010: nominated for IFTA Award for Best Director for Film, Best Film, and Best Script for Film
Color, 111 minutes

BYZANTIUM (2012)
UK
Production Company: Demarest Films, Lipsync Productions, Number Nine Films, Parallel Film Production, West End Films
Producer: Sam Englebardt, William D. Johnson, Elizabeth Karlsen, Mark C. Manuel, Alan Moloney, Redmond Morris, Stephen Woolley
Director: **Neil Jordan**
Screenplay: Moira Buffini
Cinematography: Sean Bobbitt
Editor: Tony Lawson
Cast: Gemma Arterton (Clara Webb), Saoirse Ronan (Eleanora Webb), Jonny Lee Miller (Ruthven), Sam Riley (Darvel)

Short Films

NOT I (2001)
Ireland
Production Company: Blue Angel Films, Tyrone Productions, FilmFour, RTÉ
Producer: Stephen Woolley
Executive Producer: Michael Colgan, Alan Moloney, Joe Mulholland
Director: **Neil Jordan**
Based on the play by Samuel Beckett (1972)
Cinematography: Roger Pratt

Editor: Tony Lawson
Cast: Julianne Moore (Auditor/Mouth)
Color, 14 minutes

Television

THE BORGIAS (2011)
Canada/Ireland/Hungary
Production Company: Borgias Productions, Mid Atlantic Films, Octagon Films, Take 5 Productions
Producer: **Neil Jordan**, Michael Hirst
Executive Producers: **Neil Jordan**, Jack Rapke, Darryl Frank, John Weber, Sheila Hockin, James Flynn
Creator: **Neil Jordan**
Cast: Jeremy Irons (Rodrigo Borgia), François Arnaud (Cesare Borgia), Holliday Grainger (Lucrezia Borgia), Lotte Verbeek (Giulia Farnese), David Oakes (Juan Borgia), Colm Feore (Giuliano Della Rovere), Aidan Alexander (Gioffre Borgia), Sean Harris (Michelotto Corella), Joanne Whalley (Vannozza Dei Cattanei), Ronan Vibert (Giovanni Sforza), Peter Sullivan (Cardinal Ascanio Sforza)
Gemini Awards, 2011: Gemini for Best Dramatic Series; Emmy Awards, 2011: Nominated for Outstanding Directing for a Drama Series
Color

Neil Jordan: Interviews

Conversation with Neil Jordan

Mario Falsetto / 1997

From *Personal Visions: Conversations with Contemporary Film Directors* (Los Angeles: Silman-James Press, 2000), 217–54. Interview conducted in 1997. Reprinted by permission of the author.

Mario Falsetto: Can you talk about your background, and growing up in the fifties and sixties?

Neil Jordan: I was born near Sligo [Ireland], in a little town called Rosses Point. My father was a teacher. When I was about six, we moved to Dublin. So, I'm really a Dubliner, though I was born in the country.

MF: You went to University College in Dublin, right?

NJ: I went to university because I wanted to study literature, and I quite enjoyed that.

MF: Is that when you started writing?

NJ: No, I started writing when I was about fifteen. I don't know why. I suppose I always felt a bit isolated. My mother was a painter. She taught us how to paint and she brought each one of her kids up to want to do that stuff. So I grew up in a large, bohemian household, in a very pedestrian environment. I began to write short stories and poetry when I was about sixteen or seventeen, and I just kept on writing.

MF: Were you involved in theater at university?

NJ: I did a lot of theater with the Drama Society in the University. When I came out, I got a job teaching.

MF: Who were some of the cultural and aesthetic influences on you?

NJ: Well, I come from Ireland, so William Butler Yeats, James Joyce, and Samuel Beckett, basically. It was a writer's culture; it always has been.

3

MF: Were you interested in film at that time?

NJ: Yeah, very much. I always was. When I grew up, I used to love movies, but they didn't seem to belong to the culture I lived in. Nobody Irish had ever made a film. I absolutely loved films, but I didn't think they were made by human beings and certainly not by people like me. When I left university, I tried to go to film school. I got into a place called Beckinsfield, a major film school in England, but I couldn't afford to go there, so I began to write. I published novels and a collection of short stories. I began to write for television and film scripts, some of which were made as independent movies. Then I began directing, really. That's my story.

MF: What were some of the films that had an impact on you growing up? Was there anybody particularly important to you?

NJ: I was interested in European art cinema, and American films of the forties and fifties. I was into everything I saw. Nicholas Ray, Fellini, Buñuel, Kurosawa. I grew up in Dublin and there was an art-house cinema here. I used to go and see every movie that went into that cinema. It's a thing that's gone now, that kind of repertory movie theater. When you say to me, "What are you influenced by?" I don't know anybody who's not influenced by everything they see. There's no one specific thing.

You must have seen *The Twilight Zone*, for example, which could influence you as much as anything, couldn't it? It could be as profound as anything else. When you're that age, and you're looking at movies and reading books, and you listen to music or whatever, you realize that any human being could sit down and write, or play an instrument, but for any human being to master the art of cinema, it seems a huge stretch of the imagination.

MF: How did you make the leap from writing to direction?

NJ: I only began to direct because I wrote a script, *Traveller*, which was made into a film, and some other pieces for television. I was so depressed by the experience of seeing them realized that I had to do it myself. That's the only reason I began to direct. If I had been able to write out exactly what I wanted to see on the screen, and get someone to realize it, I would never have directed.

MF: Did you become disillusioned with writing?

NJ: No. *Night in Tunisia* was the first book I wrote when I was twenty-four. It was a collection of short stories, and then I published a novel called *The Past*. And if you grew up in this country, writing was the main culture. When I began to make movies, I felt a huge internal conflict because I was dealing with a medium that had basically nothing to do with words, which I loved. A lot of people who admired my work as a writer were outraged.

MF: They felt you were betraying the art of writing?
NJ: I did myself, too, in a way, because writing is a totally internal voice and procedure, and movies are a big public fact.

MF: Music plays a big part in your life; you're also a musician, aren't you?
NJ: Well, I wouldn't say I was a musician. I had to make a living by playing music because I got married very young, and we had two young children, and I was overwhelmed, basically. So I played in a bunch of bands trying to make some money. That was it. But I used to play the classical guitar and stuff like that.

MF: You've written poetry and your fiction is also considered poetic. Do you think the idea of poetry works differently in cinema?
NJ: I think cinema's probably the most poetic medium ever invented, in a strange way. Even in the most vulgar, noisy movies, it can lead to a kind of poetry you don't find in any other medium. It's an odd thing; it's what keeps people obsessed with movies. On the one hand there are these crass vulgar facts of the world we live in, but on the other hand we've got this potential to express this extraordinary poetry you don't find in any other realm of expression.

MF: Is there something more immediate about creating poetry with film?
NJ: It's very simple. I grew up in Dublin, but was born in Sligo. And William Butler Yeats was born in Sligo, and wrote about Sligo. James Joyce was born in Dublin. So every facet of the landscape that you grew up in has been explored endlessly. There's probably more words per square meter of turf here than there are anywhere in the world, so a writer has this huge weight of stuff, of precedent in front of them. But when I began making movies, I felt this tremendous burst of feeling, because nobody had ever done this before. Not to my knowledge anyway.

MF: Was there any Irish film industry at that time?

NJ: No, there wasn't. I'd never seen a film that depicted the landscapes that I knew when I grew up. So I just got a tremendous burst of freedom. I suppose I'd been longing to do it for many years without knowing it.

MF: How did your first film, *Angel*, come about?
NJ: I was working with John Boorman. I had written a script for him and he asked me to go through the last draft of *Excalibur* with him. So I did a rewrite job of that. I had written this screenplay and Channel Four had just started up, so I sent it to them, and they said, "We're very interested in it." There was a guy called Walter Donohue there, who was the commissioning editor of projects for Channel Four, and a lovely man called David Rose, who was head of Film on Four. It was a new venture in England, to use television to stimulate independent movie making. They liked the script and they said they wanted to make it, and I told them I wanted to direct it. They were very nervous, but were interested in an author's cinema. They were worried about me never having directed before, and I asked John to produce it for me, which gave them some security, and so they let me make this movie.

MF: Where did the idea come from?
NJ: I'd been playing in a band. We'd been traveling up and down around the country, driving up to Belfast and playing gigs. It was the worst time of the sectarian killings in the North of Ireland. It was very scary, around 1979–80. You always thought, as a musician, you were safe. We'd always be driving back at three or four in the morning, and sometimes you came to a roadblock, and you'd be stopped by guys in balaclavas and all this *shite*. Then a band called The Miami Show Band was stopped and they were all machine-gunned. Seven of them were shot dead and it was such a horrible fact. The idea of music, and the kind of tawdry pleasure it gives people, and that kind of violence, was shocking. It led to the idea of Stephen Rea's character, the saxophone player in *Angel*. It was the instrument I used to play. He hides the gun in his saxophone case.

MF: What was it like directing your first film? How prepared were you?
NJ: I wasn't prepared at all, because I'd never gone to film school, or studied any aspect of filmmaking. I had no knowledge of the rules. But I had a great cameraman, Chris Menges, one of the best cameramen in the world, probably. I just kind of shot that movie out of naivety.

MF: Did you storyboard?

NJ: No, no. I was very conscious of the things I wanted to see on the screen, though. Very clear images, but I didn't know how to realize them. That's the problem with a lot of first-time directors. You get a very clear image in your head, but you don't realize that to actually get it on the screen, you've got to do all this basic preparation.

MF: Did the film change much from the written text as you were shooting it?

NJ: No, it didn't change at all. I just shot exactly what I'd written, probably to a fault. But it's a great thing to make a movie out of that kind of naivety. You've got a freshness that you'll never have again in your life.

MF: Did you feel confident?

NJ: I felt terrified! I was getting death threats because I was making a film about sectarian killing and some people thought it was about the IRA. People visited my house, and there was all this stuff in the newspaper, because this is such a small country. You can imagine a young guy making a feature film; it's a big deal. It was all over the papers back then. There was an independent cinema movement in Ireland, and other directors had only had the opportunity to make short films, and saw me, a writer, making this movie. They really got pissed off. It was hard. And I had to go the Special Branch, because we had some threats to my house, and I asked them, "Should I be worried?" They said, "Yes, you should be worried," which made me even more worried.

MF: Did you feel comfortable working with actors?

NJ: I think so. I just loved actors. I really loved watching them.

MF: Did you know how to talk to actors?

NJ: They would talk to me. When you make a film for the first time, you're surrounded by the crew, grips and electricians, all these people who've done all this stuff, probably really crap work, and they keep saying, "Who's this little fucker telling us what to do?" Yet you're employing them. The actors are your only mates in a way, so you conspire to make this thing work.

MF: So your inexperience was a disadvantage in working with the crew?

NJ: Yes, in terms of organization. But it was a blessing too. If I tried to imagine the rules of this medium, I probably would have got it totally wrong. You're better off trying to realize exactly what you see in your mind when you wrote the script, when the project was conceived. So that's all I shot, really.

MF: Had you known Stephen Rea before?

NJ: Yeah. I didn't know him that well, but I kind of wrote it with him in mind. There was a saxophonist at the time called Keith Donald, who was a very good musician, who I knew well, and he did the saxophone riffs for the score. He also taught Stephen to play. They were both from Belfast. The film was about the life that was affecting youth in the North of Ireland. So we all hit it off. But Stephen's a remarkable actor. I'd seen him on stage once or twice. I always thought he was a film actor. He reminded me of Humphrey Bogart or somebody like that. He's one of the best, genuinely one of the most intelligent actors in the world.

MF: Although this was your first film, so many of your obsessions are already in place.

NJ: Well, nothing changes. They're all there, aren't they? They're all there in the first collection of stories I wrote. I've used the same locations in about seven movies, certain places I knew as a child. We do a movie like *The Crying Game* or *Michael Collins*, and people say, "Where will we put the scene?" and I'll say, "Oh, I know where we can do it."

MF: Did you and Stephen agree on the interpretation of the character?

NJ: We agreed totally. He wore my clothes, basically, because we hadn't enough money to really work out the costume. If any piece of the costume seemed wrong, I'd take off my coat and say, "Well, maybe this will fit," and of course it did. I don't improvise. I've never done that.

MF: Do you rehearse with actors?

NJ: Not a lot. What's important to me is the central meaning of what people are doing, and either that's there or it's not. I didn't know how to rehearse then. I didn't know what it meant. We would just discuss the implications of the scene. The whole thing of photography, to me, was just such a beautiful thing. I'd never done it before, the kind of reality and accidents you're able to capture.

MF: What was central for you about *Angel*?

NJ: The story, to me, was musical. It was a contrast between the world of music and the world of the downbeat, concrete-and-clay kind of thriller. So there were these contrasts in my mind, all this glitter and colors like gold, purple, and pink, and the greys and khaki green, stuff like that. The thing to me was all about contrasts. In the end, it was about having this guy in this pink suit wandering through a rural landscape, being exposed like a peacock, being out of his place.

MF: The film has a very elliptical structure; it seems barely finished.
NJ: It's not finished at all. It makes gestures towards telling the story and the genre, and then it just goes on.

MF: It certainly makes references to European art films.
NJ: Yeah, it does. I suppose it's most like the early films of Fassbinder and Wim Wenders. It's kind of an anti-narrative, in a way, and it's there for the purpose of getting certain themes and emotions onto the screen. The major problem in that movie is that I didn't pretend to tell the story persuasively, to do the thriller bit of the story and the B-movie bit of it. I used a slight shorthand to get there.

MF: There's something very subtle about the film.
NJ: Maybe. I think it's a very beautiful thing. I haven't seen it for years. I was down in Italy years ago with Karel Reisz at some festival, and they were showing *Angel*. I had to watch it and I hadn't since I made it, because I find it very difficult to watch the films I've made. I was glad that it was such a naive thing.

MF: Basically it chronicles the main character's descent into violence.
NJ: It was about negativity, about a guy being eaten up by a black hole. There was a word I used in the movie, "nobodaddy." I think it came from William Blake, I'm not sure. It was the force of just this emptiness that takes people. It's about the attraction of violence, killing and nihilism. It was about this man, Stephen Rea's character, who, through a series of coincidences, loses his soul, and the awful glamour and persuasiveness of it.

MF: You call the film an "anti-narrative," so was the most important thing to create poetic images with emotional impact?
NJ: I was more interested in trying to use this medium to do stuff that it doesn't normally do. Stanley Kubrick was asked if the important thing was having something to say, and he said, "No, no, the important thing is actually disguising it." That's oddly true in movies, because the world wants these things to perform a certain function, but you want this thing

actually to perform a very strange kind of poetic function. You have to disguise it, because if you admitted what you wanted it to do, nobody would go see what you're doing. I wanted it to be like painting or like art.

MF: Were you upset at the controversy when the film was released in Ireland?

NJ: Oh, that was all bullshit. That was because I got money. It was because I became too well-known, too young. That's a specifically Irish thing. It's still going on. Some people hated me here. There were directors who wanted the union to stop me making that movie, because I was too young, and a writer. Anybody who did anything back then, they just literally tried to chop your head off, rip your guts out. It was a bitchy little controversy, quite unpleasant.

MF: What were the other responses to the film?

NJ: The British press were hugely generous towards it, and it was shown at festivals throughout the world. It was shown in Cannes and different places. It became a *succès d'estime*, you could call it. People in Dublin went to see it, and either they were gob-smacked by it, or they said, "What the hell is that?" It didn't get a huge release here. I finished this movie and the making of it was terribly traumatic. It was surrounded in this country by all sorts of controversy. The manager of The Miami Show Band, whose members had been killed, came to me and said, "I believe you're making a film about my band," and I said, "It's not true." There was all this stuff in the paper about me expropriating money and bullshit like this. People in the literary community were saying, "This man should not be making movies. He's betraying our language and our culture." So it was terribly traumatic.

MF: When you finished it and looked at it, did you feel you had achieved what you'd set out to achieve?

NJ: Yeah, I achieved more than I'd set out to achieve. I thought that photography was such a beautiful thing.

MF: Let's go on to *The Company of Wolves*.

NJ: *The Company of Wolves* was very simple. The guy who released *Angel* in England was Stephen Woolley. He saw it in Cannes and really liked it. He bought it because he was setting up distribution in Britain, so he released it. He wanted to be in production. I really liked this guy. He was a very passionate cineaste, and still is.

For the centenary of James Joyce's birth, there was a festival in Dublin where they invited these writers from all over the world. They had Borges, Anthony Burgess, and among them was Angela Carter. Somebody had shown me a short story she'd written, or a short radio play based on a short story, "The Company of Wolves." And they asked me to read it to see whether it could be made into a film. It would have been an amazing movie, but it was too short to make into a proper film, so I began talking to Angela, and I proposed this structure of story within a story within a story, where this old granny is telling the central story to this young girl: "Don't go into the woods; don't stray from the path," and to illustrate this basic premise, she tells her other stories, and the people within the stories tell their own stories. Angela had written this book of stories that basically went through Grimm's fairy tales, with this kind of strange Freudian, modernist take on things. So we began to write the script, and it became this strange, rather wonderful script for *The Company of Wolves*.

MF: Did you have any cinematic models in mind?
NJ: Yeah, I had. There's a movie called *The Sargasso Manuscript*, a Polish film. And Pasolini's version of *A Thousand and One Nights*.

MF: Was there anything in the horror genre that specifically inspired you?
NJ: I love horror movies, but not formally. There was nothing in the horror genre that I was thinking of, but it was definitely meant to be a horror movie.

MF: When you were writing the script with Angela Carter, how much research did you do into fairy tales and Gothic literature?
NJ: None at all. I mean, there was a popular book by Bruno Bettelheim called *Uses of Enchantment* which everybody referred to after they saw the movie. I never read it. I still haven't read it. Angela wrote the story as a feminist metaphor, really. I was following her imagination. She knew the power of the fable. She was an absolutely unique writer; there's been nobody like her since. She died very tragically. Like Gabriel Garcia Marquez, she knew the power of story to have many meanings. I was really just trying to do justice to her imagination. I saw it as a wonderful opportunity.

MF: I think Angela Carter called it a kind of "menstrual" movie.

NJ: Oh, yeah. It was a movie about little girls and wolves. There's all this blood, this symbolism, and hidden sexuality and sensuality. Even the forest itself. I worked with Anton Furst, a magnificent guy who had just designed one movie. I was trying to eroticize this forest, and he knew exactly what I was talking about. We built this set at Shepperton with these trees that had these vaginal propensities to them. [Laughs] We looked at a painter called Samuel Palmer. If you want to see how to eroticize landscape, look at his paintings; they're beautiful. It was all about sensuality and beauty, really, but one was very aware that at the heart of it, is a cautionary tale, and bloody dark stuff going on.

This was a studio-based movie. It was like going back to those strange realities of movies you saw in the forties, where artificiality was so prominent. A bit like *Black Narcissus*, or something like that. We used painted sets. We did these archly naive effects shots. I just thought it was a blast. We were actually just painting everything we saw, and finding these ludicrous means to achieve it.

MF: What was the budget on the film?
NJ: Two million pounds. To me it was huge.

MF: You never felt limited by the budget.
NJ: No, not at all. I felt limited by the imagination of the crews that I was working with. Every day we'd go out to Shepperton Studios and they'd just laugh at me and say, "Okay, it's your funeral." These guys had worked on *Star Wars*, and these big American epics, and to get me and Anton Furst saying, "Okay, now the set is going to change from winter to summer in the same shot." They said, "Well, is it winter over here, or is it summer here?"

MF: You created this very tough pre-adolescent, very strong girl, who chooses to join this "other" society, to join the company of wolves.
NJ: Absolutely. Well, it was about her embracing this beast. The only thing I wasn't happy with in that movie was the ending. That's where the limitations of budget came. The theme of the movie is a young girl's discovery of her own power, so to end it with her screaming was not enough. What we had written was her waking from this strange dream in her bedroom, standing up on the bed and diving into the floor. The floor is like a pool of water. She vanishes and this floor kind of ripples and goes back to wood again. I just didn't know how to realize it.

I think the ending now blunts the film as a whole because she'd actually mastered these wolves. She'd made them do her bidding and she ends up embracing this wolf. I had to have that little girl, Sarah Patterson, sit down there with a timber wolf and put her arms around this thing. It could have ripped her neck off, so even the actress had to kind of master this monster.

MF: The ending can be seen as a kind of fall from innocence into experience.

NJ: It was a tragic fall. That's the only way it can be seen. It can only be seen in generic terms.

After *Angel*, everybody said, "Why are you doing this strange thing?" because they got it into their brains that what I was good at was "poetic realism." You want to do these things because you actually haven't seen it on the screen: that's often the reason why you want to do difficult stuff. We opened it in the biggest cinema in England, the Odeon Leicester Square with this huge party, and everyone was saying, "You're insane to open it at this cinema," because, at the time, they only opened the biggest American movies there. I remember, we had to sit in the premiere and watch it, and the audience was going, "What the fuck is this?" I walked out with Steve Woolley, and there were lines of people everywhere, and I was saying, "What are all these people doing?" and he said, "Well, they're queuing up for the late night show." [Laughs] It was so funny, and we made a hit with this strange film, which was weird.

MF: Did it do well in North America?

NJ: No, it didn't. It was bought by Cannon and they released it as a horror movie. I don't think they actually saw the movie. I think they just saw the trailer for it or something and they paid a lot of money for it. So the financiers made all their money back out of this one sale. I went to America to publicize it, and it was appalling what they'd done. They basically pushed it like *An American Werewolf in London*, and all these slasher, gore movies. They released it this way and the audience felt cheated. I read an article about some woman describing her experience of seeing *The Company of Wolves* in Times Square on the opening night. All these people in the theater just wanted blood, and instead, they saw this strange fairy tale so they went back and ripped up the theater and everything. So it wasn't released correctly there, but it's become this cult thing. It seems to be the favorite movie for all these heavy metal bands. Every time I meet anybody who plays in a heavy metal band, like Metallica, these guys have seen that movie thirty times. I don't know why.

MF: How did *Mona Lisa* come about? What interested you in particular about this genre?

NJ: What is the genre? It's a love story, really. It was a story about the journey of one guy's soul, really, a guy with a beautiful soul, a bit like *The Butcher Boy*, like Francie Brady. He had this wonderful comprehension and openness to experience, but his experience never matched what he hoped for. It was about a naive heart, I thought. Also, I wanted to do a kind of London movie. It was the first big city I've ever encountered. I went over there when I was seventeen or eighteen.

MF: You didn't consider Dublin big?

NJ: No, no, back then, Dublin was provincial, totally narrow-minded. I went to London and it was my first experience of a metropolis. To me, it was full of darkness and mystery around every corner. I had this image of the city in my mind which I'd never seen in movies, because it's very difficult to photograph London. It's not like New York, with these angular facets to it. London's a collection of suburbs. I had this feeling, this thing in my mind, of a great metropolis with all these lovely shadows and secrets behind the public surface. That was the attraction for me to make *Mona Lisa*. Also, I wanted to make a love story about a man and a woman who didn't understand each other, a love story where somebody was just saying to their loved one, "Just tell me what the story is, dear, please." I had to model the city to make it part of Bob Hoskins's brain when he's looking for this girl. I created a version of London that people hadn't seen, because it probably isn't there.

MF: The music is very important of course.

NJ: The music is basically Nat King Cole. It's Nelson Riddle, really. A very good composer called Michael Kamen did the rest of the score. There was too much music in it. That was an argument I had with the production company, Handmade Films. I wanted to take a lot of it off, but they thought that the subject matter was kind of repellent and it needed all this music. The musical motifs in the movie, the Nat King Cole songs, "Mona Lisa," "When I Fall in Love," and all those songs of the fifties, are songs of male isolation and romantic confusion. They're very beautiful.

MF: I find *Mona Lisa* different from your first two films. It's a successful film artistically and commercially, but narratively it seems more conventional to me.

NJ: Oh yes, it was much more conventional. I wanted to make a movie about direct human emotions. I wanted to make a movie about the characters, not about artifice. I just wanted to put real emotion on the screen.

MF: You called it a film about yearning.
NJ: Yes, that's what it was about. It was about the way men misunderstand women, and have this fixation on this love object that is in their own brain, and rarely in the person they choose. Bob Hoskins wanting this woman to be something that he imagined, and she turned out to be something quite different. That's what I thought the film was about.

MF: Do you want to talk about *High Spirits*?
NJ: Yeah, we can talk about that. You should have seen the director's cut.

MF: Is there such a thing?
NJ: Well, there should be but there won't be. A comedy is like a mathematical form, and it's got a great appeal to me, though I can't actually do it. There are some absolutely magic comedies like *It Happened One Night*, or *Bringing Up Baby*.

I read this story in the paper about this guy who was running these ghost tours in Ireland. I thought it would be an opportunity to make an elegant Restoration comedy. A bit like an Irish *Whiskey Galore*, or *The Man in the White Suit*, or something like that. I wrote this little story out. *Mona Lisa* had been quite a success and I wanted to do this tiny little thing in Ireland on a low budget. Then all these Hollywood people got interested in it, and it became bigger and bigger, and in the end, it became something different. That's all I can say about that.

MF: Did you lose control of the film?
NJ: Yeah, I totally lost control.

MF: Were you unhappy with the actors in the movie?
NJ: Nobody engaged in the reality of that movie, except Donal McCann, and some of the other Irish actors, who did some thrilling stuff, but none of it ended up on the screen. It was the first time a film had been taken out of my hands. We shot some really wonderful stuff, with Irish characters, caricaturing what they imagined were the caricatures people imposed on them, and a lot of lovely, gentle stuff, and none of it was in the final movie, which ended up being very loud and noisy. If you see the film you can understand what I wanted it to be because it was about this eruption of these dead people. I thought it was a necrophiliac

comedy—that's what it should have been—all these dead people falling in love with living people, and at the end, embracing in the grave, embracing corpses.

MF: I found the reaction of critics pretty brutal to that film.

NJ: But that's what happens with films, if you get a reputation. They're pitiless when you fail. They come down with hobnailed boots on top of your head. Pauline Kael saw it and liked it. She rang me up and said, "I can see this thing has been cut to ribbons. Can I see the director's cut?" There was no director's cut because I never got to the stage of even compiling my cut. Even before we finished it, they previewed it and started chipping away at it. George Fenton, the composer, who did a beautiful score, said to me, "We've never even seen the movie that we shot." We never had time to consider it, to look at it on screen, you know.

MF: It's lost forever?

NJ: I tried to go back to the vaults in Shepperton, and I hired an editor—the editor who cut *Angel*, Pat Duffner—and I said to him, "Pat, just go back and get all the footage out, and look at it," to reassemble what we actually shot. Shepperton wouldn't release it because they hadn't been paid. I got involved with the bad end of Hollywood there. I found the experience horrible. Anton Furst started building these beautiful sets in Shepperton. I was over in Los Angeles and I could see this thing was going really bad, because I was involved with these producers from hell. I rang up my collaborators back in London, and I said, "Look, I'm going to have to call off the movie." And they all said, "We're doing this amazing stuff, you can't. You've got to keep going and make it work." And I was saying, "Well, it doesn't look good from over here." But when you should say "stop," you don't, and then you end up in manure up to your neck. You imagine you can make it right, and the more you try to make it right, the worse it gets.

MF: I quite liked *We're No Angels*.

NJ: Yeah, that I liked. That was a beautiful script by David Mamet. David was being affectionate about a cultural world to which he was an outsider. It was this little Catholic fable, a bit like *Il Miracolo*, or something like that, about these convicts who were redeemed by goodness. I was a director-for-hire on that, really.

MF: You had no input into the casting?

NJ: It was written for Robert De Niro and Sean Penn, basically. Mamet actually wrote a play about it called *Speed-the-Plough*. It was a merciless portrait of the Hollywood system. The characters in the play are trying to write this script about two escaped prisoners on the run. I think David wrote the play about the experience of the movie.

MF: Did you have input into the script?
NJ: I changed bits and pieces, and there's a visual structure to the thing that is mine, but as to the basic subject matter, it was not my property. It was the first time I'd ever been I suppose what you call a "director," and I didn't enjoy the position very much. It was a bit odd.

MF: So it was an unhappy experience?
NJ: No, not entirely. I sat with Sean quite a lot. He was splitting up from Madonna at the time, so we had this kind of love-hate relationship going on. I think Sean's performance is marvelous. Because of the kind of relationship that we had, it was slightly fractious but mutually engaged. I think I ignored Robert and should have concentrated more on what he was doing.

MF: There are sweet moments with Sean.
NJ: Oh, he's fucking great. They're both great actors, but I think Sean took a lot of my energies. The truth is, working with actors you're always trying to get them to take it down. De Niro is such an actor that if you want him to go into a mad gesture of his own, he can do two million variations of it, and that was fascinating to me. I probably did him a bit of a disservice in not reining him back enough.

MF: The film doesn't have much relationship to the film made in the fifties.
NJ: It didn't. The fifties film is terrible.

MF: So you came back and made *The Miracle*, a small film. I find it charming.
NJ: I think so. It was me just trying to get out of Hollywood, that's the truth. I wrote the script based on these Irish short stories, and weaved it around these two adolescent kids who were telling stories of the world they were about to experience.

MF: It's interesting that you frequently use people who've never acted before, like Eammon Owens in *The Butcher Boy* and Jaye Davidson in *The Crying Game*. Why do you do that?

NJ: Just because I write these parts. In *The Miracle*, I wrote these parts for kids who were about sixteen or seventeen, and if you want to cast people like that, they're often people who haven't acted before. When I cast Jaye, I couldn't have cast Wesley Snipes or Prince because everyone would know they're men. I had to find some unknown to play that role.

MF: Is there anything about *The Miracle* that you're unhappy with?

NJ: I have no idea. Well, it is this Oedipal drama, you know, there's no revelation in the story. You know the story a third of the way through and the characters don't know the story.

MF: The narrative is very subtle.

NJ: Yeah. You've got to accept it on a different level. I haven't seen it since I made it. If there is a problem with the movie, it's with the central character, the boy. You're saying, "Come on, you know the story, man, cut to the chase." To me, the film wasn't about the story. The story was like a mechanism just to explore these themes.

MF: I wonder if the characters are a bit too vague?

NJ: Maybe. It was me at that age, really. It's a very personal film. I shot it in my house, and wrote it for the actress [Beverly D'Angelo] who I was having a relationship with at the time. There's one beautiful shot in the film, where she sings "Stardust," and the boy comes up behind her. It lasts for about three or four minutes. The film is about emotion unfulfilled, or satisfaction deferred, and it's got all these characters who discover these things too late.

MF: You have good feelings about it?

NJ: Yeah, absolutely.

MF: *The Crying Game* obviously struck some kind of incredible nerve. Do you think it was just the taboo subject matter, or great marketing by Miramax?

NJ: I don't know. People liked it a lot. I think it was because it was about the exploration of identity. I don't know why it hadn't been done before, a love affair where somebody is persuasive as a woman and then turns out to be a man.

The story of *The Crying Game* was written after I wrote *Angel*. The film was a kind of inquiry. This guy Fergus [Stephen Rea] is a Catholic and a nationalist, and he identifies himself with certain parameters. He thinks this is what he is, a political animal. He's wedded to violence. He feels that he's a soldier, and is justified in killing people he doesn't know for this cause. I was interested in setting this person up with his polar opposite, someone who is so far away from his experience: a black soldier, who is gay, although Fergus didn't know it. If you throw this character on this journey, will he survive and will he change? To me, that was what it was about, really.

MF: He certainly changed.
NJ: He changed and survived. To me it had a lot to do with the IRA at the time, to see if they could they change. Could people's narrow identifications of themselves change? This country has been blighted with a sense of exclusive identification of people who see themselves as Catholic, Protestant, Unionist, or Nationalist. It was an exploration of self. That's what I wanted to do with it. If you strip away all these masks human beings wear, is anything left underneath? Is anything left of Fergus when all this stuff is stripped away from him? In fact, there is, and he turns out to be a human being.

MF: Did people criticize your portrayal of the IRA?
NJ: Oh yeah, of course they did. There were two criticisms: on the one hand I made Fergus too sympathetic, and on the other I made them caricatures. An example is the part that Miranda Richardson played. She was a snarly, psychopathic killer, and I was criticized for that. I was also criticized for daring to make a character, Fergus, a member of the IRA, a cogent, intelligent, rational human being. Did people criticize my portrayal of the IRA? Yes, they did, with great vituperation. At the time, there was this huge argument going on in this country about the issue of the North of Ireland and terrorism. That was such an emotional issue. The minute you even broached it, you were accused of being in sympathy.

MF: Does the criticism bother you?
NJ: No, it doesn't bother me. Basically people were saying, "How dare you? Representing these people as anything other than psychopaths does a disservice to the body politic at large." They need to be seen like this to be dealt with and got rid of. The problem, actually, with those kinds of organizations, is precisely that they're not psychopaths. If they

were, they'd be easy to deal with. The problem is that they are people who've got a decided political agenda and have made rational decisions to blow other people from the face of the earth. The problem is not the psychopathology, the problem is the rationality. The film was not an exploration of terrorism, or of the IRA, or anything like that. It was looking at a character who's a familiar one in the Irish landscape.

MF: I'm curious how you hit upon the twist of unveiling Jaye Davidson's sexuality mid-way through the film?

NJ: I'd written the first third of the story, and every time I took the character to London, it didn't seem to work. I'd written the story of Fergus, who kidnaps Jody [Forest Whitaker], who was black, so you've got all these cultural facts that are turned on their head. Fergus regards himself as a member of a repressed minority, yet he kidnaps a black British soldier who took the only job he could get. So you've got this strange thing of the victimized minority victimizing another minority. He inadvertently causes the death of Jody and goes to London, and he does what he was asked to do—basically, tracks down the guy's wife—but Fergus can't reveal his own identity. Every time I came to the London section where he tracks down the wife, it became a bit like a Ken Loach movie, a documentary-realist thing. I didn't know where to go with it. I wasn't really exploring what I wanted to explore.

Then I thought if I'd make the character a man, a transvestite, and Fergus gets absolutely fascinated with her, falls in love with her, has sex with her and then finds out she's a man, he'll be confronting the person he really killed. Then the story began to make sense to me and that's when I wrote the script. The first part of it is like a one-act play. People say, "There's too many issues going on here," but I think that's bullshit. I think there's such a reductive perception of cinema going on at the moment, in the last ten years. It makes me sick. I think movies should be about something, and they should be explorations of ideas, and you should be able to explore anything you want.

MF: Some critics say that the parts don't cohere that well.

NJ: Oh, they do. The first part seems to be about politics, and the second part seems to be about something else, but, if anybody thinks politics is not about something else, they're insane. The second part is a mirror of the first part, and everything that happens in the first part happens again in the second part, but in a different way. I'm sure there's things wrong with the movie, of course. There's things wrong with every movie I make.

MF: Do you think the film is essentially about the redemption of Fergus?
NJ: It's about whether this man can truly live. Can he live a truly engaged life, as a human being? Can he actually embrace humanity, even though it had a different face to what he always thought it would have? I think it's also a kind of cosmic joke. He's made a promise to look after Jody's "wife," and that's what the act of love is, making a promise, so he's bound by that promise. Will he live up to that promise? I think he will and that's what I think is heroic about the movie. And if you're in jail for twenty-five years, and you have this pretty thing coming to you, wouldn't you say, "Yeah, I do love you."

MF: We don't know what's going to happen to them.
NJ: Well, in twenty-five years, we don't know what's going to happen to anybody, do we? That's all the fun. It's not a movie about a guy discovering that he's homosexual. If it was about that it would be something quite different. It's about a guy loving another human being, that's all.

MF: After your previous experiences in Hollywood, did you have any trepidation about doing a big Hollywood movie when you agreed to make *Interview with the Vampire*?
NJ: David Geffen [the producer] is a very persuasive man. A great guy, actually, a lovely man, very powerful. I didn't know him and he sent me the script. I'd heard about the book, but I hadn't read it. So I read the script which Anne Rice had written, and it was very theatrical but kind of fascinating. It was a vampire movie that took the issue of vampires seriously. After we finished *The Crying Game*, one of the things I was going to do—because Angela Carter had wanted to write a vampire movie—was to do a similar thing to the vampire nexus of things that she did to the werewolf in *The Company of Wolves*. She had written a script called *Vampirella* which, again, was too short and not quite there. I would love to have worked with her on it, but I didn't get the chance because she died. I really wanted to get back into that Gothic stuff again; I love it. It's like going into a dark, mysterious wood.

I read the Anne Rice book and thought it was a wonderful book. I thought it was one of the best pieces of Gothic fiction since *Dracula*, and really interesting. Not entirely literature, but that only makes it more fascinating in a way. So I said to Geffen that if I could get the script right, I would try and make a movie out of it. I went back to the book and adapted Anne Rice's script, and eventually came up with something I was happy with and sent it to David. He got very excited about it and said he wanted to make it. I was very nervous about making a Hollywood movie, as you can understand. He said, "Look, I'll enable you to make it as an independent film, so you can do exactly what you want," and David is powerful enough to get the studio to do this big movie that cost about $70 million and let me make it the way I made *The Company of Wolves*. To me, it was a blast.

MF: Did you cast Tom Cruise?

NJ: Yeah. David had always wanted Brad Pitt to be in it, and at the time, he wanted Daniel Day-Lewis for Lestat. I met Daniel, but he hummed and hawed for about three or four months and eventually said he didn't want to play a vampire. We were looking around for someone we could cast, and thinking of different people, and Tom Cruise's name came up. I went to meet Tom once and then twice, and you know, I thought I'd love to do it with this guy, because he's really a fine actor. He's got a kind of pitiless logic to him that would be good for the role. It was obviously casting against type. I'd do another movie with Tom in a minute; he's really a force of nature. Then everybody began objecting, Anne Rice and all that. But in a way what happened with Tom and Brad gave us another kind of power, because the world was all against us. We had to run this closed set, and it was as if we were making a tiny movie like *The Company of Wolves*, except with big resources.

MF: Was it a difficult film to make?

NJ: No, it wasn't, no.

MF: And the controversy never really affected you very much?

NJ: I thought it was all rubbish. I mean, what are you going to say? It was on every talk show, it seems, every week in the United States. You know: "They are doing this. They are taking out the gay subtext. They are doing that," and Anne Rice is on the radio and TV saying all this stuff. But to me it was a film about guilt and longing, and if there is a fault in the movie, the fault is also in the book, because once Louis becomes a vampire, they kind of bitch through the ages, don't they? All that changes are the centuries. But I loved that in a strange way. I was aware that it was a picaresque narrative; it wasn't driven by narrative concerns. I was very happy with it because I had the freedom to make it the way I wanted.

MF: There's a kind of airless quality about it.

NJ: Of course, it's an unreality. You make a movie about people who are dead, spend two hours with people who are dead, you'll feel a need for fresh air. The problem with it was that, in a way, you couldn't scare people, and I kept saying this to David. When all your protagonists are monsters, you cannot get the scares that you get in normal horror films, because you know they can't die. So it became something different, something about the fascination of repellent things, about decay, and stuff like that.

MF: They became quite a dysfunctional little family. [Laughs]

NJ: [Laughs] In a way, yeah, to some extent.

MF: The erotic elements are interesting.

NJ: I think so. They're as interesting as they are in the book. Lestat loves Louis, and Louis loves to be punished. And he's punished through eternity, although he doesn't know he loves to be punished.

MF: I'm curious about the kind of discussions you might have had with Cruise and Pitt about the erotic elements of their roles.

NJ: What erotic elements? They never had sex, but they never had sex in the book. Their transformation into vampires is always done in a sexual way. They loved to punish each other!

MF: Did you have a rehearsal period? And did you have a lot of discussions with them about their characters?

NJ: Yes, I did. We rehearsed for about a week, but I'm not a great rehearser, really. With Tom, it was about the beauty of cruelty in a way. We had a lot of discussions about this. We watched a lot of animal footage, leopards killing rabbits and stuff like this. And with Brad it was about suffering, this beautiful soul that suffers and suffers. That book you could discuss endlessly, so we just got down and made it. To me, it was about visually trying to make this beautifully rotten fruit, in a way. It was a bit like Gustav Klimt or Aubrey Beardsley, that slightly decorative or decadent art at the turn of the century. I just read Flaubert's *Sentimental Education* and realized where Anne Rice got a lot of her stuff for the novel.

MF: So stylistically, you were going for a painterly look?

NJ: I was just trying to create something that was dead, like a funeral home. The whole thing is a series of funeral interiors. I worked with a great designer, Dante Ferretti. I mean, they always lived at night. There was daylight in the first ten minutes of the movie, and after that you're in night until the very end. It was about making their entire world like a coffin: Los Angeles, Paris, San Francisco.

MF: The Paris scenes were quite intriguing. Stephen Rea's character brings a nice humor to the film.

NJ: He does, yeah. Stephen based his stuff on the *Comédie Française*. He took these *Comédie Française* videotapes and looked at them all.

MF: Did you feel restricted in any way? You didn't even take credit on the screenplay.

NJ: No, I didn't. Nobody restricted me in any way whatsoever.

MF: Let's talk about *The Butcher Boy*. It's a great movie.

NJ: Well, it's Pat McCabe's novel. I read the book when I was doing *Interview with the Vampire*, and I bought the rights to it. Pat's an amazing writer. I commissioned him to write a screenplay, and he did a draft, and then another draft, and I did the final draft. Coming off two big movies like *Interview with the Vampire* and *Michael Collins*, the main thing about *The Butcher Boy* was a weird feeling, kind of naked. That was a difficult film to make, really hard, because it was like stripping down what we do. I wasn't making a big movie anymore, but this tiny little film, entirely about the character, and about emotions and nuances of emotion and the rawness of emotion. It's much more difficult to do than use two thousand pounds of explosives to blow up buildings.

MF: What was the most crucial element for you to retain from the book? Was it the tone or the voice-over?

NJ: It was to re-invent the novel for the screen, really. If you were faithful to the way the book proceeds, it would make a very bad movie. It was to recreate the emotional feeling I had when I finished the book; that's what I wanted to get on to the screen. There was something very cinematic in the middle of the novel, in Francie's obsession, in the way he sees himself as a cartoon character, and his obsession with cartoons. Yet the book was written in this beautifully dense language, and through the voice of the kid. It seems to happen inside the boy's head, so it seems unfilmable. But on the other hand, it absolutely is filmable. I worked with Pat McCabe the way I'd worked with Angela Carter on *The Company of Wolves*, trying to find the cinematic equivalent for his unique book.

MF: Where did you find Eamonn Owens, the boy who plays Francie Brady?

NJ: I found him up in Killeshandra. I saw thousands of kids.

MF: How did you work with him on his performance? He must be a very rambunctious little guy.

NJ: Well, he's a very sweet, lovely, but tough guy. I videotaped a lot of the kids that came in. He came in, and I got him to play the part and followed him around with the video camera, just to read through the scene. I looked at that stuff and it was really good. I called him back and we did more stuff with the video camera, and explored it some more, almost like play. Then we went out to Ardmore studios, and I photographed him again in the real environment, in the open fields and stuff like that, and so his engagement with the part got a bit deeper. That's the way it happened, really. Through that series of tests I saw that he was quite a remarkable actor, and then we started doing the film and his performance grew deeper and deeper. I realized I'd found a remarkable talent here.

It was also the way that Pat McCabe had imagined this world of childhood, had recreated it. It was so true that all those boys just stepped into it like stepping into their own suits or something. It's very difficult to be accurate about childhood, but I think McCabe wrote one of the best books about childhood ever written. So I didn't have to do anything to get those kids to act, because the parts just fitted them rather beautifully.

MF: In some ways the voice-over narration is the key to the work.

NJ: Oh yeah, of course it is.

MF: What's interesting is that Stephen Rea is supposed to be narrating from the perspective of an adult, but he's actually narrating from the perspective of a grown-up who is still a twelve-year-old.

NJ: And you feel that.

MF: Absolutely. It seems like he's actually imitating Eamonn's voice patterns.

NJ: Yeah, of course. The whole film was structured around the voice-over. There's a very interesting relationship between the narration in that film and what actually happens on screen; very funny, deeply ironic. So, the first two drafts Pat had written had no voice-over, and I said, "We've got to have the voice in here, because the voice of Francie Brady is obviously central to the book," and I wanted it to have a specific relation to the action in the film, because the voice is saying one thing, and the film's doing another. Sometimes the voice would intrude in the narrative, and talk to the boy. I just thought it could be used in a unique way for this film.

When Stephen came to do the voice-over, obviously he was finished with the movie, so he'd acted with Eamonn and seen his performance. He'd heard his voice and vocal speech patterns. By the time he came to actually put the voice-over onto film, he knew all that stuff, so he could link his own mental words right to Eamonn's.

MF: You suddenly shift tone in the middle of scenes. It's like pulling the rug out from under the viewer. You're laughing and suddenly it's shocking.

NJ: The difficulty with the tone was that you could never put caricature in. It had to be kind to its characters, because the book and the movie is longing for a villain, and if you gave the story a villain you would have messed up the whole film. Even Mrs. Nugent's [Fiona Shaw] not a villain. You see her from her own perspective, and the difficult thing about directing the movie was actually getting that tone right. If any of the actors veered into a kind of caricature, it was like a red flag; you could just see it instantly.

It's a film with a simple logic, because Francie always laughs, he always makes you laugh, and he always laughs at himself. The book actually is far more sardonic. In the book he rips out Mrs. Nugent's intestines, and all this stuff, and he walks around with her chopped up parts. What I'm saying is the book is a comic book, but about these horrific things. You couldn't actually read the book if it wasn't comic, because laughter is a great way of looking at the unmentionable. It a very simple logic: the more Francie made you laugh as an audience, the more you liked him. The more you liked him, the more you felt for him, and the more you felt for him the more you laughed with him, so it was laughter and horror. A rhythm was established in the telling of the story, and the balance between laughter and horror gets faster and faster towards the end of the movie, so by the end you're horrified one second and you're laughing the next, whereas at the start, the tone shifts, but at a slower pace.

MF: You implicate the period, in a way, because this society isn't equipped to deal with Francie: not the church, not the psychiatrists.

NJ: Even now, perhaps. Some things never change. And, in a way, I thought the guy had a soul too beautiful for the world, you know, a heart too big. And the world is inevitably going to disappoint him. I mean, it's about 1950s Ireland, but it's not an indictment of Ireland in the fifties. There obviously were no social services. Actually, the kid led a great bucolic life. He was left to run free. I'd love to have had a childhood like that. You couldn't have nowadays.

MF: But in some ways Francie also represents something we fear, this kind of irrational aspect of our psyche, or the uncontrollable aspect of the self.

NJ: Yeah, he's a human being of that culture. He's the unaccommodated man. He's somebody who refuses to learn the rules of disappointment. He refuses to civilize his feelings because that would do his feelings an injustice. Pat McCabe struck gold with that character. I suppose it's a bit like Holden Caulfield. You can explain who he was, or what he was, but you don't know why or how.

MF: Stylistically, you deliberately went the way of surrealism, or at least non-naturalism.

NJ: Well, the book is like that. It happens in the boy's imagination, and real events and unreal events have the same weight to him. The Virgin Mary [Sinead O'Connor] appearing in a field is as real to him as a bog-man wolfing down his potatoes. He hadn't learned to separate these things into different categories.

I saw that movie *Heavenly Creatures*, which I didn't like. They had these claymation figures going on, and they didn't seem to have any emotional resonance or connection with the world of the characters, and it seemed wrong to me in some way. I wouldn't have done all that imaginary stuff in *The Butcher Boy* if it didn't come directly out of the character. It had to come directly out of his voice and his mental world and his soul. I don't like movies where they strain for significance. It seemed to come out of the perspective of a child's world, and particularly Francie Brady's world. You've got to lead the audience through this film, and they follow the journey with this boy, so halfway through the movie they realize they're watching somebody go mad in front of their eyes. All the connective tissue is broken and separated, but it's the same things you were looking at in the beginning of the movie, except they're in a different place now.

MF: What is your perspective on Francie at the end of the film, when he comes out of the hospital?

NJ: Has he changed? Yeah, he's changed. He knows he's done a bad thing. He does! [Laughs] He says, "No more chopping up." He hasn't changed his language, and he doesn't regret, but he's changed. He's a sinner who's finding redemption in the only way he knows. The sinner never regrets their sins, do they, really? Regret is not the same thing as repentance.

MF: What's been the response to the film in Ireland?

NJ: They absolutely loved it.

MF: And your portrayal of Irish life?

NJ: It wasn't an unkind portrayal. It was deeply sympathetic to all, even to the priests, the old priest that Milo O'Shea played. It wasn't unsympathetic, and it wasn't untrue. I think they saw that it wasn't untrue. There's a lot of caricatures you could make of those figures, like the town drunk, or the parish priest, or the pedophile priest, or the suicidal mother. I think they were portrayed accurately and with sympathy, and I think people saw that. They also saw an aspect of Irish experience that they never thought was worthy of fiction, and how fascinating it is, that small town thing. You think, "Oh, if you make movies they should be about more obviously dramatic aspects of our experience," whereas when they saw this, and they saw how true it was, they liked it.

MF: What is your relationship to Hollywood exactly? Do you consider yourself an independent filmmaker?

NJ: Yes, I do.

MF: You've somehow worked it out that you can work for the studios and retain your independence.

NJ: Well, I think it's more simple than that. I've got a very visual imagination, and sometimes some of the projects I want to do involve creating stuff that you can only do on large budgets. So unlike Mike Leigh or Ken Loach, I'm condemned to have to encounter the system to explore the things I want to do. Mike Leigh can quite happily work in London, because his artistry expresses itself through the fabric of real people's lives, whereas I do movies like *Interview with the Vampire*, or *The Company of Wolves*. I suppose I've got large tastes every now and then, as well as small tastes, so I'm condemned to be there or not be there. But it's not a bad place to be. I don't make commercial movies, really. I'm only a marginally successful director commercially, but for some reason they continue to allow me to make films. It's silly to pretend that you've no relationship with Hollywood. Every director does, anywhere in the world, even independent directors, because in the end their films have to be distributed by that system. But I won't make a movie where I haven't got the freedom to do what I want to do. I won't do that ever again.

MF: Are things wrong with the film industry?

NJ: Oh, dreadful. But things are wrong with the culture, not just the film industry. The film industry reflects the broader culture we live in, very sad times. If there was a way of measuring the state of the soul through the cultural artifacts any culture produces, I'd say we're in a pretty bad way. You've got to realize I'm also a novelist. People bemoan the state of the film industry, but they haven't ever encountered the publishing industry; that is appalling. What's happened over the last twenty years, since I began writing fiction, is shocking. It's a justification for major violence, if I was that way inclined. The publishing industry is dominated by numbers. It's in as appalling a state as the film industry. It's the culture that's fucked, I think.

MF: As an Irish artist, do you ever feel the weight of your cultural past?

NJ: No, I don't think so. But you only know what you know, don't you? That's what I know. I grew up in a Catholic country, with a strange pagan kind of Catholicism that you get in Ireland; it's different from elsewhere. It was very superstitious, but a lot of that's gone now, thank goodness. It's a world that teaches you the value of fables. I suppose it teaches the rules of imaginative behavior, in a strange way. The only thing Irish people are good at is imagination. They're not good at football; they were never good at painting; they haven't got great architecture; they didn't build great empires. All they're really good at is their wit and their brains, redeeming the world through the way they imagine and perceive it.

MF: What gives you the greatest pleasure in being a filmmaker?

NJ: The whole thing is a great pleasure and I should do it more. I could probably do it better, because it's a great gift to be allowed to make a movie. I like the whole thing. Most of all I like the activity of doing it, being engaged in some fiction which, in many ways, is more rewarding than life. You can aim at a certain kind of perfection in fiction that you can never achieve in life.

Face to Face with Evil

Michael Open / 1982

From *Film Directions* 5, no. 18 (December 1, 1982): 3–5, 16. Reprinted by permission of the author.

In spite of the controversy it caused at the Festival of Film and Television in Celtic countries, held in Wexford, with its inane boycotts, walkouts, and similar childish protests by members of the Association of Independent Producers (who ought to have known better), Neil Jordan's *Angel* has burst upon the Irish cinema screen as its major cinematic achievement of recent years.

The film was given a screening in the film market at Cannes and was greeted with euphoria by all of those who saw it. I went into the film expecting to leave before it ended and catch up with its ending when I returned to Ireland, however, it was so impressive I stayed to the end. As soon as I returned I contacted Neil Jordan to record the interview which I had been asking for since he started production of the film and between one thing and another, had never materialized.

After a smash-hit run of many weeks in Dublin, *Angel* was by that time something of a phenomenon. It tells the story of a young and talented saxophonist player (Danny, played by Stephen Rea). In the course of a dalliance with a deaf teenager after a dance at which he had been playing, he witnesses a terrorist bombing and the killing of both his band's manager and the deaf girl. Using only his wits and the information he has observed during this traumatic event, Danny becomes both private eye and angel of death and pursues the perpetrators of this outrage to a shattering climax.

The following interview was conducted in Neil Jordan's Dublin flat.

MO: You've written a number of things before you started into making films, and *Angel* is your first fiction film, had you actually been holding it back to make yourself for a considerable time, or was it just the next script that you'd written?

NJ: It was just the next script that I'd written.

MO: So there wasn't anything that was particularly more personal in *Angel* than in any of the others?

NJ: No, nothing—except I suppose the fact that the main character is a musician.

MO: One of the things that struck me about the film when I saw it at Cannes was that it seemed to be very exterior, there's a great deal of movement in the film. Was that a conscious thing that you put into it?

NJ: I've written three or four films now and I think in all of them the character has gone on a journey, and part of the appeal of film for me as a writer, and someone who has been used to sitting in a room, is the fact that you can take your mind and your concerns and your obsessions and imagination on the same kind of journey. So I think that's reflected in it really, it's just a kind of a bedrock. It's one of these tendencies that people who tell stories have.

The journey, the actual physical journey in some sense echoes the metaphysical journey that's going on inside the main character, and I suppose too there's an element of the road movie type film in it.

MO: What about the practical details of how it was financed? How did the finance come about?

NJ: Really by persistence, and a kind of manic assault in all possible areas and finding out where there actually was money. I always outline the script first and write a thirty-page outline, in terms of what actually happens. It's a help to show people what your intentions are. And I showed that around to several people, and myself and John Boorman showed it around to the major companies, none of whom were interested! I had worked with Walter Donohue (I'd had some contact with him at Channel 4), and I sent him the script and he liked it and they were interested in making films of that type and it was from Channel 4 that the finance of the film came.

All you do is get your script and send it round where you can and if you find somebody who needs this type of film and wants to back it, you follow them.

MO: There was no opposition to you making it yourself as a first feature film?

NJ: There was quite a lot of nervousness. But I decided when I wrote the script that nobody else was going to direct it but me, so anyone who was interested in it, I just said to them, "Well I'm going to direct it, so if you don't want that, you can't have the script!" John Boorman's position as Executive Producer gave people a lot of confidence.

Then we budgeted it, and we couldn't make it on the amount of money Channel 4 came up with . . . it would have had to constrain the film if we had to stay with the budget they could afford. It would have limited the film too much, and so we began to look for co-production money which we eventually got from the Film Board here. That's basically the financial story of the film, it's quite simple. I was told that it was the easiest passage anyone has ever had to get finance for their first film!

MO: When I first saw the film, my first reaction was that the reference to Antonioni was very significant and I saw lots and lots of parallels with *Blow Up*, whereas a much more insightful colleague then saw it and pointed out that there are lots of things from *Point Blank* in the film. How do you see the progenitors of the film?

NJ: I don't know, because I'm really not that cinematically literate, you know? I've never gone to college and studied film. I've seen and eaten as many films as I can, but they've gone into my mind in a jumbled kind of manner. I think there's very little of *Blow Up* in the film. If there is something in the film I think it's more of *The Passenger*, in other words the kind of obsession in the central character, in somebody who assumes the identity of (well in *The Passenger* it's the case of a dead man) but you know, this kind of transmutation of identity. I think there's a lot of the mood of Antonioni, particularly *Blow Up* and *The Passenger*, they've just stuck in my mind.

But the simple truth about that little Antonioni reference is that in the script what I intended to do was—because I knew an old cinema in Camden Street that was going to put a play on. In the projection room there were huge life-size cutouts of people like Cary Grant. I wanted that scene to be surrounded by these dusty life-size cutouts, I just wanted it to be surrounded by some reference to the cinema, and we couldn't get them! We went through all these films magazines and saw the picture of Anna Magnani. It did strike me as quite apt really.

There's quite a lot of *Point Blank* in it too. My urge was to do something with a thriller. There's two things you can do with genre, you can either abstract it, so that it becomes an abstraction of itself and it becomes about the genre rather than about anything else, which is in a sense what *Point Blank* did, in a kind of very light-hearted and very fruitful way. But a film like Walter Hill's *The Driver* is almost a total abstraction. That is one way you can treat genre, and what I wanted to do with this was I wanted to take the bones of the thriller genre, of a revenge story, and add certain kinds of metaphysical concerns and obsessions and try to make it about evil. I would love to be able to construct a story about a detective who is trying to solve a series of crimes and trying to find the heart of evil and actually he comes to the conclusion that the evil has no heart and he faces something that is even beyond the confines of the film. One could not construct a story like that. What I wanted to do in this, I wanted to take the bones of the genre itself and to fill it in with some more philosophic concerns really.

MO: In the film, the central character, Danny, goes through a kind of transmutation in the sense that he starts out apparently aimless, and in the course of the film becomes totally animated and at the end he is stopped short.

NJ: Central characters are always to some extent anonymous I think, that's the problem with central characters because an audience views things through them, particularly in a film like that when everything that happens is basically either seen by him or seen with him. The problem is in giving character to a central character like that, particularly if you want them to be to some extent emblematic, and I wanted him to be totally ordinary, to be a person. He's a totally ordinary human being who doesn't know his own desires; he plays music very well, that's perhaps the key to his life, and he fancies the girl singer. He's not even sure that he fancies her, he's willing to be seduced by this deaf and dumb girl, he's willing even to take advantage of her. He's a human being with all these foibles and failings

Now I wanted to put him through an event that would act like a chemical solution on that mass of undifferentiated humanity and define it in some way. I wanted him to be presented with situations whereby he had to make a moral choice. If he had made a moral choice in any point of the film, the story would have ended there. I wanted to show the process whereby the fact that he doesn't make moral choices allows his character to be fired by something outside himself, something that is very violent and that's basically in the end a negation of the life he represented at the start. That's what I wanted to show. To do that, you do that the way that somebody does when they invent a character, they just try to picture them and fill in the little blank outline with as much color as you can.

MO: That's interesting because you don't see then that his vendetta is in fact a moral judgment?

NJ: No. I think it's a feeling of outrage. I mean the question is always raised, the question Hitchcock talked about is why didn't he go to the police. This question has some point in this story. Hitchcock always said they don't go to the police because it's boring to go to the police! But in this case there is a point, because if he was motivated by anything as defined as moral outrage he would have gone to the police, and perhaps would have found quite a simple solution—I don't mean that in literal terms he would have gone to the police, what I wanted to do was, I wanted to show the process. (I suppose it's a very dismal outlook on human beings really, in other words, that we are masses of responses who are conditioned by events that happen to us without any choices on our own part.) I'm saying that we have a choice, but I'm trying to posit what happens when those choices aren't exercised. So in the first place he sees the girl shot and the manager shot. This event traumatizes him in a very basic way and he happens to go into this orthopedic shop to meet somebody who he thinks may be one of the assassins. He follows him home, goes into his house and finds a gun there. The very fact of him finding the gun there leads him to shooting the assassin himself. The way I tried to shoot that scene was that his actual discovery of the gun, this fascination of the mechanism of the gun and the very fact that he allows himself to hold it and allows himself to be fascinated by it leads inadvertently to the killing. So he becomes a killer by default and even by surprise. I suppose I just wanted to show the kind of sinister ease with which these things happen.

MO: And so in other words he's a victim of his own logic, in the sense that the first killing inevitably has to lead to another.

NJ: Well he's a victim of his own lack of logic, he supplies no logic himself, but the relentless logic is supplied to him by forces that are outside of him. And these are the forces of politics, sectarianism, the forces of social hate really, and I think they are forces which assume a momentum that is larger than human beings. And that's the terrifying thing I find about the world at the moment, that ideas and ideologies and common constructs that are created by human beings assume a power that is actually larger than the sum of those human beings. And that is really what I wanted to show in the film.

MO: On the more stylistic side of the film, you seemed to have hit on a very articulate style in the sense that there are lots of occasions in the film where it is very evident that your camera placement for example, very firmly emphasizes certain relationships between characters.

NJ: The only thing I could work on was instinct. The only film I'd made before was a documentary film, with a documentary crew, and it was influenced by everything that you're influenced by when you're just trying to follow the action! There were just two things I knew I wanted to do the opposite of what one expects of a thriller. I wanted the pace of it to be poetic rather than aggressive. My instinct is for long takes and for camera movements that encompass quite a lot of the action and not so much cutting. I think sometimes it's very difficult to conceive a shot, unless you choose an obvious landscape that is chosen directly for that shot and there were quite a few cases of that, but you have to try and get the actors to feel the mood of the scene and you have to try and find out the certain truth in the scene—even through their movement and the way they walk and the way they turn and then through the way the camera follows them.

People say there are two thousand ways of shooting one scene—I don't think there are really, I just think there's one way, and that's the right way and that has to be found. There is a kind of poetry there and I think that's the most basic job of a director, to actually find that series of relationships which express the whole scene.

I deliberately did not study any mentors. I didn't look at films . . . I tried not to look at movies for the few months going up to it and I tried not to make references to other shots in other films that I'd seen—I wanted to be able to shoot blind so that the movements of the camera and the texture of the lighting would be as particular to this film as it could possibly be. So in a way I was taking a risk because I suppose if the instincts weren't right, it could have been a disaster. I think there are an awful lot of influences in the film, and they come from a lot of places, there's quite a lot of Bertolucci in it too.

The only thing I can say stylistically, is that the one thing I wanted to do was push for the poetic dimension rather than the visceral excitement of films of action.

MO: It struck me that you handled the scene in the dance hall at the beginning exceptionally well. Those kinds of shots are really very difficult to pull off; did that bother you at all?

NJ: It was very difficult for me because we were dealing with playback, and when you're using playback you can be stuck to a tune and to the rhythm of that tune. I shot very few cutaway shots of the guitarist playing. That scene was done in the middle of the shoot so I wasn't camera-shy anymore.

It seems to me in films that there are so many elements that influence a film. I've been reading a series of interviews by Francis Bacon with David Sylvester and they're brilliant about the creative process. What Bacon always says is that he tries to find out the element of accidents that would give the image this added kind of charge and reality. And my experience in shooting that film was that there were so many things that entered into the process of making the film that were basically outside anybody's control. And as a director, what you have to do is to try to attempt to make them benign influences rather than malicious ones.

MO: What about directing the actors, that seems to me to be an area where a lot of filmmakers fall down. What approach did you use? Presumably this is the first time you've directed actors and you haven't done stage work?

NJ: I have actually. That's the area I was most at home with because I've written several plays and I've directed several productions. I genuinely do like working with actors. That was one of the most satisfying things of the production, the relationship you can build up with actors and share the truths of the film. In so far as possible I always try to get the basic concerns of story and character. I didn't try to deal with any theories of acting. In a way it's like the planning of shots, discussions were always around that central theme which was at the heart of the scene.

There's such a great potential of wealth of acting talent here at the moment. Particularly the young actors. They're so aware and just instinctively seem to move for the camera. The old type of garrulous Abbey acting is dead.

MO: Regarding the iconography of the film, you have the gun and the saxophone—interestingly the publicity for the film makes a great deal of play for both of these objects—do you look upon the saxophone as creativity and the gun as destruction? Is that opposition the pivot of the whole film?

NJ: Yes, it's the exteriorization of the theme that I was talking about really. I wanted on one level the character Danny to be someone who was fascinated with the saxophone as an instrument, then he finds the gun and the mechanics of the gun are as fascinating as the keys of the saxophone. I wanted to counterpoint the horrific nature of the attraction of the gun against the quite beautiful nature of the attraction of an instrument of music. I wanted to maintain that tension all the way through the film and to design the scenes of music and celebration in a way that was the polar opposite of the scenes of grimy realism and death. Those two principles of light and shade I wanted to get right through the film.

MO: Following that on, there would seem to be something rather special about the scene in the middle of the film where he gets the sax back.

NJ: It's as if he has actually forgotten—he goes back to his Aunt's house and there he finds the old soprano sax and it brings him back to the world of his uncle and he plays this tune which belongs to that world, an old blues tune and when you've gone through a trauma like that, you go like a dazed dog and you're drawn towards what you know. So he's drawn back to his Aunt's flat and finds the saxophone there, and after the actual explosion and his hospitalization I imagine him in a kind of womb of cotton wool and he comes out and he encounters every single thing that led to that event—he encounters the world of his uncle, the music, the band again and then he encounters the character with the damaged foot and eventually he encounters the gun.

So, the first twenty minutes of the film, in balance, they hold all the elements of the whole film, they hold the music, they hold the violence, they hold the characters. Then the next twenty minutes really are his encounter with each object of that whole world from a totally different kind of perspective. Everything looks strange to him, the saxophone looks strange to him, the singer looks strange to him, all his relationships are seen from this slightly warped perspective.

MO: At the end, do you think that we should believe that he would go back to the sax?

NJ: I didn't want to answer those questions at the end—in real terms I suppose the character would be changed. The way I wanted the end to function was—the metaphysical language in which the film speaks is a very Catholic one, it's to do with sin and guilt. It's a language that I know and one that is rich in some strange way, but that I don't agree with—and in the last scene his response to each of these things, the way he meets that gun the first time, is exactly the way Catholic priests tell you the process of actual sin happens. In the end, I wanted that language to be the language of that triad of guilt, sin, and redemption to be presented to him there. But it does not. Within the language of his own mind, his inner thoughts, the only thing that could show him the way out would be something like the metaphysical idea of some kind of redemption. I wanted to place all those things in context and to show that actually even that in itself does not provide a solution; basically the only weapon that one has against the forces encountered is the weapon of reason which is the one that he hasn't admitted into the world of his thoughts.

I find something very appealing about the idea of a faith-healer who presumes he has the power of healing magic and yet who sells his power at £1.50 a time and his uncle dresses him up in a flashy suit. I suppose from Danny's point of view it's as if he encountered the childhood innocence just before the story of the film itself.

MO: Have you got any other projects going?
NJ: Channel 4 would like me to do another film. Basically I would like to do another film on a roughly similar budget to attempt to do it a little better this time. I've several scripts written and several things outlined. One is a historical subject which could be very expensive and difficult to get finance for, but which I hope to do someday. But in the near future, I hope to do a film on roughly the same budget and the same kind of set-up that we've used in this case, maybe I'll be shooting it in the spring. I'd also love to do a children's film, a pantomime or musical which takes the world of forties and fifties music and transposes it into outer space. It's about a young girl, a tap dancer, wandering around the universe looking for her father who was a comedian.

Beauty and the Beasts

Neil Jordan / 1984

From *Time Out* (September 13–19, 1984): 18–21. Reprinted by permission of Neil Jordan.

Novelist turned film director Neil Jordan describes the metamorphosis of Angela Carter's eleven-page short story "The Company of Wolves" into a full-length English Gothic horror movie.

"At night, the eyes of wolves shine like candle flames, yellowish, reddish, but that is because the pupils of their eyes fatten on darkness and catch the light from your lantern and flash it back to you—red for danger; if a wolf's eyes reflect only moonlight, then they gleam a cold and unnatural green, a mineral, a piercing color."

On the set we place a light box in front of the camera lens, with a pea-bulb encased in a two-way mirror, which throws the beam from the bulb towards the wolf's eyes, which indeed fatten on the darkness, catch the light, and flash it back to us. So the wolf's eyes gleam, sometimes red, sometimes yellow. All of which shows me that imaginative fiction can sometimes have the precision of science.

It was this precision that first drew me to the story. Angela Carter had been commissioned by Channel 4 to write a short script based on her short story "The Company of Wolves." We had met, quite by accident, during a week of festivities in Dublin to celebrate the centenary of James Joyce. Jorge Luis Borges read a speech to a thousand or so of Dublin's finest in a plush hotel. No one seemed to know who he was. Halfway through, a Ceilidh band struck up next door, drowning him out completely. No one seemed to notice. I asked the head of the Irish Tourist Board to get the band turned off, and found myself thrown out on the street. Angela had wandered through this baroque extravaganza in a state of bemused wonder. I remember a night's drinking with an Irish lecturer in mediaeval philosophy and a gay priest, the conversation of which consisted mainly of a discourse on farting and the problems of erections on buses. And Angela proved herself to be a model of tact in the face of these, and other, manifestations of the national temperament.

A week after that, her script arrived. It was quite short, but all the splendor of her story rippled off it. A series of tales told to a small girl by a wonderfully wicked granny, all culminating in her own encounter with the legend of Red Riding Hood; sensual and brutal, like the fairy tale you dreamed of as a child, but were never told.

I brought the script to Steve Woolley of Palace, who rapidly put together a development deal which allowed for a fuller script to be written, and some preparatory production work. I came to London and cycled out to Angela's house in Clapham every morning, where we would spend the day on the script.

We would drink large quantities of tea, and proceed through the script in quite a businesslike manner. I was reminded of the surrealist painter Magritte who would dress impeccably each morning, pack his briefcase, kiss his wife goodbye, then walk round the block, return home and begin to work. Angela maintains a similar sense of order, a certain Scots puritan rigor which belies the wicked nature of her work. The script began to sizzle after a while, like an old stew. The whole world of fairy tale proved to be of infinite suggestiveness. Little Red Riding Hood led us towards intimations of Tom Thumb, which led via Beauty and the Beast back to Little Red Riding Hood.

"A witch from up the valley once turned an entire wedding party into wolves because the groom had settled on another girl."

It was fascinating to me how an allusion like that, just part of the texture of the story, could become a whole sequence in the script. One tries to picture the valley, muses on the look of that wedding-party, expand on the tale of the groom, spoilt scion of the landed classes and the peasant girl he wronged, her bewitching pleasures and the pale, hemophiliac visage of the bride he chose.

Writing is normally an isolated process, quite painful most of the time, and it is only when you work with another mind that you realize how exhilarating it actually is, stretching the imagination like a set of unused muscles. After a while, though the pattern of the day maintained the same order, the script lost all touch with common decency.

It became gothic and sensual, acquired a special kind of horror. Images began to come from nowhere, lurid and illogical, but somehow perfect for the tale. Though Angela was pregnant at the time, I didn't realize it, until after two or three weeks we took a cold look at the finished script and found that almost every episode contained a pregnancy.

So I had a script then, which I took to Palace. They liked it and Woolley began the game of finding the finance. If it isn't quite a game, he approached it as one. There are probably a total of nine or ten sources in the whole of Britain for real film finance and Woolley adopted the sensible tactic of approaching them all at once.

Wolves are shy creatures, difficult to get a coherent reaction from and dangerously unpredictable. Just at the point you think you have gained their confidence, they turn and bite your arm off. Not too different, really, from the kinds of people who put money into films—their reactions impossible to gauge, their decisions quite unpredictable, and just when you think they're eating morsels from your palm, you get bitten. Meetings are the order of the day, meetings where prevarication is generally expressed through comment upon the script, or by discussion of that unpronounceable French concept, genre. In the meetings about "The Company of Wolves," though, I realized that we were blessed with luck, for we had a script that had an inbuilt resistance to any kind of comment. It was a deeply irrational piece of work, outlandish in the way the story moved and simple to the point of naivety in its characters. Quite mad, perhaps, in the end. And madness has the characteristic of either convincing totally, or not at all. So we were spared those endless delays that could so easily take the freshness from a project.

"The forest closed upon her like a pair of jaws . . ."

Anton Furst is a designer who has done things as various as London's first hologram shows and the eggs in *Alien*. Like many people now working in the British film industry, he is a combination of fastidious technical expertise and a roving, eclectic visual sensibility.

We needed to create a forest for the film, a forest that would have the sensual detail and wonder a child could respond to and was yet immense and brooding, like a cathedral of huge limbs. People who work steadily in large-budget films suffer from a kind of madness, the madness that comes from too much work in too little time, and the results that are too intangible for all that expense of effort. Anton assembled a team of people who worked mainly on large-budget American films, but relished the chance of doing something more personal—creating a fabricated landscape using old-fashioned studio techniques to make effects as convincing as those nowadays done with blue-screen or matte-work.

We had to make the forests and the dwellings of the film awaken as many associations as the story did itself. We began to sift through reproductions of Breughel, Gustav Dore, Richard Dadd, and Piranesi, making a kind of rapid dash through the history of European painting, and found our bible in Samuel Palmer, a humble British exponent of the art. There was a quiet madness to his landscape, the trees swollen erotically, a church spire listing slightly to one side, as if melting under the painter's gaze.

Since our budget was limited, we decided to spend most of it on the trunks of the trees, creating the illusion that they were soaring to a sky that can rarely be seen. We could afford eight or so three-dimensional trees, with assorted stumps and root structures thrown in. We built these on rollers, so they could be moved at will to create different areas, the illusion of space being created by a combination of cut-outs, dioramas, and painted backings. The tale came to find itself repeated in the shapes of the forest. We built a well, like a remnant from some lost age, in the center of the village. The well acquired levers, strange hydraulic arms, shafts that stretched into the bowels of the earth, which seemed propelled by some secret principle of perpetual motion—such a good well, in fact, that it cried out for an episode all to itself, which Angela and myself duly wrote.

"That long-drawn, wavering howl has, for all its fearful resonance, some inherent sadness in it, as if the beasts would love to be less beastly if only they knew how and never cease to mourn their own condition."

The transformations as described in Angela's story have a sadness about them, and a sensuality as if the heroes cannot resist that wolf inside them, and as if the wolf always longs to be human again. Christopher Tucker, a onetime opera singer with a fascination for pathological diseases and a genius for animatronic effects, was in charge of them. It was here that the largest problems lay, since we had to execute three major transformation scenes, each of which had to satisfy an audience already primed by *An American Werewolf in London,* the central sequence of which took nine months to prepare. We had to avoid that hybrid, the werewolf, and somehow simulate the transformation of a man into an actual wolf. We had also to avoid that delight in repulsion that special effects films indulge in.

The imagery in films like *Alien* and *The Thing* conveys a very deep hatred of sexuality, a pathological disgust with the human form. This is possibly because the most obvious use of animatronic effects—a term which basically means the building of articulated dolls and models to simulate real actors—is to tear the human shape to shreds, to have heads burst like melons and chests explode, releasing the gore which covers a multitude. *The Company of Wolves* was to be about sex, not about hating it. A wolf that crawls out of the skin of a man covered in various red and yellow liquids wouldn't hold much attraction for a thirteen-year-old girl. So we began to study Leonardo's anatomical drawings, Francis Bacon's portraits of screaming heads, and saw that the muscular structures underneath the skin can have a kind of beauty. We began a series of tests which involved peeling skin, the muscles revealed beneath it precise and visible, or a mouth open in an anguished cry and a wolf emerging through it.

"She is an unbroken egg; she is a sealed vessel; she has inside her a magic space, the entrance to which is shut tight with a plug of membrane; she is a closed system; she does not know how to shiver. She has her knife and she is afraid of nothing."

We began shooting soon after Christmas. Neither myself or the producers had any experience of studio filming. What was a delicate, tight story of eleven pages had three sound studios at Shepperton and two full camera crews. The whole thing seemed as innocent as the heroine, which was a great advantage since only a kind of benign ignorance could carry you through, with problems so outlandish and a budget so tight. The real delight, though, lay in the mixture of artistry and technical expertise that British camera, design, and special effects crews brought with them. In a world where a Covent Garden baritone can end up designing monsters, I suppose anything can happen.

Since each episode in the script demanded its own fresh environment, the rapid turnaround of sets meant that a whole new set of problems presented themselves before the lethargy set in. To move the camera at all demanded meticulous redressing of the sets, and a microcosmic examination of the holes behind them. To coax a wolf out of a well, over a bridge, or on to the bough of a tree seemed to take days. For a scene that involved thirteen wolves dressed in immaculate eighteenth-century costumes we first tried to move the wolves, kept by a gypsy in Nottingham, down to the studio. On the way, however, one of the wolves was eaten by the others. We then built a cage and tranquilized several of them, on the presumption that we could dress them while they slept, then observe the great effect of their waking—tearing their elegant clothes off and leaping to freedom. After twelve hours, however, they had merely shifted and yawned.

The schedule you set up, though, and even the problems it gives rise to soon develops its own momentum. The texture you are looking for becomes common property, the precise mixture of sensuality and savagery so beautifully conveyed in Angela's story becomes a hidden password to success or failure. When that essence isn't there, one knows very rapidly the set-up isn't working and moves on to something else.

"Naked, she combed out her hair with her fingers; her hair looked white as the snow outside. Then went directly to the man with red eyes in whose unkempt mane the lice moved; she stood up on tiptoe and unbuttoned the collar of his shirt. What big arms you have . . ."

From the first, we had wanted to use the resources that are normally the exclusive preserve of big American productions, to subvert them and put them to the service of a fantasy that is as rich as the fairy-tales themselves. Beauty and The Beast can teach something about life, but not much about morality. The sugar-sweet coating that Disney and, more lately, George Lucas's generation have given to such material is in many ways akin to the way the Victorians, and even the Brothers Grimm, tamed the brutalities and washed out the sensuality of their sources. Angela Carter's instincts are far more iconoclastic than that and, in the end, probably far truer. When we showed the finished film to the censors, though, we found the absence of a moral lesson created some outrage. A film with little nudity and less sex was seen as an erotic enticement to teenage girls. Image after image from the film was banned by the London Transport Authority. We had to content ourselves with an 18 certificate, though the film was made with a teenage audience in mind.

I was used to the puritanism of the Irish censors, to that odd mixture of moral rectitude and monkish insistence in seeing a sexual dimension to objects as innocuous as the needle of a compass. I had assumed those battles had been won in Britain, but it seems that somewhere between the battles against video nasties and against the advertising campaign for Pretty Polly tights, a few freedoms are quietly sinking.

Wolf at the Door

Steve Jenkins and Paul Taylor / 1984

From *Monthly Film Bulletin*, September 1984, 264–65, published by the British Film Institute. Reprinted by permission.

Down in the Woods

Neil Jordan: I met Steve Woolley when he was keen to distribute *Angel* after seeing it in Cannes. He told me that Palace wanted to get into production and that he would like to see anything I was thinking of doing. Then Walter Donohue of Channel 4 commissioned a series of short films, about fifty minutes or so, one of which was an adaptation by Angela Carter of her story "The Company of Wolves." I had met Angela briefly when I won the *Guardian* prize in 1979 and she was on the jury, and then again in Dublin during a centenary week for the birth of James Joyce. So I showed her script to Steve Woolley and spoke to Angela, whom I'd already talked to about films, and we thought of ways of making it into a larger feature film. Steve then got the development money and we sat down and wrote the script quite quickly, in about two or three weeks.

The single most important factor that drew me to Angela's work—which to me is like nothing else—is that it's both so dramatic and so graphic. She has this iconoclastic, very steely intelligence, which I don't often find now in writers. She's an intellectual in the old sense, from the twenties and thirties. But she also has this incredibly fertile imagination and thinks very strongly in terms of imagery. The first script was full of things like "a man turns into a wolf in front of his family, he gets his head chopped off and it falls into a bucket and comes up as his own head." You just don't find that sort of thing very often in British movies. That script was quite a direct transposition of the story. If you take a short story and put the narrative down as a screenplay, you get one thing. But if you look at all the little bits in between the sentences, the atmospheres and the tiny bits of description and the references, you get other things. I was really trying to pull out these little things that Angela just hinted at, saying, "Well, couldn't this be a big sequence?" It was very instructive with regard to the way that people adapt things, which is usually scaling down rather than up, because the story is only a few pages. She says things like "It was rumored once that a witch walked into a wedding party and turned the entire village into wolves." In the film that became an entire sequence.

We found the shape—of stories within stories, and the portmanteau device of the girl dreaming—and then we built the script up by association. Instead of the forest meaning danger, the wolf meaning sexuality, and the granny authority, we tried to let images and types of stories come to us in an associative way, and follow them for the pleasure of it. I think that the meaning emerges from the pleasure, rather than in any straight-forward interpretative way. I particularly wanted to avoid that rather obvious, pedestrian approach. When I was a kid, the pleasure I got from Disney films, or from *Night of the Hunter* or *The Wizard of Oz*, was more to do with recognition than interpretation. We tried to build each set so that it reminded you of something you had seen but weren't quite sure what it was. You feel that you're visiting somewhere that you've been before, like Hansel and Gretel's cottage. In that sense, I wanted the culmination of the film to be the recognition that this is the story of Little Red Riding Hood. Angela had built her original story around that, and she had alluded to werewolf lore at the beginning and end of it. We also took a bit from a story of hers called "Wolf Alice," and I drew a lot of images from my novel *Dream of a Beast*, which I'd just finished; things like the little babies coming out of the eggs, some of the stranger imagery.

I also wanted to play a game with the perceptions of the audience, in the sense that you are led through one sequence, and think you are at home, and then someone tells a story and you go into another world, and so on. I wanted it to be like a puzzle which people would enjoy in the way that they enjoy unraveling a thriller. It may be that people are very literal-minded nowadays and don't allow themselves to take straight sensual pleasure from things. For example, when we were doing the music with George Fenton, we tried to construct the score so that at certain points—like when the girl is running through the forest—you could just sit back and eat it up. With a lot of the sequences, we were just trying to wring the sensual pleasure out of them.

It's quite difficult to know how to end a film like this. Originally we had the idea that the girl just woke from the dream and it was a proper waking up. But with this kind of fantasy film, it's a little bit boring for her just to wake up and go downstairs. Then we had another thought, that she woke up, dived through the floor, and vanished. But that was very difficult to realize in concrete terms. So then I shot the ending we have now, which is actually more in keeping with the rest of the film, with the dogs coming through the house and the wolf jumping through the painting. But if you go for the spectacle and that emotional feeling, the problem is that it does get confused. If you just go back to the Alsatian scratching at the door and the girl waking up and letting the dog in, at least people could say, "Ah, it's ended now." But I wanted to make it an ambiguous ending, with the final scream and the poem—which I'd always wanted to use—and the girl's voice to strengthen the ambiguity. I didn't want the film to end with the girl under threat; it's a liberation in a way.

Back in the Studio

All along, everybody felt that it should be a studio film. In the end it was a matter of logistics. You have to play a wait and see game in that regard. I mean, if we had found an extraordinary forest . . . I did actually look, and the only one that was close to it was down in Lyme Regis, with strange trees and pools, but then one wouldn't have been able to light it properly. The fact that you don't return to the "real" world was scripted from the start. It was written so that there were just trees leading up to a real house, and then a nightmare sequence in a fantasy forest, with large mushrooms and teddy bears and things like that. And then there was a forest which was out of a Grimm's fairy-tale, which at a push could have been real, if you had had a lot of money and it happened to snow. But in the end, when I began to work with Anton Furst, the designer, and we began to enlarge the whole thing conceptually, it was clear that he could realize things much better with the studio look than by using a combination of studio and the real thing.

I wanted to do it with a bit of cheek really. It was the feeling of, why do Americans have all the fun? Why are they allowed to have people's eyebrows pop out, and people going into space, while over here we have to film people on the streets? I wanted to make a film that had all the production values of those American films, but that was actually subversive, that offered a more intelligent and perhaps more real pleasure. The question of whether it would be commercial or not never really arose except at the level of the effects. The effects had to be hugely satisfying, and they had to be things you had not seen before. And the sets and the feeling of the forest had to be immense and full of wonder. But if it didn't work as a story, there was something wrong. Because if you examine the films that are actually breaking ground visually and technically, their content is terribly depressing isn't it? Hugely clever people like Spielberg and Lucas have brought back the story—with a beginning, a middle, and an end—with such a bang. And I think that's a little bit depressing. So I wanted the film to have the visual challenge of the American films, but also to be narratively rich and full and adventurous.

We had no generic sense of it in terms of cinema while we were writing it. I didn't want to have any sense of reference for it. When you are writing, particularly in Ireland, everything is referenced to something else. People talk about their influences before they've written a line. I went into making films hoping that it was free of all that, and suddenly you find that there's even more of this baggage to take with you. That does bother me quite a bit. Genre is a critical way of looking at films, but it's also a way of marketing them, and I would like this film to help free people from those straitjackets. It's odd that nowadays every film has to belong to a genre. *Angel*, despite what people said, wasn't a film noir. It was a story of revenge, but stylistically it was very brightly lit, very colorful.

If you look at silent movies, where a lot of people came into film from theatre, acting, and different disciplines, they didn't really create the genres as we know them now. That happened in the thirties and forties. And when the cine-literate generation came along and began to tear films apart, they did it in terms of genre again. Godard was always referring to different types of movie. Now they're doing it in America. Ridley Scott made a haunted house movie in space, and George Lucas made a Second World War aeroplane movie in space, and they are quite simple transpositions of things. But I think if you got someone who knew very little about films, or who had seen only silent films, and they made a movie, you wouldn't be able to tie it to any genre. So for us, the early silent horror films, and the sets they used to build at UFA, were an influence, but atmospherically rather than generically. There's a bit of *Night of the Hunter*, but it's not a matter of references. It's just using devices that were used there, like people being looked at by little creatures. If you were to make a film that referred to "Beauty and the Beast," you'd be invoking the fairy-tale rather than the Cocteau film version of it. And that was the real reference: fairy-tales.

Sweetness and Light

Jonathan Romney / 1990

From *City Limits*, May 31–June 7, 1990, 16–17. Reprinted by permission of the author.

When his debut feature *Angel* was released in 1982, Irish director Neil Jordan found his colors being nailed, by default, to a tentative "British Renaissance," fuelled by Channel 4's modest coffers. *Angel*—cofounded by Channel 4 and the Irish Film Board—saw Jordan bracketed with such diverse non-novices as Peter Greenaway, Jack Gold, Mike Leigh, and Stephen Frears as one of the supposed "new" hopes. They've gone in wildly different directions since—Frears to be an international journeyman of mixed repute, Leigh to plough his determinedly solitary furrow, Greenaway to be even more obsessively Greenaway . . .

But four films later, still no one's sure what to make of Jordan. With his new film *We're No Angels*, he seems to have settled quite contentedly into a Hollywood niche, reaping the benefits of a star cast (Robert De Niro, Sean Penn, Demi Moore), a prestige script (David Mamet), and modestly De Mille-esque production values. In time-honored style, he's lost a fair measure of his personal touch in the process. It's more fuel to his detractors, who claim he was never so hot in the first place, but this fading of identity has taken time, and with each new film, you've had to strain to remind yourself just who Neil Jordan is, and why his career's been such a strange one.

For a start, there's a paradox of this Sligo man being generally cited as an example of the odd fate of *British* directors, a result not only of the "Film on 4" connection, but of the overtly English nature of the films that followed *Angel*—a deceptively fey version of Angela Carter's fireside fable "The Company of Wolves," and *Mona Lisa*, with its Dantean vision of London's low-life inferno and its projection of the definitive Bob Hoskins persona. Perhaps it was a surfeit of Englishness that persuaded Jordan to return to Irish imagery, although in the event, he did it in the most disastrous way possible, with *High Spirits*, a grotesque and embarrassing Auld Country romp that makes Jordan wince when you mention it.

Stranger still, he's an unlikely candidate to be working in movies at all, since he made his name as a writer, winning the Guardian Fiction Prize in 1979 with his collection of somberly impressionistic stories *Night in Tunisia*, as overt a homage to Joyce's *Dubliners* as you could find. That was followed by two novels, *The Past* and *The Dream of a Beast*, the latter crystallizing his talent as a miniaturist with a flair for disturbing and ambiguous fine detail—something that's scarce indeed in *We're No Angels*.

So why has a contemplative, ironically inclined literary cove like himself made a glossy production like *We're No Angels*?

Trailing stray threads, Jordan attempts to shrug himself into the shirt and out of the "Hollywood director" role. "It's important to me to work with comparative freedom, I wouldn't like to become a Hollywood director. I wouldn't want to be stuck there . . ." His relationship with Hollywood has been ambivalent to say the least—a trip there to sell the idea of *High Spirits* resulted in a wittily bitter narrative poem for *Producer* magazine. Today, as befits the promotional task at hand, he's equivocal.

"Well, it's a rather generous place, and it's a merciless place, it loves you and it hates you. But if you want to make movies on a certain scale you *have* to go there. Even if you spend your life making films like *Sammy and Rosie* or *Mona Lisa*, you have to have some relationship with it—you can't have a budget of two or three million pounds without getting an American sale or an American partner."

For *We're No Angels*, Jordan built a monumental outdoor set—a plankboard shanty town, complete with a thickset whitewood monastery—from scratch in British Columbia, an upmarket echo of Robert Altman's creation for *McCabe and Mrs. Miller*. The film carries a sense of place, certainly, but at the cost of dwarfing its actors.

This is the first product Jordan has accepted as a straight commission. The film was already conceived as a vehicle for Penn and De Niro—Jordan had already approached the latter for a possible version of Dashiell Hammett's *Red Harvest*—and came complete with a David Mamet script. Jordan happened to find the concept right up his alley.

"I was very surprised that a script like that should have come from Los Angeles, and from David Mamet as well—it dealt with Catholicism, Madonnas—and that it dealt with *sweetness* to a certain extent. I connect his work with a lot of savagery, with dark premises leading to even darker conclusions, and this was like a little fable. There were themes that I'd dealt with before myself. It was very melodramatic in its shape, it had a Madonna that wept, a deaf girl that spoke, two convicts with bruised exteriors and warm interiors, a whore with a heart of gold . . . so I decided to do it."

"Sweetness" is clearly a quality close to Jordan's heart. "Robert De Niro's the best actor of his generation, and a very sweet man to work with. He's obviously a big star, and there's procedures that follow big stars around on Hollywood movies, but it was a good experience. Sean is a more a . . . *brooding* personality, but he's got a lot of sweetness that has never emerged, that the world at large has never perceived, and I wanted him to play that sort of person, who has a sweetness inside that he didn't even know existed."

Unfortunately, *We're No Angels* overdoses on sweetness, with a tear-jerking, redemptive conclusion, and its unshakeable belief (is this *really* David Mamet?) in people's deep-down niceness. This is not a carry-over from the 1955 Humphrey Bogart film of the same name, whose central premise (runaway crooks get mistaken for priests) it shares. "It's *not* a re-make," Jordan insists, "it's just using the title. The basic idea of two convicts grappling with goodness, that's all there is to it, in a way."

But there's something strangely amiss with the handling of this simple premise. It's close enough to the tawdry drag dramatics of *Nuns on the Run*, but where Idle and Coltrane wholeheartedly don habits and post-Python shrieks to pass as "such devoted sisters," Penn and De Niro never for a second stop acting like lamebrained hard cases, furrowing their brows and jutting their jaws in a clumsy approximation of what two tough cons might do if *half-heartedly* posing as priests. In terms of narrative (these guys are running for their *lives*, for god's sake), it makes no sense, and the one-dimensional acting blows the joke entirely. Unless, of course, it's calculated ambiguity?

"Well . . ." Jordan argues, "most of the humor comes from the fact that they make no attempt whatsoever to behave like priests. But it's one of those scripts where if you don't accept the premise, then you don't accept the movie. But, having accepted the premise, the film is about different things. It started as a genre movie, like *I Was a Fugitive from a Chain Gang*, a prison escape film, then it becomes a film about mistaken identity, then it becomes a fable. And the critics that haven't accepted the movie haven't been able to accept that kind of movement. Which surprises me, because mostly large budget films operate on the simplest of premises, which is why a lot of them are so bad, because they follow one simple high concept line."

But the problem with *Angels* is precisely that it settles for one "high concept" line—two tough guys in skirts, the oldest gag in the Good Book. Jordan's problem seems to be that he starts out with high intentions about genre-juggling, and then—perhaps because genre doesn't *really* exist in movies any more—the intentions get lost, as does the joke.

"I've been playing with different genres. *Angel* is a thriller and a musical, *Company of Wolves* is a horror film and a fantasy, *Mona Lisa* is a love story and a film noir, *High Spirits* was *meant* to be a lot of things . . ."

Mmm, yes, *High Spirits*, Jordan's Waterloo. Made under the auspices of British production house Palace, but defiantly Hollywood in its appeal, this frenetic necrophilic romp starred inelegant American leads (Steve Guttenberg, Daryl Hannah, Beverly D'Angelo), tossed in a little "authentic" Irish spice (Peter O'Toole, Mary Couglan), and became a farcical farrago about a rip-roaring, peat-sotted Haunted Ireland that could have been seen as offensive tourist stereotyping, if it weren't so crass. A prize example of Jordan's genre-mixing misfiring, it was an own goal in every sense, and its director seems fated to sigh in despair whenever it's mentioned.

"I'd like to recut it and see if there was a film there. I was actually striving for something rather elegant, believe it or not, and it turned out to be the noisiest film ever made, every minute was a crash. But basically it was cut to shreds. As conceived, there was a logic to every character, but as it ended up there was very little logic to it at all.

"It was a very risky thing to do, that's one of the reasons I did it—the basic joke being you have a bunch of Irish people making themselves comic figures to Americans, and the Americans are cardboard figures to these Irish people. But what the film seems to be about now is a bunch of Americans coming to a strange little place where there are a bunch of thinly drawn Irish characters . . ."

Although he swears that *High Spirits* was well liked in Ireland, it would seem to provide ground for a general mistrust of Jordan in his own country—and ill-feeling that set in when he first got into movies, by way of a "creative consultancy" on John Boorman's *Excalibur*.

"I found it was like committing an original sin with the Irish literary community. Films have always been regarded as the worst slumming for writers—Scott Fitzgerald lost his sanity in Hollywood, and Faulkner used to take the money and run—so it was regarded as the grossest form of betrayal. And no one had made a feature film there for a long time, so the film community was outraged that a writer should presume to do that.

"I'm regarded as an anomaly because the things I do are rather personal, but they're seen to be rather big and to belong to the world of Hollywood and international finance. I'd like to produce some things over there for younger filmmakers but I'm regarded as a rather dangerous figure to mess around with."

Now based in Dublin again, Jordan feels ready to complete work on his next novel, which till now has been interrupted by transatlantic shiftlessness. He's also ready to work on a smaller scale again, on a film that premises a return to the more distinctive idiosyncrasies of *Angel*. "It's a small film about sex, a bit like those stories in *Night in Tunisia*. It's an oedipal tale about incest. It's rather dark, and the whole thing happens in a series of unraveling dreams."

Unraveling dreams may after all be Jordan's forte. If not the lurid nightmares of *High Spirits*, or the too-wakeful fancifulness of *We're No Angels*, then at least the febrile, skewed realism of *Angel* or *Mona Lisa* . . . And now seems the right time for him to step off the Hollywood ladder, and return to working out a personal style that seems to have been stifled in its development. "I know it would seem," he says, building an invisible ladder, "that I've done small, larger, *larger*, LARGER . . . There are certain dangers in that, which is one of the reasons I'm going back to doing a tiny film."

And if that suggests that Jordan's niche is as an art-house director, a parochial visionary, maybe the fine-tuned observations of his written fiction bear that out in a way that the generously but impersonally ladled-on sweetness of *We're No Angels* doesn't. What is clear, though—and pretty encouraging—is that Neil Jordan is a director who still has everything left to prove.

Neil Jordan's Guilty Pleasures

Neil Jordan / 1992

From *Film Comment* 28, no. 6 (November 1992): 36–39. Reprinted by permission of Neil Jordan.

When I was a kid I grew up in a rather strict Catholic household in Dublin. I saw a lot of religious films—that was all I was allowed to see. I was brought along to *The Robe, King of Kings, Samson and Delilah*. I remember only fragments: Victor Mature demolishing an entire cast with the jawbone of an ass . . . They probably made a dreadful confusion in my mind between the church and movies.

The Song of Bernadette is religious kitsch taken to its ultimate extreme. It concluded with a scene of a lot of French peasants climbing up a hill on which the Virgin was supposed to have appeared. Jennifer Jones played this young girl who had seen an apparition of the Virgin Mary; nobody believed her except the local curate. Every time I see it, it moves me without me wanting to be moved; it has this kind of disgraceful effect, probably because I saw it so young. It's a film that's basically like those trashy kitsch pictures of Jesus. It gets me every time.

There was also a Spanish movie from the fifties, *Marcelino/Bread and Wine*; it was like *The First Communion Suit*, with the same kind of dreadfully exploitive effect. There was this boy whose only private pleasure was to go into church and the statue of Jesus would come down off the cross and wrap his arms around him. He would have private conversations with this statue. When I saw it as a kid, it actually terrified the life out of me.

Whistle Down the Wind, directed by Bryan Forbes, also belongs in this category of religious films we were all trooped out to see in school. When I was a kid, Hayley Mills—a sexier version of Judy Garland, really—did a whole string of films like *The Family Way*. She plays one of these kids who find this tramp (Alan Bates) and think he's Jesus. It's a very affecting film.

In Cannes a few years ago I saw a film not a lot of people have seen called *Therese*. It's a French movie, shot by Philippe Rousellot, and I think it's the best piece of photography I've seen in my life. It was all done in a very spare, theatrical way, as if it were theater, and the atmosphere was great. It's based around a real saint, Saint Therese of the Little Flower or something, in nineteenth-century France. This poor unfortunate man had about eight daughters, and one after the other they joined a nunnery. The director, Alain Cavalier, made a genuinely erotic film about all these women in this nunnery who had the same lover, Jesus Christ. He gave it an edge of eroticism that was quite extraordinary: you'd see these nuns wake up in the morning and say to each other, "Did he visit you last night?" and one of them would give a secret smile of pleasure, as if this creature had crept into her bed and spent the entire night with her. The others would be like, "You bitch, what the fuck is this—where is He?" It was done so beautifully and subversively, and reminded me of the effect those other films had on me when I was a child.

Darby O'Gill and the Little People: one of the first films Sean Connery was in. It's Disney, a piece of Irish kitsch, part of that vogue for Celtic, misty kind of things, like *Brigadoon* (although that was Scottish). Sean Connery played a young man who transgressed some rule or other, and this leprechaun (Jimmy O'Dea) appeared to him. And there was a banshee, a ghost that announces the death of somebody in a community—this magnificent green creature who would appear in the Irish landscape at night and howl. That is my first memory of a truly horrific, frightening experience in the cinema. And it was the first time I became aware of special effects. It's actually quite a good movie. I took it out before I did *High Spirits* to watch it again and was surprised. Connery was a bodybuilder at the time and he sang this song . . .

The Rising of the Moon: I love John Ford's Westerns, but I could never stand those bits of Irishery he'd shove into them. They always irritated me because the movies were so great and these bits of light relief stuck out like a sore thumb. He came to Ireland with the Abbey Players in the fifties and did this film that was three little vignettes based on Irish stories and plays. The central one, based on a Percy French song, was called "A Minute's Wait"; it's about this train that never takes off from the station and never gets to where it should be. This was one time Ford's Irish sentimentality paid off for me. A couple of years ago I tried to search it out in Hollywood; somebody managed to get their hands on a print and

I looked at it with [English producer] Steve Woolley, again when I was doing *High Spirits*. It's wonderful.

I've got two daughters, and there was a period when I began to get out films for them when they were between the ages of seven and fourteen. I developed a great affection for *National Velvet, Meet Me in St. Louis*, and all those films Molly Ringwald made with John Hughes, especially *Pretty in Pink*. It was a genre of movie almost like the stories you get in girls' magazines, all about roleplaying among adolescent girls, and dresses and teenage angst. They raise these issues and then don't do anything with them. I actually began to admire them—I thought Molly Ringwald was so perfect. In *Pretty in Pink* Harry Dean Stanton played her father and she had to make her own pink dress; it was so clever in a kind of horrible way. Andrew McCarthy played this dreadful upper-middle-class twit who fell in love with her, and she didn't want him, and he turns out to have a good heart in the end and there's this awful cloying conclusion. I really thought it was a masterpiece of a certain kind of dreadful genre.

As my daughters grew older, the acme of the form was *Dirty Dancing*, a truly awful film. My youngest used to watch that bloody thing endlessly, and as I watched it I actually began to appreciate certain qualities in it: basically it's a subdued sex movie, a piece of very effective and well-disguised porn, and parts of it aren't that bad. The girl who's from the wrong side of the tracks has an abortion and Patrick Swayze helps her, and you've got all those confusions, and they all end up happy.

As for movies from my own teens, I think *King Creole* with Elvis Presley, set in New Orleans, is very good. I was a big Elvis fan. *Catch Us If You Can*, directed by John Boorman, is a fascinating mixture of the good, the bad, and the trashy. It had the Dave Clark Five and some young model from the mid-sixties. It was John's first movie, released in the States under the title *Having a Wild Weekend*—a kind of teen journey through what was presented as the superficiality of English upper-middle-class life. They were looking for some idyllic mythical place, and reached what they thought was an island. At the end the sea retreated and they found it was connected to the mainland after all. Very John Boorman; a lot of the things he's been trying to express lately are there in an unstrained form—though he could never get Dave Clark to act.

I often feel it would be great if there was a category or genre of filmmaking that was like pornography but not quite porn: the erotic movie, the equivalent of the painter's nude—a perfectly acceptable subject to address as a painter, the female or the male form presented in an erotic light. *La Marge/The Streetwalker* is with Sylvia Kristel and Joe Dallesandro and was directed by Walerian Borowczyk, who made *Blanche*, a very beautiful medieval movie, quite a respectable arthouse piece of work. *La Marge* was a pornographic film basically, but done by a master. Every now and then he'd cut to an old lady staring through a keyhole at Sylvia Kristel's goings-on. It bears looking at, a good example of the genre that could be, if the categories of censorship allowed it.

I once saw a Japanese movie when I was about fourteen or fifteen which I've never been able to trace. It was shown in Dublin under the title *The Lost Sex*. A superb melodramatic story about a Kabuki actor who had been wounded in Hiroshima and had lost his virility, and in between bouts being a star of the Kabuki theater, he'd go to this tiny village. His housekeeper was a woman who never spoke to him, after whom he lusted, though like the Hemingway hero in *The Sun Also Rises*, who has a war wound so he can't have sex. The housekeeper tells him about a village custom that happens every year, where every woman in the town stays at home, every man goes out and wears a mask, and in disguise they can creep into the bed of whomever they want. So he puts on this mask and dresses up, creeps into her house, and makes love to her—when he's disguised he can actually have sex, there's a great irony in that. But while he's having sex she mentions the name of somebody else, whereupon he gets instantly jealous and retreats. Apparently we're meant to believe the woman doesn't know who he is. She comes in to clean his house the next morning, and they're looking at each other in this wonderfully pregnant way. Eventually he's driven mad with jealousy by this name she whispered in her sleep; he becomes very cruel and fires her. He goes back to Tokyo and doesn't return for several years. He returns to find that she's dead, and he asks about this ritual and people say, "Oh, that was an old tradition that died out fifty years ago:" So he realizes that she knew all along. It's a terrific love story.

The Barefoot Contessa opens with a magnificent, beautifully set-up scene of an Italian graveyard, with all these umbrellas, and Humphrey Bogart standing in the background talking about this elusive woman who turns out to be Ava Gardner. It's a wonderful piece of Europe reinvented by Hollywood. It's also got a castrated Italian count who's been war-wounded, like *The Lost Sex*. It's one of my great pleasures, every time I see it. It means absolutely nothing; it's like an epic without a subject and without a style, but with the longing to be a great piece of epic storytelling. But there's nothing there whatsoever except the desire to create that feeling.

Trapeze: I think the one director who hasn't been revived sufficiently is Carol Reed. I love circus movies like Cecil B. DeMille's *The Greatest Show on Earth* and even Alexander Kluge's *Artistes at the Top of the Big Top: Disoriented*, a very labored allegory. It's just something of mine—every time I see a circus in a film, I can't resist it. I just thought *Trapeze* was the best circus movie I'd ever seen. The way Reed photographed the trapeze sequences was extraordinary, and of course Burt Lancaster was a circus artist originally. And it had Tony Curtis in tights, and Gina Lollobrigida. Again, obviously a piece of pure kitsch about these two performers and the woman who comes between them, and it all ends in tragedy. I took it out to watch it again when I was doing *The Miracle*.

Another movie Reed made that I liked was *Outcast of the Islands*. It's a bit like that British fascination with its imperial outland. Trevor Howard drifts into this area in the South Seas and goes native, falls in love with this native woman. Quite an amazing portrayal of emotional obsession. Both wonderful films that aren't seen that often.

I like nonsense in films, films that approach nonsense verse like Edward Lear: "Last night as I went up the stair/I met a man who was not there/He was not there again today/I wish, I wish he'd go away."

I'm a big Minnelli fan. *Ziegfeld Follies*—not one of his best films at all—has a magnificent sequence in which Judy Garland plays this starlet who's being interviewed about her current plans, and she's been asked to do a film about the woman in Belgium who invented the safety pin— as if she's been asked to be in *The Barefoot Contessa*, a serious Hollywood movie about Europe. She does this number in her dressing room, the most sublime bit of nonsense I've ever heard: this song turns into scat halfway through, this kind of wonderfully empty-headed jazz. You find a lot of sublime nonsense in musicals.

Beat the Devil is a great piece of nonsense where you can see all these lovely actors going through a totally nonsensical plot that for some reason is totally gripping. They're in this splendid location, an Italian hotel with a lozenge-patterned floor. *Cry-Baby* is also great nonsense, and a great American musical. Terrific jailhouse scene.

The Night They Raided Minsky's: now that is a film that is rubbish—but I like it. A kind of backstage musical. It was obviously so cheap, and they created a sense of the period by cutting in black-and-white stock footage. Norman Wisdom was in it, with this tall guy who did this fall-down act. When I was a kid, my favorite actor was Norman Wisdom. I used to go and see every film he was in. Always cried. He mugged dreadfully. There was one where he was in love with a girl, he had to bring her something, there was this huge society do in a ballroom, he's in there and he does everything wrong, and the entire party stops: they're all laughing at him for his gaucheness, and then he makes this heartfelt speech about laughing at somebody like me. That is one of those childhood attachments that doesn't bear examining.

El Topo: a truly shameful pleasure out of the late sixties, ridiculous to like because it's actually dreadful. That strain of Pasolini madness taken to its ultimate, it's a Western set in some mythical terrain, probably somewhere in Mexico, and it basically ends in a blood feast. It means nothing and everything. A very bad movie, but I miss that kind of excess in contemporary filmmaking.

Celtic Dreamer

Marina Burke / 1993

From *Film Ireland* 34 (April/May 1993): 16–21.

Marina Burke: You have elsewhere described yourself as not a political filmmaker. But don't you think that the use of Northern Ireland as a background in *Angel* and *The Crying Game* is an implicit political statement in itself?

Neil Jordan: Yes it is, of course. I haven't anything particularly political to say, and I haven't any particular political solution even in my own mind. Most Irish people wind up jaded and a bit confused about the whole thing. Except that in this film, *The Crying Game*, I did want to make something that came out of the nationalist point of view. I wanted the Stephen Rea character to have a certain coherent set of beliefs. I didn't want him to be a psychopath. I didn't want him to be someone who was bruised by circumstances or whatever. I just wanted him to be someone who had a pretty good perspective himself, you know? So I suppose I wanted [him] to represent that aspect in the film.

MB: Was that film an extension of the story in *Angel*?

NJ: Yes. *Angel* was about that period around 1982 when all those sectarian killings were going on in the North and which mostly came out of the world of the UDF and the UDA. It was criticized here at the time for showing that the violence was kind of mindless. But I've never understood people's attitude towards that film, the way people criticized it.

MB: Actually I wouldn't have seen it like that at all. What struck me in the film was the way you were treating the violence there as a kind of nameless entity. You know, how there's a line in the film about violence—"it's evil, it's everywhere." It's all very nebulous, and even the investigating characters are very hard to place, very ambiguous.

NJ: I deliberately didn't make anything at all in *Angel* specific, because I wanted it to be about somebody who is increasingly taken over by the attraction of violence. I wrote the story for *The Crying Game* around 1983, but when I wrote the script [last year] it struck me that there were different realities at play and now there's a situation where, I suppose, the revisionist ethic is the one that everyone subscribes to.

MB: Well, nearly everybody.

NJ: Yeah, nearly everybody . . . well, "all right-thinking" people. Now there's a consensus that any sympathy with the nationalist community in Belfast or Derry or South Armagh, or wherever the case may be, is misplaced. There's a very strong sense of a witch hunt going on, that people are "fellow travellers" or whatever, you know what I mean? That's an equally erroneous assumption. I just wanted to see what was going on here. I wanted to see how the hell this Stephen Rea character would react if he was faced with the human consequences of what he was doing, if he was put face to face with any of his victims. But that's the extent of my politics.

MB: You're obviously aware of the situation?

NJ: I'm aware of course. But it's just an urge to tell the truth, that's all, and to look at the thing accurately. It's the most difficult thing to do in [these] circumstances.

MB: Yes, perhaps, but I found that the other IRA characters, the leader, and the woman in particular, were portrayed in very stereotyped terms as cold-blooded killers.

NJ: I didn't think they were stereotyped at all. I mean Adrian [Dunbar's character] was the person who could do what the Stephen Rea character couldn't do. He could allow himself to do things without considering the emotional consequences. He could follow the line and stick to it, as simple as that.

MB: Yes, the Stephen Rea character was the kind of sensitive one.

NJ: He wasn't particularly sensitive, he was just a human being. I mean he was the one who let himself become aware of the consequences of what he was doing. The film is not about the IRA, it's about other things too, different kinds of things.

MB: It's like two different films in fact, the Northern Ireland bit and the London bit.

NJ: It is, yeah, it's two different things. And one goes back to the other. In the first half there's a series of events, and in the second a rather similar series of events takes place, except they're in a totally different context to the first half.

MB: How do you mean?

NJ: Well, in the first half there's the kidnapping, and a kind of seduction between the two guys, and in the second half it's a similar situation between Fergus and the Dil character. He finds himself tied to the chair, he finds himself the recipient of violence. I wanted the second half to be a mirror of the first half.

MB: The portrayal of Jude—the Miranda Richardson character—struck me as being very peculiar, misogynistic almost. In the portrayal of the women in the film, it was as if the only acceptable face of femininity was the transvestite, Dil. The Jude character was this cold-blooded monster, obsessed with "the cause," whose only function it seemed was to act as bait to trap the Jody character and then to make tea for the lads.

NJ: Well, she was a tough girl. She made tea too, yeah.

MB: The Dil character on the other hand was very stereotypically feminine in the way she was worried about her make-up running, masochistic—she says at one point "I'll do anything for you."

NJ: So which do you say is the offensive one? I've heard that, I mean, why do people say, only in Ireland actually, that the Miranda character is offensive to women, that she's a retrogressive image or whatever? Why is that offensive to women? I mean, she's the strongest person in the whole film.

MB: The most frightening maybe.

NJ: She's stronger than Stephen Rea's character.

MB: She gets killed in the end though, in a particularly bloody fashion.

NJ: Yeah, of course she gets killed. What's wrong with that? I don't understand this argument, you know, I really don't. It puzzles me. I wrote her quite consciously as a monster, a monstrous part, because all the men who survive make female choices, and the woman makes male choices. It's very consciously done.

MB: Could you elaborate on that?

NJ: Well, Stephen only survives by becoming a woman, in a way. I mean, only survives by not becoming a woman but by taking on what you would think of as feminine virtues, you know, more understanding, compassionate. The corollary of that is that the woman would become more like a man. I don't understand what's offensive about it. I read this argument in the *Irish Times* and it is just so naïve because nothing that happens in the film is unconscious, you know? I wrote this monstrous Joan Crawford kind of figure—do they say that Joan Crawford or Bette Davis, the images of women they portrayed, are offensive to women? I don't think they do.

MB: Maybe it's that they're such extremes.

NJ: Well, it's not even a woman in peril. This is a woman who imperils other people. I think what women find threatening about this movie is that the men make choices that exclude them. The central character rejects the woman, the Miranda Richardson character, and chooses a man in the end, and the film creates a more viable and more attractive image of a woman through a man than through a woman. That's what's so offensive, but they don't say that.

MB: You mean the Dil character?

NJ: Yes. She's the romantic interest, you know? What I'm saying is that in this movie you've got a man who chooses to be with a man who dresses like a woman rather than be with a woman, and that's what women find offensive, but they never say that, they say the Miranda Richardson character is what you said and that kind of argument. Whereas if people would just come out straight and say "I found it offensive personally that a man should choose to be with a man rather than with a woman," then I could talk about it. But it doesn't make sense to me to argue that the film was an unconscious denigration of women. The part of Miranda is in many ways the strongest part in the film. She's winning all the awards in America anyway. It's a great woman's role. Miranda wouldn't have played it otherwise. I can't think of anyone more committed or politically more aware of the implications of the parts she plays than Miranda Richardson.

MB: Well, people are going to react to your films in different ways.

NJ: No. I'll tell you what it is. That kind of argument here is still in the kind of state that it used to be elsewhere in the world around 1976. The battles that are being fought here are the ones that were being fought in the United States or England or Europe ten years ago. I show this film in America and I'm interviewed by the gay and lesbian press or something like that and they can take it as a statement for what it is. The kind of sexual joke in the movie, the series of sexual ironies, they can take as them as ironies and they can enjoy it, they're really delighted with it. It's only here that people find if threatening because that kind of dialogue is still going on. Because this society is so fucked up really.

MB: I wouldn't agree that in that sense we're so far behind.

NJ: Okay. That's what I found anyway and I just find it kind of odd. I talked to a gay woman journalist in the United States about the movie and I was never once accused of being sexist. It's only here that I have those kinds of problems. I mean my sister Eithne said that to me when she saw the movie first, but she said it straight.

MB: She didn't like it?

NJ: No, no, she liked it. But she said she found it disturbing that the center of the story was a man choosing a man rather than a woman, that in many ways it was about the rejection of women by men.

MB: This is not the only film where you've been criticized for your portrayal of women, is it?

NJ: No! But only here. They said it about *Mona Lisa*, they say I create, you know Madonnas or whores. I've never created a Madonna or a whore. Well, yes, there was a prostitute in *Mona Lisa*. And they say . . . actually, I just don't understand the argument. The truth is that nobody writes roles for women, or very few people do. Woody Allen is the only person really. I do write roles for women. *Mona Lisa* was about a guy who thought that there was this kind of angelic soul in the woman he was driving around as a prostitute, he thought there was this thing I could redeem in her. And he was so wrong, because she didn't want to be that at all. She was quite happy in herself, and she had a lover who was a woman. It was about how he got this character wrong, it wasn't about my image of women Madonnas or whores.

The Miracle was about this young boy who has a fantasy about his mother. I've got Beverley [D'Angelo] there and I've photographed her beautifully, she's a beautiful woman. Is that what's wrong? That must be what's wrong.

MB: Aren't you being a bit defensive?

NJ: No, but it does piss me off, particularly if people all say the same thing, if they use a current phrase from the politically correct thing.

MB: I'm very suspicious about this wielding of the stick of political correctness. Anyway, let's move onto something else. You've used Stephen Rea a number of times in your films. Do you identify with him in some way?

NJ: Yes, I suppose he's my alter ego in some ways. He's a great actor because he's such a chameleon, like Jean Pierre Leaud or Marcello Mastroianni. With Mastroianni you can read a lot into his face. You see Stephen Rea and you can read an awful lot into his face, can't you? I've only made two films with him—no, I've made three, he was in *Company of Wolves* too. But I do [identify with him], yeah.

MB: You have recurrent images of churches in your films, which could only occur in the work of an Irish, or perhaps Italian, filmmaker. To what extent do you consider yourself an Irish filmmaker?

NJ: In that way, you know, in the Catholicism and in the things I write about, I suppose, in the way I've got fantasy. I like to take stories that have a realistic beginning, that start from the point of realism and go to some other place that is surrealistic. I suppose there's a certain impatience with reality. That sort of thing, that's Irish.

MB: Do you think that's specifically Irish?

NJ: I do, yeah. I think Irish people are terribly impatient with the real world. I think Irish literature has been like that. You don't have a realistic literature, you have a tradition of fantastic literature here. I mean Colm Tóibín has written that book [*The Heather Blazing*] about an Irish political family, which is a kind of realism that has never been in Irish literature.

MB: There's something else I've just remembered before we get off the subject of *The Crying Game*, and perhaps *Mona Lisa*. You use black actors quite a lot in those two films. Any particular reason?

NJ: Well, only in those two things. Cathy Tyson was black because Bob Hoskins in the film was a racist. Basically he was a working-class, English, unconscious racist. She was black because she was the furthest possible thing from what he would consider acceptable, and the film was about his growing fascination with this woman, whom otherwise he would have rejected. And I used Forest Whitaker because just about every black British soldier has been to Northern Ireland, where they're subjected to a lot of overt racism. I suppose because Irish people have never liked other minorities. So there was the irony of a guy from an oppressed situation in England being in an oppressive situation in Northern Ireland.

MB: Do you think that by using that kind of irony you were letting the British Army off the hook in a way?
NJ: Because he was black?

MB: Not so much that he was black, but because he was in the army because it was a job for him, it was one of the only jobs available because he was part of an oppressed minority. It was hard not to sympathize with him.
NJ: Oh, is that letting the British Army off the hook? I didn't think so. Maybe it was, but he had to be a sympathetic character. If he'd been an officer from Sandhurst with blond hair there wouldn't have been a movie. It would have been a different story.

MB: I actually felt that the whole film was really about the relationship between him and the Stephen Rea character.
NJ: I conceived of the film in terms of classical tragedy, and there's always homoerotic feeling between men in conflict. Through the woman [Dil] he wants to re-embrace the dead man.

MB: Anyway, you're probably sick to the teeth with that film by now?
NJ: No, no, not at all. I think it's interesting the questions it raises in an Irish context, you know. The things I'm asked about, like the Provisional IRA and feminism. It's interesting that all those questions here are so charged. Obviously the IRA thing, and the feminist issue . . . the discussion becomes charged here in a way I find surprising.

MB: I find it surprising that those kinds of questions are only raised here. The IRA thing I suppose is bound to be charged here, and you've had reactions from very opposing sides, but the feminist argument . . . ? Maybe it's the link between the two, in the Miranda Richardson character?

NJ: Maybe.

MB: How do you feel about the success that *The Crying Game* is currently enjoying?

NJ: It's great because it's not an easy film. It's not a film that says how great the Irish are and how wonderful it all is. It's not like *Hear My Song* or *The Commitments*, or those kinds of films which show this rather vital eccentric kind of place. That's what's thought of as the Irish movie now, and that's the temptation of filmmakers here, to make films that would sort of seduce international audiences by the charm of their "Irishness." What I found pleasing about *The Crying Game* is that it's actually rather a challenging movie and it's getting across to a huge number of people.

MB: Did you expect this kind of success?

NJ: Yeah, I did, yeah. Well, I hoped it would be, but you always do. I thought that if people could approach the story at all, if you could make the story work as a film, it'd be a captivating experience if only on the level of a yarn, what was going to happen next, that kind of thing. With most movies nowadays you know what's going to happen after the first five minutes. So I thought that if we could get them in there it would work. The problem would be getting them in, because you've got the IRA, you've got race, homosexuality, all these issues. How do you publicize this kind of movie? But it's doing phenomenal business in America.

MB: And carrying off all kinds of awards.

NJ: It's not the awards, it's the fact that so many people are seeing it. And that's good.

MB: It should make it pretty easy to finance your next film anyway?

NJ: Yes, it will. Yeah.

MB: Did you have trouble financing *The Crying Game*?

NJ: Yeah, this one was the hardest. Because nobody who saw the script would accept it. I tried to get some money here. I tried to get money from America. People read the script and they said "no, we don't want to touch it." They either found it offensive or they said audiences would find it offensive, or that it just wouldn't work as a film. So Stephen Woolley put it together, really—with the help of his credit card and Channel 4. So there was no Irish money in the film at all. Like most Irish movies it was financed from England.

MB: Talking about Ireland, who do you think is promising here?

NJ: Promising? Alan Gilsenan, and I always thought Cathal Black was a very talented man, and what's-his-name who made *Clash of the Ash*, Fergus Tighe. But there's something in Irish culture that steps on young people that pisses me off. In the United States, if you're nineteen and you've got ideas and scripts, it's wonderful, but here you have to wait until you're forty-five. But I think there's a lot of talented people here, like your man who made *Shellshock Rock*, John T. Davis. I haven't seen a lot of these shorts, but in those I have seen the one thing I do notice is the lack of a strong narrative drive. Like when that movie *Joyriders* came out I thought, oh great, this is going to be about joyriders, all these little kids driving these cars. I thought it was going to be like *Rebel without a Cause* or something like that. Then I saw this strange movie, and I thought this is just too strange, it's nothing to do with joyriders. There's a lack of narrative excitement in the stuff that you see that is noticeable. That was why I thought Fergus Tighe's film was so good.

MB: Do you have any ideas on the future of the film industry in Ireland?

NJ: You mean if I was in charge? Well, the first thing I'd do is break up RTE. If you want to stimulate the film industry here you need to disestablish the entire RTE organization. I would take every producer off the payroll. I would try to make it work along the lines of Channel 4. I don't think the station works at any level, even as a news service. But if you did that you'd have a beginning, if the place was set up to commission programs, maybe some hour-long movies. Also, I'd set up a Film Board, though I don't know how much money you'd put into it. There's the European Script Fund, but I can't see a Film Board providing more money than they provide [for script development].

MB: But a lot of scripts which win those awards never get made at all. They just never find any more money . . .

NJ: I know, but that's the nature of development, isn't it? It was the same when the Film Board was there before. They put a lot of money into development and scripts, but that's what you have to do. You get twenty-five film scripts developed and one of them becomes a film. It's the same in Hollywood. I don't know how much money the Film Board would be given, but at least if there was an agency there with authority over the whole issue of film, and how it impinges on RTE and the Arts council, and how it could be helped by private money and the Government sector, at least there would something there, it would be a start.

MB: I believe you're working on a script from an Elizabeth Bowen novel at the moment, written by John Banville.
NJ: No, I'm still working on this Michael Collins movie. It's with Warner Bros., you know, and basically Kevin Costner is trying to prevent me from doing it . . .

MB: Do you think he's actively trying to prevent you from doing it?
NJ: Well, he's moved his enterprise to Warner Bros. now, they have my script and they've kind of buried it, it's as simple as that. So I don't know what to do about that.

MB: You could move it to somewhere else.
NJ: They won't let go of it. They were going to give it back to me but then a couple of weeks ago they said no, they wouldn't. They didn't want to offend Kevin. So that's a piece of cultural imperialism that I have to contend with. But if that was free that's what I'd be working on now because it would be the most logical progression for me.

MB: Do you have a longstanding interest in Michael Collins?
NJ: Yeah, I'm interested in Irish history. I'm interested in the foundation of this State, the problems of violence in Irish society. I've written a script which goes from 1916 to 1922, which is about two guys, Collins and Boland, who basically disestablish the British Empire, and the implications of the violence they had to engage in for their own lives and for the society they lived in.

MB: It would be interesting if the two versions were made, don't you think?
NJ: There's no way that guy would play Collins. I mean, can you imagine Kevin Costner playing Michael Collins?

MB: Who did you want to play Collins?
NJ: Liam Neeson, or maybe Mel Gibson. But Liam would be my ideal choice. The problem with it is that it's a film of such scale that you do need stars of that size.

MB: Is it a project dear to your heart?

NJ: Of course it is. I've tried to do it many times. It's a pain in the arse because I was originally commissioned to do it by David Puttnam in 1984 or something like that. Then Eoghan Harris wrote a script that Michael Cimino wanted to make, which I think was unmakeable really, and that just basically collapsed. It's one of those films that I don't believe that any major company in Hollywood is ever going to make. It's too politically alive, and it's also going to be expensive to make. Every time I do a movie I come back to try and make it. Something else always happens though.

MB: Would you see yourself making it on a much smaller scale?

NJ: No, because I can make things on a large scale for not an awful lot of money. I can see a way of making this film as an epic that wouldn't cost $100 million, and I don't believe that anybody else would have the same kind of—what would you call it?—moral authority, with the perspective that would justify making it. There's another thing I've got called *Jonathan Wilde*, but every time I finish a movie I come back to the Collins thing and try and do it.

MB: So you're working on other things?

NJ: Yeah, I've got a few other things. *Jonathan Wilde* is by a friend of mine called Don McPherson, about an eighteenth-century gangster. It's good.

MB: A last question. Are you happier to be working here rather than in Hollywood?

NJ: It doesn't matter where I work really. If you stay here too much you can get very strange, very weird. It's a strange country, it's not particularly conducive to activity.

MB: Are you happier working on a smaller scale?

NJ: No. I'm lucky to be able to work on a smaller scale, that's the thing, because what happens to directors like Alan Parker, say, is that they make a movie that doesn't cost that much, then they make a more expensive movie, then they make a Hollywood film, and once they make a Hollywood film they never get out of that system. Whereas I made that thing *We're No Angels* and I just got sick of it all and I came back here to make a smaller movie. If I couldn't do that I would have been stuck.

MB: As arguably Ireland's most successful filmmaker do you see a role for yourself in the Irish industry?

NJ: I don't think I'm Ireland's most successful filmmaker. Anyway, do I see a role for myself in the industry? Yeah, if I was given one. I'd like to be able to help to put people in touch with finances and resources. If I could do that, I'd do it.

MB: Definitely last question, and going back a bit. The fuss about *Angel* at the time, in 1982, do you think that has affected your relationship with other Irish filmmakers? Do you think there's still any kind of bad feeling?

NJ: I think some of them don't particularly like me. I don't lose any sleep over it though. I think there's still a bit of bad feeling somewhere.

MB: Do you think it's justified?

NJ: On what level?

MB: Well, the objections to how the film was financed.

NJ: The objection then was that I got money from the Film Board. John Boorman was the chairman of the Board, and I was given—I think it was £80,000—I think it was 7 percent or percent of the budget. People objected to it because they didn't think that I should be making a movie because I was a writer. But I'd written the script and I'd sent it to Channel 4. They agreed to fund it to the tune of £400,000 and I needed an extra bit so I brought it to the Film Board, which had been set up specifically to make movies. Channel 4 were a bit uncomfortable with me as the director because I'd never made a movie before, so I asked John if he'd be the executive producer, which gave it some kind of insurance. So I brought it to the Board which the Minister at the time had asked John to be the chairman of—I think everybody objected to that in itself, you know. I mean John was trying to help the film business here. He was involved in trying to help Joe Comerford to finance *Traveller*. But the truth is that there had been nobody that had made movies. There were several projects brought to that Board which they'd backed. I think *Angel* was the biggest of them, it was the only one with financing, so it was a commercial proposition to them really. So there was a huge outcry from a lot of people, letters to the papers and all that kind of stuff.

MB: What about exactly?

NJ: One of the things was that I shouldn't be making movies because I was a writer, that the film should be made by a director. So I think that created a lot of resentment because I'd gotten a lot of money to make a feature. You see, the first thing I wrote was *Traveller* and I wrote that because I thought, wouldn't it be great to make an Irish feature film. And Joe made it into a story that was shorter than I thought it would be. Joe took the script and made it into something else, because he has his own concerns in filmmaking. I thought it was a very interesting film, but it was not the film I wanted to write. So I said okay, I'll write one myself and I'll direct it, because I wanted to make a film that would be shown in the cinemas. So then I wrote *Angel*, and the only way I could see of getting it made properly was if I was to make it myself. And a lot of filmmakers objected to that, some of them actually said to me they'd prevent me from doing it. It was amazing. When we got the money from the Film Board a lot of people said that John, as chairman of the Board, should not have given money to a film that he was the producer of, so John resigned from the Film Board. It was one of those very negative sequences of events which can only end in arguments, roars, and shoutin' all over the place. It was a bit crazy. It was just indicative to me of the difficulty there was in trying to get anything done here.

Interview with Stephen Rea

Carole Zucker / 1999

Extract from an interview originally published in *In the Company of Actors: Reflection on the Craft of Acting* (London: A & C Black, 1999), 113–14, 115. Reprinted by permission of the author.

Working with Neil Jordan: *The Crying Game*

Neil and I have an almost unspoken relationship, because we know each other very, very well, and he knows what he can get. He knows I'll do the script; I don't have any other agenda than to do the script as well as possible. I know all actors say that, but not all of them are entirely truthful about it. Anyway, I'll tell you why it's fun, because his sense of narrative is so highly developed that you're very secure as an actor. The story is being told; you don't have any other responsibility than just to be the person that you're supposed to be. Sometimes, when you're doing a script that's less polished, less thought-through, you're having to make it work as you're doing it. You don't with Neil; it works. A crude example is you're walking down the street; you don't have to do anything because everybody knows that someone you thought was a woman, is a man. But his movies are always like that; you only have to walk down the street, everybody knows who you are. Sometimes, in other cases, you feel you have to be offering information, you're helping make the thing work, but you're very released when you're working with Neil. In terms of composing the shots, he really does make it up as he goes along, so every scene is shot the way that scene should be shot. He doesn't predetermine, he doesn't come and do master shot, reverse, reverse, reverse, tighter lens, he doesn't run through the lenses in that way. He maybe does one really interesting developing shot, and does a reverse on it, to match it, and some closer stuff, but you feel very involved in it, because you know you're contributing. The completeness of whatever you have to offer is used. That's why you don't get bored working with Neil.

I always knew *The Crying Game* would be a good film, but it had a huge success, and how could you anticipate that? You couldn't. Miramax marketed it very successfully, and that contributed to the whole thing. It was a good movie, it caught the moment. It caught the whole gender thing, and it caught it in a way that was humorous as well as touching. And it was such an unusual setting, a very unlikely story of a transvestite and an IRA man. Almost anyone else you can think of would have done that very clumsily. If you read a treatment for it, you'd say "What? A tranny meets an IRA terrorist? Please. . . ." But, as Neil said at the time, the last taboo was gender. All the class divisions had dropped, and racial divisions—although he had an element of race in it as well—but that's gone as a kind of barrier to relationships.

It was very clever of Neil to maintain the ambiguity of the relationship between Fergus and Dil. I mean, Fergus is definitely heterosexual, that's why he had the relationship with Miranda (Richardson). I remember at the time, Neil saying "I don't know if we need to have this scene outside with Miranda," and I said "You've got to see him kiss her, because you've got to be sure that he's heterosexual."

But I think it is an ambiguous relationship between Fergus and Dil, and deliberately so. After he knows that Dil is a man, they never consummate the relationship. They kiss, but it's never actually consummated. That's Neil's way of avoiding the potential prurience and squalor of it. But, when he kisses Miranda, it's definitely in the audience's mind that they're lovers. Part of the deal, why she comes after him, is that she's a spurned lover, as much as Fergus's running away from the movement.

Fergus is completely naïve. There may be gay bars here now, but there weren't many at the time that movie was set. Around the north of Ireland, he wouldn't have seen a gay bar, and it wouldn't have occurred to him. Actually, the first time he goes into the gay bar, it's not as apparent as when he goes in the second time. It's much more ambiguous. The second time he goes in, it's apparent; they've got hairy chests, and all that. That's the filmmaker tampering with the material to help the audience, so that the audience feels the way Fergus feels when eventually it's revealed that Dil is a man. And then when he goes into the gay bar the second time, the audience laughs, they say, "Jesus, how did we not notice?" But he didn't notice.

Building a Character

I don't have any fixed idea or method, or a fixed approach to acting, because I don't think you can. Each role is a different project. Sometimes you just have an instinct about how it should go, and it works. Other times you have to do a little more probing and a little more work. I respond to scripts. If you read a text like *Translations, Dancing at Lughnasa, Someone to Watch Over Me,* you know it will be sustained right to the end; I have known that about certain pieces of work. You know that unless the writer has had a nervous collapse before he's finished the play, it's bound to work.

I wouldn't create a backstory for a character like Fergus. Some people might, but I think it's too literal. You can make it work just by saying, "Yeah, I know where he would have come from," but you don't work it out. I wouldn't work out who his cousins were, brothers, his granny; it's not necessary. The text already exists with Neil, and you have an emotional understanding which you bring to the piece. If you were doing Shakespeare, you don't work out Othello's auntie, you know what I mean? I think you do whatever you need to do to make the thing real for you, as the actor. I'm not challenging anyone who wants to work out a backstory. There's a current fetish for research; everybody says "How did you research that role?" Sometimes you just read the script, and if the scenes are really well written. . . . If I was doing *Streetcar Named Desire,* why would I have to research it? The fucking stuff eats you off the page; the poetic language is so intense, Williams is such a poet, what's there to research?

The emotional journey is that Fergus realizes that you can love anyone. He goes from being a man who's got a very rigid code about who you can offer love to, and it doesn't include British soldiers, it doesn't include black men, or black people. So by the end of the movie, he knows, and we all know and all feel it, you can love anyone—race, gender, nationality, are all meaningless. That wasn't a challenge to me, because I believe that with all my heart. It's wonderful to be in a movie where it really happens. I think that's what everyone responded to.

Working with a Non-actor

Working with a non-actor is tricky, you know. It's not that they're not talented, it's not that they're not conscientious, but it'd be like a professional footballer working with a non-professional footballer: it doesn't matter how good they are, they're bound to slip out of position. They don't have professional standards; they couldn't have. So what non-actors sometimes do is pick up your tone. Like that scene at the end of *The Crying Game* where I'm tied to the bed and my character says he's sorry. We started doing that, take one, and I started to fill up with tears, right? So take two, Jaye (Davidson) starts to fill up with tears as well. Take three, he's crying more than me, so that's the un-discipline that happens, because you don't just start a scene and go wherever it goes, you go into a scene thinking. You go in with a conscious notion of where you want to go with the scene, and you don't let it knock you about all over the place. That's a football analogy as well; when they talk about the team losing its shape. What happens with a non-actor is that a scene more quickly loses its shape. That doesn't mean they're not brilliant—and Jaye was absolutely brilliant in it—but when they're being brilliant, you have to get it right then. The professional actor will get it, be able to do it again, and develop it. If I was doing a scene with Miranda, the scene would automatically develop, because she's a fine professional actor. It might go in the wrong direction, and then Neil would say "Well, pull it this way." But with a non-actor, it doesn't happen like that. You need to tinker a bit more. Not in all cases, but that is one of the dangers with an inexperienced actor.

Michael Collins:
Treaty Makers and Filmmakers

Séamas McSwiney / 1996

From *Film West* 26 (Autumn 1996): 10–16. Reprinted by permission of the author.

Michael Collins is, or will be, a successful film on at least three levels. Firstly, it is a fine "historical movie" in the sense that it makes historians of us all. It provokes a spontaneous desire to go to the bookshelves to check the facts as they are presented in the film and to investigate the omissions. Whatever Tim Pat Coogan may feel about the historical inaccuracies, he will not be able to complain about the renewed commercial success of his Collins biography. Read the book, see the film, and check the book again. Go further and cross-check with Frank O'Connor's book. The dry discipline of historians will become both fashionable and fascinating! Secondly, the film itself will be a commercial success internationally because it tells a compelling story and tells it well. I'd wondered if this condensed version of Irish history might not be too much for non-Irish audiences but there's enough to hang on to for entertainment buffs. Along with the historical content, it has all the action, emotion, and passion of popular movie drama. Some journalists express reserve and critics may occupy an aesthetic high ground, evoking their disappointment at the film's classic linear narrative, but the audiences and especially the jury in Venice belie these fears. Add to this Warner Bros.' commercial expertise and the movie is short odds for success. Thirdly, and most intriguingly, it's a success with the Tory press and opinion. Having feared the worst, they were extremely relieved that the British got off so lightly in the film. We see the 1916 executions that are an ingrained part of our martyr ethos and we get a taste of the "Tans," but none of this is dwelled on in any indulgent depth. Unfortunately,

we never get a crack at Winston Churchill, a prime candidate for sophis-
ticated movie villainy, not even a whiff of his cigar. But, as Neil Jordan
explains, that was not the film he wanted to make. He wanted to make a
film about Mick and Dev.

This explains the palpable relief emanating from Fleet Street, Murdo-
chville, and Westminster. However, there will still be some hack-attacks
on this level, like for instance, the London journalist (it's not important
to name him here), who, like some lone sniper, went off to Venice without reading the latest dispatches from HQ. At the packed press confer-
ence, he pulled out the old chestnut whereby such films rattle the collecting tins of IRA fund-raisers in the U.S., "where ignorance on the Irish
question is bottomless." He went on to evoke the film's "failure to give
any kind of sympathetic portrayal of the British dilemma or of the position of the Protestant minority in the North of Ireland." Neil Jordan answered in a reasoned way and when the journalist persisted in his credo
of American ignorance, Jordan replied sharply that it was "kind of an
insult to Americans in general to presume that they are a bottomless pit
of ignorance about any event . . ."! This provoked a spontaneous burst
of applause, led presumably by the contingent of American journalists
responsible for informing their public. The newsman in question would
have saved himself some embarrassment had he consulted the elders of
his tribe, like Quentin Curtis of the *Telegraph* or, our favorite, Alexander
Walker of the *Evening Standard*. Curtis is very enthusiastic about the film
and, while regretting certain omissions, regards the notion of *Michael
Collins* (the film) being a pro-IRA film as "an absurd leap." He also seems
enamored of Michael Collins (the man) and even justifies to a certain extent Collins's violent choices. Curtis coyly quotes a British signatory of
the treaty, who recalled Collins as being "full of fascination and charm
. . . one of the most courageous leaders ever produced by a valiant race,"
before revealing, like a talented screenwriter, that the words were of
David Lloyd George. Equally jubilant, but in a stranger way, Alexander
Walker had led the chorus of approval. He savors with relish the anec-
dotal anti-Brit quips and, both rightly and righteously, he condemns the
Black and Tans as being the dregs of WWI trenches (let's not dwell on
who sent them!). He isolates the factual inaccuracies in the representation of the Croke Park shootings, not to quibble with them mind you,
but to better defend the director's tasteful choice of rendering the British army faceless. Like many of us, he also seems to regret the omission
of the treaty negotiations while recognizing that "Collins's guerrilla

warfare had brought the Brits to the bargaining table, which had the unfortunate effect of partitioning Ireland. . . ." (!) One could mischievously stretch the subtext of this statement to believe that, for Alexander Walker, it might not be too late.

Michael Collins succeeded in bringing the British further than they had ever envisaged. *Michael Collins* does likewise. Chameleon-like, Jordan absorbs the tonalities of Collins's approach, bursts of sudden violence and a readiness for pragmatic compromise. By focusing on the Irish coefficient of the "Irish problem," he seems to have made a diplomatically correct film, one which appeases the Brits and West Brits alike. So, like his hero, Neil Jordan will receive the bitter flack from his own. But the film should not be condemned outright for its obvious politics. Instead, Neil Jordan should be congratulated for bringing some refreshing input to the ongoing debate. Historically, or perhaps geographically, he has cleaned the moss from a signpost to a past when "bandit country" was West Cork, the southernmost region of the disputed territory, thereby metaphorically twinning it with South Armagh, which it is today. Politically, he has offered a cinematic demonstration of an effective, if impure, negotiation strategy. Agree with it or not, it is not less useful for being simplified. It's only a movie.

Likewise, other films, other voices, treating similar subject-matter with differing perspectives, should not be condemned without discussion and debate. It is unfortunate to witness an emerging tendency among opinion makers to dismiss out of hand one political-cinematic point of view in favor of another. This is to reduce the advantages of cinema to the intransigence of party-politicking and illegal armies. Another regrettable fact is, whatever their point of view, all of these films seem to be made from one side of the Irish divide. When will we see a biopic of Edward Carson, for example? Apparently, he spoke good Irish and there are surely many other interesting facts that even some of his most ardent followers are not aware of. In the charisma department, there's also "Ian Paisley: The Movie" and as for ancient history there's the possibility of making a *Braveheart* of King Billy. Great stories. Any takers?

Séamas McSwiney: The political controversy around *Michael Collins* seems to have disappeared in a puff of reassurance. Can you fill us in on that?

Neil Jordan: Yes. Some of the more right-wing newspapers in Britain were publishing articles before they'd seen it. Since then, Warner Bros. have shown it to some of these people and they've revised their opinion.

All I can say is that I tried to make it as objectively as possible. I wasn't trying to make *Braveheart* with this movie, I was trying to show what actually went on. The events that happen in the film are very well documented. The massacre of Bloody Sunday is very well known. The activities of the Black and Tans are very well known. I think that when English people see it, I think it might be instructive because any of the screenings we've had in London, public previews and things like that, people found it very moving because they didn't know any aspect of this history. They didn't know about the establishment of the North of Ireland, they didn't know about the treaty, partition, and all those things. I'm looking forward to the film opening in Dublin and I think it will do very well in England because I think English people do want to know, they do want to know about this period, they want to know about the problems they've been dealing with for the last twenty years.

SM: Can the film claim having the same value as historical document?
NJ: No, I don't think it should even attempt to. I mean it's not a work of history, it's not a historical document. It has not got the exhaustion or the detail. . . . Before I began making films and writing books, I did a degree in Irish history myself. The film is as accurate a dramatic reconstruction as I could make.

SM: Can you comment on the difficulty of making historical cinema?
NJ: Well it's almost like a distillation process, like making whiskey out of barley or making brandy out of wine . . . (but) there is one advantage of making a movie about historical events because you can show the confusion of those events as they occurred to the characters themselves. I mean people don't live history, they live their lives and people don't have the objectivity of historians when they're living their own lives. A dispassionate work of history could never show the emotional impact the events have on the characters themselves as a movie can do. I wanted to tell the story from the point of view of the protagonists themselves. You have Eamon de Valera, Harry Boland, and Michael Collins who are republicans who set out with certain aims to make the British Empire unworkable in Ireland. I wanted to show what that led to in their own words. So, I share their point of view and share the confusion and in the end perhaps share the tragedy of it. We were taught a version of history that stopped at 1916 basically that said that these great heroic men, Padraig Pearse, Thomas McDonagh, and all went out in this glorious revolution and died for Ireland and that was it and they were wonderful and

they were pious and they were holy and they were saints. We were taught nothing about the War of Independence, the Civil War, the brutality of that period, nor the complexity of the politics or the issues. Because of the continuing troubles in the North of Ireland, for the last twenty years that period has been suppressed in our minds, people didn't want to talk about it, think about it, discuss it. It is part of our past, part of our history, it deserves examination.

SM: Do you think the film might have a therapeutic effect?

NJ: I hope so; psychoanalysis teaches us that we shouldn't bury things in our past, that we should bring them to life, bring our traumas out to the surface. We should stop blocking, we shouldn't be in denial. So if making a movie about these subject matters does this, then I think it should have a certain cathartic effect.

SM: Do you think the film itself is a vector for correcting a misinformed version, that it revises a view of Irish history?

NJ: Obviously, I'm only an individual, I've been lucky enough to make this film, I've certain opinions and a certain point of view. Everybody wouldn't share them.

SM: The film will be more accessible to the Irish people . . .

NJ: Yes, and I think if the film has a fault, it may be difficult for perhaps American audiences to approach it because it doesn't see things in terms of good and bad, it doesn't see things in terms of good heroic Irish men and nasty, brutal British people. It shows how much the struggle was involved among Irish people themselves. That was what attracted me to the story; because in many ways people don't realize the history of that conflict is really a war among Irish people; I mean most of the people Collins assassinates in the Castle are Irishmen working for the Empire, working for the Crown.

In many ways, the War of Independence was a war amongst different interpretations of what it means to be Irish. Some people wanted Ireland happily to be a member of the commonwealth or stay in the Empire forever. Others didn't. The difficult thing was—some people did say to me at the time I was writing the script—that there is no coherent British villain protagonist kind of geezer; there's no Winston Churchill thumping the table, Lloyd George, stuff like that, because the characters never met during the period of the struggle. I mean dramatically it didn't seem justified to bring them in so I just made the decision to actually show that struggle from the point of view of the protagonists themselves. . . . The movie is not *JFK* for example which was, you know, a conspiracy theory. We're still quite close to these events in Ireland. Instead of the inaccuracies, what people should argue really is not what I've put in but what I've left out, I mean that's what you should take issue with.

SM: A big chapter that's left out, which would have been a very juicy one for Irish people, is the negotiations in London. Was that a difficult piece to leave out?

NJ: I had to make a choice really, because the negotiations were so complex and so tortuous. There was this series called *The Treaty* made by RTE (in which Brendan Gleeson plays Collins; he plays Liam Tobin in *Michael Collins*), and even that didn't manage to explain it to me properly so, I made, I suppose, an authorial decision: I just decided that the dramatic issue of the historical information that people needed was that Collins didn't want to go, he went under duress, and that he came back with what was inevitably a compromise and the compromise involved an oath of allegiance and the partition of the country.

SM: We do see the change in him when he comes back. This is the period where he got another vision of what the solution had to be . . .

NJ: Yeah, well he had to learn the art of politics, he was attempting to learn the art of politics. (We see the transformation but we don't see the process. . . .) There is another movie to be made on that whole London section.

SM: And the Kitty Kiernan story?

NJ: That story is based on truth. Both Harry Boland and Michael Collins were in love with the same woman and it was a very old-fashioned, rather naïve kind of courtship. Their letters do exist and I quote from them quite extensively. Collins was shot on the day that he had originally planned to marry Kitty. She was not Rosa Luxembourg, she wasn't involved in politics, so, in many ways, people might find the part slightly underwritten but that's what the character was.

SM: Do you personally think that this deepened the intransigence between Harry Boland and Michael Collins?

NJ: That's the puzzling thing when you do read the letters when Kitty finally chose Michael. It kind of coincided with Boland's rift with Collins so it's difficult to know to what extent emotional disappointment played. It did break Collins's heart, that his best friend actually left him. But, to do Harry Boland justice, I think he took the anti-treaty stance based on ideology.

SM: Yet it made it more difficult for them to communicate afterwards?

NJ: Yes, it did, terribly. That aspect of the story is true. As are all the others.

SM: Can you expand on what you say that Collins was the founder of modern guerrilla warfare (which later inspired the likes of Mao Tse-Tung and Yitzak Shamir) but would never be a proponent of terrorism as practiced today?

NJ: I think that when he was in 1916 and he saw the carnage that went on there, in terms of the participants themselves and the people of Dublin and the destruction of the whole city, he said he never wanted to fight a war like that again. He devised a whole new bunch of tactics, the idea of urban guerrilla warfare, hit and run, the idea of a non-uniformed army and basically he set out to make the British administration in the country unwanted. . . . And he had popular support. . . . (But) he did not involve himself in the campaign against civilians. In fact, the tactics of the Black and Tans and the irregular forces that the British employed, basically, were the proponents of terrorism as we understand it today. Collins's war was very selective. He shot agents of the Crown, he fought a war that was fought out of uniform, which was shocking at the period but it was a different period and I make that clear. Michael Collins himself had to arrange many, many unpleasant events and many unpleasant assassinations. The accounts of those who knew him are quite heartrending in terms of the effect it would have on him. He was a very conflicted man and on the night of those Bloody Sunday assassinations the reports are that he paced up and down all evening because what he had ordered to happen was deeply unpleasant.

The reason I structured those scenes the way I did was because I wanted to ask the character Collins himself certain questions about what he was doing and see if the character could answer those questions. It was a dialogue within Collins's head basically and perhaps a dialogue between myself and a depiction of Collins I was creating. . . . I look at the events through the eyes of Michael Collins basically. He was a pragmatist, to achieve any measure of independence he knew a certain amount of violence was inevitable because that was the nature of the rule in the country. I think, historically, the British Empire were never going to give up the first little piece that broke away. When all had been achieved that could be achieved through warfare, he actually genuinely tried to substitute it with politics. We see the conflict between a fighter and a pacifist really. He was a very conflictive human being and the very conflicts in his own nature were a reflection of the Irish situation of the time.

SM: Did Michael Collins use torture?

NJ: No, I don't think so. I mean he ordered the assassination of many people in cold blood. I'm not saying the guy was a saint, just that he was a remarkable person. That the outcome of the war of independence in Ireland was genuinely tragic and one of the main elements of that tragedy is that he was shot, because I think he had the capacity to solve the problems that were left afterwards. For me, the fact that a man aged thirty could actually be prescient enough to see that there would have to be some accommodation within the island and that it could not be the pristine republic that they all talked about. The argument between himself and de Valera was actually over that, it was over an issue of do you keep on fighting until you get absolutely everything or do you agree to compromise? Do you agree to use ordinary political means to achieve what everybody wants? I find him a very heroic, a very touching, a very tragic figure. I grew up under the Ireland of Eamon de Valera and I wasn't too happy about that.

SM: How about the acceptability of guerrilla tactics nowadays?

NJ: I suppose guerrilla tactics are inevitable in certain situations. In the present-day world, in the West, it doesn't seem to be acceptable, we don't live with empires anymore. In South Africa, I would have supported the ANC as with the situation in Ireland up to the early part of the twentieth century. People only resort to violence when politics fails. A Home Rule Act had been promised for thirty-five years prior to the 1916 revolution and, when WWI broke out, the Home Rule Act was once again put on the backburner. It was the failure of politics that led to the War of Independence in Ireland.

SM: But you chose to focus on the rivalry between Collins and de Valera, as it evolved.

NJ: That to me was the integral part of the story. . . . The film is not sympathetic to de Valera, but they were his worst years, those years between 1918 and 1922. He went on to become a statesman and dominate the country for the next forty years, so he had better days than the ones we show of him in the movie. What interests me was the opposition between the kind of cold-hearted political strategist and the pragmatic humanist that Collins represents. There was an element of fanaticism in de Valera's character that I would find unpleasant.

SM: Can you elaborate on not being happy growing up in de Valera's Ireland?

NJ: The death of Collins extinguished a certain thing in Irish public life because the Free State that he had established—that he helped to establish, that he negotiated with Britain, with Lloyd George and Winston Churchill—came to be dominated by a very rigid authoritarian view of Irishness. The Catholic Church was given a special place in the constitution and was given command of all sorts of areas of Irish public life, education being one of them, and it became quite a repressive country. I mean, I grew up in the fifties and when I started writing in 1968–69, books were banned, like Jean Genet's for example. There was quite heavy censorship.

SM: Do you think de Valera was responsible for the civil war?

NJ: Yes, I do. Directly responsible. The speech that he gives to that big crowd where he says "We will have to wade through Irish blood, and if it takes a civil war to get our independence, then let's have a civil war." That is a direct quote from a speech. De Valera always accepted partition, his only argument with the treaty was over the oath of allegiance. Basically the civil war was fought over nothing, and that's the tragedy of it really. It was fought over principle.

SM: Which group in Ireland is likely to be the most offended by the film?

NJ: I think the portrait of Eamon de Valera will upset some people. My mother thought I was a bit hard on Dev, but she's still talking to me. . . . De Valera was an Anglophobe, he was a very anti-English man.

He kept Ireland neutral during WWII. From de Valera's point of view he didn't want Ireland involved in a war on the side of Britain even though it was against the Third Reich, the greatest evil this planet has known. He was a very odd man and he did dominate the country until 1973 when he retired as president. The quote that I have from de Valera is from 1966 ("It's my considered opinion that in the fullness of time, history will record the greatness of Collins and it will be recorded at my expense"). It was when some relatives of Collins came saying it was time to build some proper gravestone for Michael Collins in Glasnevin cemetery. They had to go and ask permission to build this gravestone and de Valera refused them permission.

SM: So the censorship that existed about Collins is via Dev?
NJ: The victor wrote the history.

SM: How about de Valera's implied involvement in Collins's death?
NJ: The only thing I've said in the movie is that Michael Collins was shot on his way to a meeting or while attempting a meeting with Eamon de Valera. Collins was trying to stop the fighting. Now that is true. I do not say in the film that de Valera arranged his assassination. . . . De Valera was in the area the morning Collins was shot in an ambush in that valley, Béal na Blath, by a group of what were called Irregulars at the time. So out of that I've constructed this drama of Collins's attempts to meet with de Valera and de Valera's inability to talk with him and then, a young activist, on his own initiative, setting up an ambush. That is a dramatic reconstruction, that is my own responsibility. I'm not saying it happened like that but a conclusion that I've drawn from all the facts that are known.

SM: What if Michael Collins had lived?
NJ: I think he would not have allowed the state to develop into this kind of Catholic monolithic thing it did. I think he would have reached some accommodation with the Unionist population in the North of Ireland. He would have understood the British mentality far better than anybody that succeeded him. I think the country would have been entirely different, a bit more like what it is now. . . . Everybody who came after him seems like minnows in a way. I think he was quite unique in that he didn't have any rancor, he didn't have any racism in his blood. He wasn't Anglophobic, he didn't hate English people. When he went to London, he became a kind of a star in the social circuit there. The only thing wrong with the guy was that he had an appalling capacity for violence.

SM: You first wrote the script in 1983; how would this film be different if you'd succeeded in making it earlier?
NJ: Other films I've made, say like *The Crying Game* or *Interview with the Vampire* or *Company of Wolves*, I can see my paws all over them. If I had made it twelve years ago, perhaps I wouldn't have had the confidence to be as objective in an authorial way. It's hard to explain really, but I think I didn't want to intrude on this story in an interpretative way, to make it

a Neil Jordan kind of thing. Perhaps I wouldn't have been able to let the story tell itself.

SM: What about the casting?
NJ: When I wrote it in 1983, I said to Liam if I get to make this I'd like you to play the part and luckily his star has risen over the years. I also discussed it with Stephen Rea at the time. Aidan Quinn, I met, and I was so glad he wanted to play Harry because it needed that kind of intensity, that humanity that Aidan brings to the part. I was considering various people for Kitty Kiernan and I got a call from Julia Roberts that she was interested. I had no idea she knew anything about Irish politics or the period but she was one of the few actresses that I met who actually did know. She goes to Ireland and reads Irish history and literature. It's actually Julia singing ("She moves through the Fair") during the film. She knew that song and instantly I said "OK, I'm casting you now." At the end of the film, it's Sinéad O'Connor singing the same song.

SM: Can you also talk about the photography and editing choices?
NJ: The photography is by Chris Menges, one of the greatest living cinematographers, who came out of retirement to do it because it was very important to him. (Menges, now a director, notably of Cannes prizewinner *A World Apart*, was also cinematographer on *Angel*.) We decided to use silhouettes quite a lot. It's because Chris is a master of available light. Cameramen can get very worried about not necessarily seeing the details of people's faces. We just decided to go for that, because it needed a very graphic kind of dramatic quality to the image, and as well to highlight the kind of documentary base in which it's set. We used a process called ENR, which is a process that Vittorio Storaro developed with Technicolor in Rome, which basically introduces a slight element of black and white dye into the printing that desaturates the colors very slightly and builds up the contrasts which would enhance that silhouette feeling, the contrasts between light and dark. We were trying to achieve a kind of elegiac realism—I could call it that really—and the story itself does deal with bursts of violence and long bursts of discussion. The story would intimate or would suggest sequences of very rapid editing and sequences that are quite languorous and quite operatic and more open.

SM: How would you situate *Michael Collins* in your work?
NJ: The first film I did was called *Angel*, about the North of Ireland, about a saxophone player who witnesses an assassination and is taken over by

the idea of revenge. I made the *The Crying Game* about a character who came out of an environment of political violence and *Michael Collins* is about the roots of that situation really, so I suppose the three of them can be seen in some way as dealing with the same issue.

SM: How does the period contrast with the present?

NJ: Northern Ireland at the moment defines itself in terms of Catholic and Protestant because that was the way the state was set up. It was set up with an inbuilt Protestant majority. During the period of the War of Independence, many of the protagonists were Protestant, many of the protagonists were British. Erskine Childers, who some would see as a great hero of the independence movement, was an Englishman. Countess Marcievicz was from ascendancy Sligo background. That period did not define itself in religious terms. People made political choices not on the basis of their religious beliefs. It was about republicanism and its opposite, really. Because the North of Ireland was set up specifically to cater for the Protestant majority there, the conflict there has expressed itself in terms of Catholic versus Protestant—because that's the way it was established. The film is also an examination of conscience. I think it's just that we should examine the roots of what we are in Ireland, why violence is still a part of the political life of the country. I really wanted to just make the movie. I didn't want to make a political statement, but as an Irish person growing up with these legends around me, it was relatively important for me to examine them quite objectively. The film is about a man who set up an army to achieve a certain end and then tried to disestablish it and found it very difficult. The force that he set up consumed him in the end. There is an object lesson there. I would hope that it shows that whatever is going on in Northern Ireland now, that it would show that it needs patience, how difficult it is actually to take the gun out of politics and replace it with dialogue. At the time we were making it, it was just quite eerie because every development in Irish politics seems to be reflected in the film. The peace process had begun and Gerry Adams and Martin McGuiness were being met by various people. Martin McGuiness went to London to negotiate. The parallels were a bit uncanny really, and then they had signs in Belfast saying "Gerry Adams remember Michael Collins."

SM: How do you feel about that parallel?

NJ: There is no connection between the Irish Volunteers that are presented in this movie and The Provisional IRA that was set up in 1969.

They have nothing to do with the organization that Collins led but with regard to the issue of the continuing presence of the gun in Irish politics there's a very obvious parallel.

SM: Is Gerry Adams following the same path as Collins, trying to find a way to renounce violence and head towards a diplomatic solution?
NJ: Yeah, well it's a constant movement in Ireland where anybody who tries to compromise is shot, is accused of the compromise, which the country needs.

SM: Do you think the film will provoke controversy within the IRA?
NJ: I don't know. I don't know anything about that. I doubt it. I mean Collins is regarded as a traitor by the IRA. He is regarded as the person who is responsible for the establishment of the North of Ireland. The film does show the genuinely tragic consequences of involvement in violent action and I think to that extent perhaps if people are involved in diehard republicanism, they might be moved by it. I don't believe the peace process is entirely dead in Ireland. I think that all the parties of that conflict in the North of Ireland do want to find some way of disengaging from it and I think this film shows the story of one man who tried do disengage.

The Butcher Boy

Ted Sheehy / 1998

From *Film Ireland* 63 (February/March 1998): 14–15. Reprinted by permission of the author. Interview conducted at the Cannes Film Festival.

Ted Sheehy: Are you sad they couldn't show *The Butcher Boy* here?
Neil Jordan: Well, yeah, but you know these festivals have their rules so that's the way it works . . .

TS: That's Berlin's rules, is it?
NJ: Yeah, well it's them.

TS: Can I compliment you on it, I think it's the best thing you've done.
NJ: Thank you.

TS: I noticed you seemed to be very nervous in Galway at the premiere last July, and I wondered was it particularly . . . am I wrong in thinking you were nervous?
NJ: No, no, it was a bit of a . . . you normally don't show a film like that at such a small festival, but I was very glad I did actually because I didn't know when the release would be and it was a very good way to show it. Normally when you show a film at a festival for the first time you show it at an international one in Europe, like Venice, you know. They were all people that knew me, that's probably why I was a bit nervous.

TS: It's probably the closest I've seen to the Irish imagination captured on screen, in all its wildness . . .
NJ: Well that's what's marvelous about the book, actually.

TS: And was it that in the book that grabbed you or the strength of the narrative . . . ?

NJ: It was the whole quality of the book, the challenge of putting the book on screen into a movie. The book is very much about cinema in a way, it's about these influences in the kid's head, he saw the world in a cinematic way. So I felt it could be made into a movie, I just didn't know how. It was a matter of two things really, the script and the principal actor. So when we finally got the script right I said, okay now, the movie can be made if we can find a child to play the part. So I didn't put it into production until we found the kid.

TS: And for Warner Bros. to hack it, because it's a fairly small picture for them, did they give you carte blanche, effectively?

NJ: The way it went was this, they said to me, "What are you doing next?"—and I had it set up independently, I'd bought the rights to the book myself and paid for the script myself—so (after doing *Interview with a Vampire* and *Michael Collins* with them) I said, "I'm doing a small Irish movie and it really is not for you," and I meant it. But the more I said that the more they were interested in it, you know that kind of thing. I said, "Look, it's not the kind of film you release. Sure I could make it with you, but you wouldn't know what to do with it when we finish it." And they said, "No, no, no, we want to do this film. We can make small films as well as big films," and so, eventually, I said, "Yes." So it was the odd position of probably the biggest studio in the world doing this very idiosyncratic, very . . . I can't think of a more non-mainstream film than this film, you know. When I showed it to them they kind of said, "What the fuck is this?" as I'd predicted. I said, "I told you you'd say that." They've been quite good about it, they don't understand it so they're asking what to do with it . . .

TS: Are they following your lead on it?

NJ: They are, at the moment. We're releasing it first in Europe as they don't know what to do in America. They love the movie, they really genuinely like it—I've been shooting another film, *In Dreams*, in America—we were going to release it in November and I hoped the actors would be able to do all the press but they said no, they needed me to do press, but I couldn't because I was shooting a film so we put it off. So then I decided to open it here because their international branch is far more used to handling small movies so I'm working with Julian Senior in London and he's marvelous, really wonderful. We're working very carefully on it, showing it to critics and we're getting an amazing response both in the United States and here, so I think they'll all be very happy in the end.

TS: What was the cost of it?
NJ: About $10 million.

TS: Small for them.
NJ: Small for them but not small for an Irish movie and there were expensive elements in it, like the nuclear wasteland, the effects, it needed a bit of money to do it.

TS: At the heart of it, for me, is Francie's discovery that the idealized notion he was clinging to is gone. Were they lies he was telling himself or . . . ?
NJ: No, he was remembering his father's comments, "I wasn't always like this, son." He really believed what his father was saying, that there was a time when he wasn't an alcoholic, when he wasn't a brute, when they genuinely loved each other. He wanted to know that he came out of love, so when the woman at Over the Waves says that to him it really does destroy his last connection with reality.

TS: Am I right in thinking in that, and in the music, and in so many other little things that reverberate through it—that it goes right back to central concerns of your own, in your earliest writings?
NJ: Yeah, well the book is an amazing book, it does reach people all across the world in a very personal way. As Pat McCabe says, they say "I knew that puddle," you know, hacking at the ice. I grew up in Ireland in the fifties. I grew up in Dublin, was born in Sligo, that rural/urban background. I knew that small, strange, same world quite well.

TS: And the thing about being a boy . . .
NJ: Well everyone knows that don't they, unless they're a girl.

TS: You know what I mean, the relationship between the two of them?
NJ: Yeah, that age of childhood when you think these relationships will never change, that they'll last forever. And of course they do change. Francie's a kid who . . . in a way he's almost too pure, he doesn't want to ever feel less, but to survive in the world you've got to teach yourself to guard against your emotions, to guard against pain and anguish. He never learned that lesson and that's my feeling about why he goes over the top in the end.

TS: To go back to what I was saying earlier about the Irish imagination,

I think the way you've rendered the story has that positive madness and openness of the Irish imagination.

NJ: Well that's the unique thing about the book, or about Francie—he's always an optimist. It was very difficult for people to grasp when we were making the film—they'd think of it as a depressing thing but no, it's not, you've got to realize this kid is so optimistic it would almost break your heart. And it emerges in the movie in the same way in the kid's performance. You know, he's always got somewhere else to go to, hasn't he. He's always got the freshness and hope of a child, and when we were putting music on the film, the music editor chose very somber stuff as a temporary track, so you could see it for the first time, and it made the whole thing very dark and depressing. When Elliott Goldenthal came on I kept saying to him, you've got to realize that this kid is such an incurable optimist and the music has to reflect it in some way.

TS: I think the opening title sequence is outstanding—whose idea was that?

NJ: That's my idea, a guy in London designed it. The idea was just to take comic books and make the opening with them.

TS: I think it brings you into the story, subliminally, before you know where it's taken you. How did you go about the casting, how do you do that?

NJ: We had to find a child from a rural background who had all that secretive, imaginative thing going, and who was also able to demonstrate it and that's a very difficult thing because so many kids in the rural area were painfully shy. It just happened we went into this little town, Killeshandra, and we found three of them—they were all these wonderful kids, they began to feed on each other really. They didn't even know that the camera was there, Eamonn had never been in a cinema before.

TS: Did that help, do you think?

NJ: I'm not sure if it helped or not. If you got a kid from an urban environment they'd be far more demonstrative, far more streetwise, far more able to display themselves. Once we found Eamonn, everything was there, he's a remarkable young actor . . .

TS: How do you direct him?

NJ: I've no idea, I don't know how I direct. I know he imitates me, he began to imitate me. A lot of his mannerisms are mine. I wouldn't show him how to do things but I'd be explaining stuff and subconsciously (all actors do it) he'd do it.

TS: And actors generally, how do you work with them?
NJ: I just want them to be open. You want an actor to respond to the material and to be open to every facet of it, with every part of themselves. You don't want any bit to be closed. That's all I ask . . . which is a lot. You've got to ask them to be totally fresh and to go wherever the part will take them. Some of them don't want to do that and those that don't want to do that, I don't work with.

TS: Tell me about the writing, because this is the first Irish project that you've sourced outside your own head.
NJ: Yeah, well, the writing, basically myself and Pat wrote it. Pat wrote two drafts and they departed from the book too much so I went back to the book and wrote the final draft.

He was called away at this point to officiate at the opening of the Irish cinema retrospective which amounted to some fifty films shown over a fortnight. He is currently in Ireland doing sound postproduction on *In Dreams* which has a provisional release date this autumn in the USA. He has bought the rights to Pat McCabe's forthcoming novel *Breakfast on Pluto*.

In Dreams

Douglas Eby / 1999

From *Cinefantastique* 31, no. 1 (February 1, 1999): 8–9. Reprinted by permission of the author.

With a tag by DreamWorks of "dark psychological thriller," Neil Jordan's film stars Annette Bening as Claire Cooper, a woman with nightmares involving the acts of a killer, Vivian (Robert Downey, Jr.). Speaking from Dublin, Jordan said that, despite the title, this film has nothing to do with a novel of his called *The Dream of the Beast*, but is rather a script that Steven Spielberg had commissioned from Bruce Robinson, whose writing credits include *Return to Paradise, Jennifer Eight, Fat Man and Little Boy*, and *The Killing Fields*. "David Geffen, with whom I'd worked, showed me Bruce's script, called *Blue Vision*, that Steven had developed," Jordan said. "It was fascinating but I wanted to take it in another direction, so I did some rewrites on it, and it became *In Dreams*. Basically, Bruce had written the story about a woman who's psychic, who is being invaded by the dreams of somebody she doesn't know. That's what intrigued me."

Jordan said another of his films that has some of this kind of dream plot is *The Company of Wolves* (1984), written by Jordan and Angela Carter, with a story constructed as a dream occurring in the mind of an adolescent girl. One reviewer called it "a surprisingly successful example of a sinister, contemporary fairy tale. Jordan conveys a sense of the fantastic, of otherness. One of the problems in adapting full-blown fantasies is that fantasy is often best left to the imagination of the reader, rather than being subjected to the 'realism' of the screen."

For this film, Jordan said he again wanted to "make it a realistic plot, on one hand, and a dream plot on the other hand, and they both interweave." The idea of having one's dreams manipulated or influenced in some way by an outside person is intriguing, Jordan agreed, and is a central element of *In Dreams*. "Basically, I wanted to make a psychological horror film, he said, "but of a kind that hasn't been done for quite a while, because it's not Wes Craven, and it's not *Scream*, and not a slasher movie. It's one that takes the subject quite seriously, and is deeply disturbing, quite scary."

The basic situation that drives the story, Jordan said, is that the central character Claire "has these dreams which she cannot interpret. Some of them are premonitions, but she only gradually realizes that. So each time she dreams, she has to kind of work out what it means, and they become increasingly more terrifying." The dreams turn out to be resulting from a psychic connection with the killer, Vivian, and "eventually to find this guy, she has to dream her way to him, because he's killing children. It's quite spooky that way."

Jordan agrees that most of his films involve in some way the idea that fantasy can make reality more bearable, but this is not one of those films: "No, her dreams are not a solace for her," he noted; "they're terrifying, nightmares, and she dreams at night and dreams in the daytime, so her reality is invaded by the reality of somebody else. So it's kind of like a perverse love story. This man is obsessed. He knows there's another dreamer out there, that's why he's doing this to her."

Jordan's filmography also includes *Interview with the Vampire*, *The Crying Game*, *High Spirits*, *Mona Lisa*, and *Michael Collins* which was based on Jordan's longtime interest in the central character who played such a part in Irish history. In this case he took on the project based on the quality of the story by Robinson: "Bruce's script was quite intriguing, and he's someone I admire as a writer and director. And I kind of made it my own. It has some personal things, except it's set in America. My last film, *The Butcher Boy*, was set in Ireland."

Annette Bening has commented about acting roles for women, and has said in a published interview: "In fact, the greatest roles for women, the profoundest and cleverest portraits of women, are found in Shakespeare. . . . He is a profound doctor of human nature, a psychological genius in exploring and fleshing-out our complicated nature." One of Jordan's main casting choices was Bening, and Jordan agreed not many of her roles have allowed for an exploration of her emotional depth, but thinks this film does: "Absolutely. This is a wonderful part for an actress, because it's her film, really. It's kind of unique in that. There are so few parts out there for women. Actually, many people wanted to play it because the part is so good. It's driven from the woman's point of view, the woman's psyche. And it's a horror movie, a bit like *Don't Look Now*." That 1973 Nicolas Roeg film was the story of John and Laura Baxter (Donald

Sutherland and Julie Christie) who are vacationing in Venice when they meet a psychic who claims she sees the spirit of the Baxters' daughter, who recently drowned. John resists the idea, but starts having waking-dream flashes of their daughter.

In a previously published comment about making another of his films, Jordan spoke of Ireland being a country formed from ghosts, and he agreed that the choice of New England as a location for *In Dreams* was, in a related way, "a perfect place to shoot the movie. It's genuinely spooky up there. That weird kind of Dutch tranquility you get. Very strange. And it's quite beautiful, quite isolated." Another main location proved a considerable challenge: "We had to build an underwater town for the movie," Jordan noted. "You know that kind of thing in America where they flood a valley to create a reservoir? That's one of the central motifs in this movie, so I spent about a month shooting at the studio Jim Cameron built for *Titanic*. It had all these wonderful water systems, and it's basically an underwater sound stage. It worked out very well, it was very beautiful."

Another main casting choice was Robert Downey, Jr., in the role of the "madman killer" and Jordan praised the actor as "one of the best actors of his generation." His character, Jordan noted, is "not very nice. He's not nice at all. He's a character who was abandoned by his mother when they evacuated this town. The mother left one child in his bedroom, chained to the bed. So he saw the entire town flooded, and he was totally alone there and saw the water rise outside, and eventually the water bursts through his window, but he slips free. Quite a traumatic experience in his life. And it led to a very twisted adult life, you know? He becomes a killer, then realizes that somebody is dreaming about his activities, and psychically seeing what he's doing. And then he becomes obsessed with them, but the obsession, for him, becomes like a love story. That's as much as I can tell you," Jordan concluded.

He said this has been a gratifying project: "It was wonderful. But it was very difficult to work out, the logic of it, because it's a very unusual movie, a very unusual horror film. But it's quite beautiful. And I think it's about time we took our nightmares seriously. We've had a lot of jokey horror films of late. I think it's time for one that expresses a deep kind of disturbance and terror." Asked if there is a chance for the audience to come away with some kind of resolution to that terror, Jordan said, "Oh yes, it's quite a ride."

A Look Over Jordan

Ted Sheehy / 2000

From *Film Ireland* 74 (February/March 2000): 16–18. Reprinted by permission of the author.

It's a peculiar setup to begin with. Over the course of a long day a snake of reviewers, interviewers, critics, columnists, and photographers uncoils itself from the lobby of the Merrion Hotel in Dublin. It eventually passes, in bite sizes, through a suite on an anonymous corridor upstairs where Neil Jordan gets on with what may be one of the more arduous aspects of being a film director. I have my own crammed page of questions and I hope some of them are new. We start with a question each about *Michael Collins*, *The Butcher Boy*, and *In Dreams*.

Ted Sheehy: Firstly a question (or critical hypothesis) about *Michael Collins*. The film is to some extent a reading of history and character but it also, it seems to me, could only have been made by someone who lived at a formative age through the 1916/1966 commemorations in Ireland, and then through the beginnings of conflict in NI, and who asked themselves serious questions about political violence at that time. Is that a valid point?

Neil Jordan: It is a valid point, yeah, absolutely. It was basically because of there being a persistence of political violence in the culture of the whole island . . . the appeal to me of the story was when you examined that story everything that is still an issue was so perfectly expressed in that period.

TS: The one niggling and perhaps only criticism of *The Butcher Boy* as a film is the ending, and the casting of Stephen Rea as the grown Francie—it presents a credibility issue to the viewer at the end.

NJ: That was Pat's conception when he wrote the original screenplay, in a way. That in the end Francie, in the mental hospital, had become the image of the father. I discussed it with Stephen, because I suppose they weren't that physically like each other. And he said, well, the only alternative is that you play him because you look like him. I didn't want to do that because I always thought it's a bit embarrassing, doing the Hitchcock bit. But the point was that Stephen was the voice, so it had to be him that played the older Francie at the end.

TS: To what do you ascribe the negative reaction to *In Dreams*, in the US especially?
NJ: They didn't like the movie, it's very simple!

TS: I know they didn't like it! Do you think there are things about the film that justify their not liking it?
NJ: I don't think the story made a lot of sense to them. The story justifies everything in a way. The story had been developed by Steven Spielberg himself, at Amblin, and he'd commissioned Bruce Robinson to write a screenplay. I read the screenplay and the images were fascinating, the premise of the entire story was absolutely fascinating. It went into this strange territory. I did a version of the screenplay myself, you know, in an attempt to solve that [story] problem. But lo and behold when I finished the movie that problem was still there. It's impossible to end that story . . . dealing with the death of a child in the middle of a film like that creates this huge narrative hole, you don't know where to put your emotions. . . . There are certain rules in the genre, in a way, you start with a female character, you know, being pursued by irrational forces . . . you expect them to survive or triumph in some way. It was a film which destroyed all the rules of the genre. But I think it's more complicated than that, I think American critics objected to me making a movie like that because they loved *The Butcher Boy* so much. They said this guy shouldn't be doing this, really. I was not unhappy with the film at all but there are holes in it. The problem is it wasn't my story.

TS: To come on to *The End of the Affair*—I'm not a great reader of Greene but (as a Catholic convert) he's said to be preoccupied with "redemption through degradation"—which is simplistic, perhaps, and doesn't address his strengths as a stylist, but there's some truth in it and he's "out of fashion" as a result. And I wondered if it were thematic, character (writer as narrator/protagonist), or stylistic (time play) concerns which drew you to the book?

NJ: What drew me to the book was quite simply the fact that the same relationship was seen from different points of view. There are multiple interpretations of a series of central events. And at the end of all those interpretations there was something inexplicable to all the characters. Greene had come up with a beautiful story—I don't know if you've read Walter Benjamin, *The Work of Art in the Age of Mechanical Reproduction.* It's collected essays and in one of them he talks about the power of the story—somebody has taken over Rome and the Emperor has to stand there and watch his entire entourage being humiliated. He sees his wife come through in chains, he doesn't move a muscle. He sees all the dignitaries, all the loved ones in his life, children, being dragged through. He doesn't move a muscle. Until the end, he sees this old, broken-backed guy, this servant who used to bring his breakfast, something like that, and he breaks down and weeps. Benjamin examines that story and says the reason it's powerful is because—and he examines different interpretations of it: someone says it was because he loved that servant best of all, someone else says it was because this was just the tiny drop that made his grief overflow. And Benjamin says the power of the story is that it's not explained by any of those explanations and yet it's amenable to all of them. I think Greene came up with such a story in this.

TS: My own feeling about it, as a novel, was that at times it's little more than a thesis . . .
NJ: Well that's the fault with it . . .

TS: And the protagonist narrator is a very unlikeable, very prickly, unpleasant character in many ways. Did you feel that you had to moderate that?
NJ: No, no I tried to make him as unlikeable as he was!

TS: Ralph Fiennes [as Maurice Bendrix] has given the audience more to empathize with in the film than there is in the book.
NJ: Yeah, perhaps there is more. The basic dynamic of the character, Bendrix, is that the more he says he hates, the more you know he has loved. The thing that I changed was exactly that kind of theoretical argument, that sense of philosophical argument towards the end of the novel which I think just overwhelmed the characters and the story itself. I think if there is a fault in the book it is that.

TS: The film I was reminded of by *The End of the Affair* is *Breaking the Waves*. Would you agree there are affinities . . . ?

NJ: To both movies, yes there are except Emily Watson is in this portrait of this tiny little community in Scotland which was deeply Presbyterian; the entire logic of all their lives was to do with religion.

TS: It was, yes, but you could say that she gave her life for Stellan Skarsgaard's character in the way, perhaps, that Sarah Miles does for Bendrix . . .

NJ: Equally irrational in a way, wasn't it?

TS: . . . and one of the consequences of adapting the novel was the issue of the possibility of his being dead on the stairs becomes more of a probability in the film.

NJ: Well the novel is entirely subjective, you know, until he encounters her diary, so he's speaking as himself. But he does say, when he's hit by that door that falls on top of him, he felt free of all pain and all jealousy and I used that voiceover. But in the movie you can present different perspectives, you can almost have present a God-like perspective. I wanted it to be a decided possibility that he actually could have died in that event. In a way he did die because his emotional life was over after that moment. He walks upstairs and she leaves him and he doesn't see her again. His life is stopped there and then, you know? And when we meet him at the start of the movie he's like a dead man, a ghost of what he was, in a way, and he's haunted by the meaning of that event. That's why he takes Henry's suggestion. And all the characters are emotionally haunted.

TS: There's something going on which allows for the possibility that there's something happening on a metaphysical plane and it's something you've intentionally enhanced in the film and I wonder where . . .

NJ: Where that comes from?

TS: Yeah . . . 'cause it's there in other female characters in a few of your other films.

NJ: Like in what?

TS: Well, it's there in *In Dreams*, there's the girl in *Angel* . . .

NJ: Yeah, yeah, I suppose so, you're right. Well it's like . . . she says something happened in that room, yeah, you know? If you're filming an event from different perspectives—his perspective, her perspective—there's another perspective too, you know? Which is the perspective of absence, in a way. I think the reason certain filmmakers have been quite mystical, or expressed oddly mystical things—I'm not sure that Kieslowski did it well in *Three Colors: Red* but he definitely did it in his *Decalogue*. He expressed this mysterious perspective where something is happening between the logic of ordinary events and the logic of mathematics, like when the kid is playing chess with his father, and the computer sends this message, and then the kid dies. There's something about filming things that makes you think of those things. Light in itself is mysterious.

TS: As a filmmaker you create that on celluloid . . .

NJ: Well it's not that. For example, me as a director, I've got to present his [Bendrix's] point of view—bitter, jealous, priapic, obsessive, needs to possess all the time and wants to reclaim, basically that's one thing. Then you present her perspective, whatever that should be—you have to make the camera more gentle yet you can't in a way. But to be making a film with the idea that there is another perspective, there's another way of looking at things which is beyond all the characters, in a way that's what the camera does in a strange way.

TS: There's a kind of ambivalence to Sarah's character in the notion of redemptive action on her part, in withdrawing from him, denying herself and then her death. Is she going from being a morally bad person to becoming a good person?

NJ: No, I don't think so. That's why the combination of sexual rapture and mystical rapture is . . . you feel they're one and the same thing, don't you? The only pictorial or physical way of presenting mystical rapture is in sexual terms, that's what Renaissance painting always did. There seems to be a rightness, really; emotionally it seems to be terribly appropriate that she is so carnal and from that she can actually be so . . . you know, so . . .

TS: Are you saying there's a purity in carnality which transfers . . .

NJ: I think there's something we deny nowadays about the whole idea of sexuality, the whole idea of any kind of rapture, you know what I mean. That's why it seems to me to be absolutely true and obvious. But people say, ok this is a very old-fashioned idea, a religious idea, but I don't agree. If there was, for example, (I'm talking about painting and portraiture) a tradition of the nude like there was when Rubens was painting and a tradition of religious portraiture, then the same elements would come into play. But all those things don't exist in our culture anymore. We've become terribly grey in our understanding of things. To me it makes absolute sense.

TS: So it's not a morally guilt-ridden thing . . .

NJ: No, not at all. I think that's the simplicity with which Julianne played it. It's hard to explain it to anybody, particularly to an actress. If I was to say, look, the emotional intensity that's put into the sexual scenes leads directly to your abandonment of this man. They're both an expression of love really, they both are exactly about the same emotion. To me it makes absolute sense.

The End of the Affair

Gerry McCarthy / 2000

From *Film West* 39 (February 2000):12–15.

Neil Jordan arrives on the set of *The End of the Affair*. "What'll we do today?" he asks. A crew-member pipes up: "Well, sir, we could do a bit of typing . . . or we could do a bit of shagging. . . . or we could do shagging and then we could do typing. Or we could do them both together, sir . . ."

He laughs. The film is about to go on release and he is telling the story against himself, with a self-deprecating humor that was not always so apparent. "It was quite funny really. But that is the reality of the writers' life, you know that, don't you?" I know that Jordan wasn't always so relaxed. I remember interviews ten years ago where he was a prickly bundle of reflexes, constantly on the alert for danger. He used to answer questions with questions: "Why do you want to know that? What do you mean?" He would begin to say something, then trail away into silence. And he had a brooding, almost menacing quality that made those silences nearly unbearable. We had some very interesting conversations, back then, but interviews were painful for both participants.

Today's Jordan, the twenty-first-century model, is much more relaxed. He can laugh at himself, and can even tolerate the in-built absurdities of the interview situation. As a writer, he's never been entirely happy producing impromptu ad-libs for others to turn into prose. He still jabs and spars, interrupts himself to look for feedback. At least he hasn't taken the route followed by some serial celeb interviewees: there are no polished anecdotes repeated ad nauseam, no chunks of copy in neatly parsed paragraphs. I suddenly remember that he directed *Interview with the Vampire* since our last meeting, recall Christian Slater as a cocky hack terrified out of his wits by his undead subject. There are ironies in there, layer upon layer of them . . .

Which, in a sense, is the Jordan trademark. He is not an ironist in the literary sense, but his films invite analysis and multiple readings. He has made a dozen features now, and managed the rare feat of covering diverse subject matter yet regularly returning to familiar themes and obsessions. There is what he calls "the transcendental power of love," seen in *The Miracle* and *The End of the Affair*. In *The Crying Game* and elsewhere we see the elemental power of sexuality, its capacity to surprise and bewilder those who think they understand it. His treatment of supernatural themes, from *The Company of Wolves* to *Interview with the Vampire* to *The End of the Affair,* range across a vast area between gothic horror and Christian belief. The transcendental, the mysterious, the unknown: whether the impulse is religious or sexual or something else, it all forms a continuum. And Jordan's films probe that continuum from an alarming variety of angles.

Michael Collins is, on the surface, the most secular of his films: a historical narrative, with no hint of the supernatural beyond the enduring power of myth. One could easily situate that film in a discourse outside the rest of Jordan's oeuvre, see it as a specifically Irish project that had gathered its own momentum even before he arrived on the scene. Where many had tried, he happened to be the one in a position to get it made. I think there is some truth in this—*Michael Collins* diverted him from the things he does best—but the film, with hindsight, sits comfortably with the rest of his work. That recurring belief in the power of words, the idea that promises really matter, that things said come back to haunt you—it has the ring of truth, and covers all the ground from love affairs to pacts with the devil.

When I suggest this to Jordan he is initially unwilling to analyze his work in this way. It's the artist's defense: you do what you do, and others dissect it. Then suddenly, he says: "Never make a promise—you may have to keep it." He has dredged the line up from somewhere, and for a moment can't remember if it is one of his own or one of Graham Greene's. So I ask, who said it? "I don't know. Somebody in something I wrote. It was in this movie, wasn't it? It was in this movie but I cut the line out. It wasn't one of Greene's lines, it was one I wrote . . . wait, no, when Henry tells Bendrix she's dying, I think he does say that. Never make a promise . . . he does, yeah, that's true." This is another Jordan trait: rapid switching between acute intelligence and studied vagueness. When I mention his high work-rate—four films in three years—his first reaction is surprise. He counts them back: "*The End of the Affair, In Dreams, The Butcher Boy* . . . that's three. Oh, yes, and *Michael Collins.* Four. Yes, that's four in three years. Well. Mm."

So what, being the implication. He points out that he's had plenty of free time, that he's started another novel as well, and that an average of just over one film per year isn't anything to brag about—"Fassbinder used to make four films in one year." But Jordan does seem to be working at a higher pitch, at a new level of creative intensity. It is true that he has reached a point where he can make pretty much any film he likes, and that the world is full of tempting projects in the unlikely event that he ever runs short of ideas. But if you cut away all the problems, the waiting, the stop-go lifecycle, the money hassles which other filmmakers struggle with, how many of his peers would sustain such a constant flow of imaginative ideas? And that means his peers in Europe and America, not just in Ireland.

As he talks about *The End of the Affair,* I notice something unusual. His accent stays in Dublin, but some curious turns of phrase stray into it. He says things like "it was decidedly odd" and "it was rather alarming" and "quite curious, really." It's not anglophilia, and definitely not hyper-correction—the linguistic quirk which makes people try to sound more English, and miss by miles. It is more like osmosis: something of the quintessential Englishness of Greene's novel has seeped into him. It's a perfect example of the writer as sponge, always ready to absorb what it encounters. The linguistic nuances interest him. "I'm less comfortable making American movies because I don't know them so well. But actually making this film was a bit like making a film in a foreign language. Our relationship to language as Irish people is decidedly different to the English. Our relationship to language and the expression of emotion. It either comes out in great splurges of words, or it's a dead silence. The kind of understatement that Greene wrote is actually terribly beautiful, and, in a way, the emotion is expressed tangentially. It's like making a film in Portuguese or something. It's like observing a foreign culture, that was the most intimidating thing. Not so much getting it right, as not letting it be the whole thing, not letting it become the whole point."

But, I point out, he has "done" London before in *Mona Lisa.* "Yes," he says, "but *Mona Lisa* was different, that belonged to a genre. It was a crime story, dark streets, film noir. The movie was in that noir language. But in this film we're talking about actual speech." Ralph Fiennes, playing Greene's novelist alter-ego, Bendrix, gives a remarkable performance. He lets us think that he is playing a wronged lover, then gradually subtracts portions of his character, deconstructing himself on screen. We see that his selfish obsession with sex and dominance is the antithesis of love. Throughout, Fiennes comes across as a flesh-and-blood figure from the 1940s: his features, expressions, gestures appear rooted in wartime London. He is like a reincarnation of some forties movie star who never was, a distant, seedier cousin of Trevor Howard. Jordan agrees: "Ralph has that quality, he has it effortlessly. He has it to a fault, in a way, in that you can't imagine anybody better. It was kind of worrisome, actually, we discussed it—he was worried and I was worried. He had done *The English Patient*, and here he is with a woman who dies, and all that sort of thing. In the end we came to the conclusion that you can't find another equivalent to play that role. He has a sense of disenchantment with things that is perfect for the part. It's not just the aura of an English intellectual, it could be the figures that Camus wrote about. That European intellectual of that period. Any certainty has vanished."

Jordan talks about his characters in a very specific way, whether they are his own conceptions or are inherited, as in this case, from a novel. Even before casting, throughout the writing process he juggles different factors: the need for each character to be plausible as a human being, credible in their context, making choices that resonate. But there is also a larger scheme, a greater pattern, in which each component plays a part. It is a tension between naturalism and formalism, and Jordan ultimately tries to retain both modes. "Characters have traits planned in advance, but must always be more than the sum. It really had to have the quality of the period. It had to be directly understandable, I suppose, timeless. If you compare Ralph as Bendrix to Stephen Rea's Henry—Stephen's conception of that man, his character, was quite brilliant. He didn't want to play him as some dreary little cuckold—which he was in the book. Greene was quite cruel about the real Henry Walston. In the film Henry himself, his construction, is that of a very achieved man, a senior civil servant. He was dressed with some style. If you look at his costume, it's got far more finish and style than Bendrix's has. Stephen presented him as a man who had actually vanished beneath the style, beneath the exterior."

As a further case of attention to detail, we have Bendrix the writer. His apartment walls are lined with books. At the film's opening and closing scenes we see him at his typewriter, banging keys, trying to make sense of his life. We even catch a glimpse of an authentic period Penguin paperback: *The Vicarious Lover*, by Maurice Bendrix. Jordan invented it. "I came up with a whole series of titles for Bendrix, it was very funny. The art department asked me to do that, to write that stuff. One was called *Dogs and Other Monsters*. And *The Vicarious Lover*—I mean, you've got Bendrix attempting to tell the story of his relationship. And as he's telling it, he's discovering it. And he hires a private detective, because he wants to know the bits of her life that he hasn't got access to. He makes assumptions, and his assumptions are wrong. With sexual betrayal, asking who's taking off her underwear now, who is messing with her shoes, who has got her soul now? So the detective is also a kind of novelist, and they're all in this position of intrusive inquiry into this woman's life. To find out what the reality of it is. What's intriguing about Greene's story is that there's a mystery at the very heart of it. A mystery I think is appropriate to anyone's life. If you examine anyone's relationship, their commitments or their failures, there's always something mysterious. Some mysterious attachment or some mysterious area of longing that persists."

The question, as so often with Jordan, remains open. Do events have a rational explanation or is there evidence of something more? Somewhere, grubbing about in our everyday lives, trying to make sense of it all, we encounter the human condition. Faith leads to faith, reason to reason: the precession of simulacra. But the really interesting stuff happens in between, and keeps asking questions. As Jordan does: "The big question is, did Bendrix die or not. In a metaphorical way, after he wakes from that bomb, he is emotionally dead. His emotional life is ended. It's taken away from him: he may as well be dead. And if the state of being in love is the state of living, he's out of that state now. It's a kind of living death. And for me, the question is, okay, if anybody attempted to examine their own relationships, their own connections, their deepest contacts with anybody else—and they push that examination to the most uncomfortable extent possible—would they come up against the same block, where rationality ends. And where something else either begins or doesn't begin."

And the writer/lover, by pushing too hard to know, destroys the relationship? "Yeah, it's a bit like quantum physics, isn't it? Heisenberg. If you observe a particle you've already disturbed it. Yeah, that's probably true." Bendrix, novelist and obsessive lover, is also informed by Jordan's experience as a fiction writer. "It was a situation I knew very well, somebody typing, trying to make sense of their life through fiction. Trying to reclaim their life through fiction. In a way, you always write about the stuff you know, and you're always trying to reclaim bits of your own past. I think it's an attempt at reconstruction, in a way."

Jordan's next move has an unlikely twist: he plans to film Beckett's *Not I*, with Julianne Moore playing the encased female figure. His ideas on Beckett are ambiguous: great respect for his imagination, real attachment to the work, but a suspicion of their value as theatre. "Beckett seems like a jailer—his work is so much about the confinement of actors." As he sees it, *Not I*—despite the strictures of the Beckett estate—can be widened to include the process of confinement as well as its result. "The question is very interesting. I think, if Beckett is the greatest playwright of the twentieth century, there's something rather sad in that. I think he is anti-theatre, in a way. But I'll be absolutely faithful to his text, while showing how one had to arrive at these peculiar circumstances."

Happy Days

Ted Sheehy / 2001

From *Film Ireland* 79 (February/March, 2001): 14–15. Reprinted by permission of the author.

At the launch of the Beckett on Film season in Dublin, Anthony Minghella, Damien O'Donnell, and Neil Jordan spoke with Ted Sheehy about filming Samuel Beckett's plays.

Ted Sheehy: Is it just that it's Beckett's work or can you conceive of yourselves otherwise wanting to make short films that are formally experimental?

Anthony Minghella: I think you'd get a different answer from every director but in my case it was entirely connected with a long-held admiration for Beckett. I studied Beckett, I tried to do a doctorate on Beckett's work, *Play* was the first play I ever directed—it was a very particular reason to go into the world of short films and I'm not sure that anyone else would have got me into that arena. Having said that I suspect that Michael Colgan and Alan Moloney can persuade anyone to do anything so the likelihood is that we'll all be back here next year doing some project they have up their sleeves.

Damien O'Donnell: It depends on who initiates it really, if you're talking about inspiring established filmmakers to work in the short medium FilmFour have a website and they did something in association with *Dazed and Confused* where they got a load of artists, including people like Harmony Korine, to make one-minute films on digital for broadcast on the web. I think, if someone has any sort of drive, filmmakers are open to experimenting and the thing about short films is you don't make a huge investment of time and if someone else is looking after production of it, it's fun really.

AM: Well you're doing a thing with Mike Figgis, aren't you?

DO: Yeah, I'm working on a website for Mike Figgis's film, *Hotel*, because I'm interested in all that kind of thing and he's invited me along to work on it, to develop material. It's five weeks work and what I like about it is I don't have to think, is this a year of my life? It's only a couple of months and I think people should always make room for that kind of work.

Neil Jordan: Any opportunity you can get to do something that makes you think of the form, that's what it made me think about. You've got this strange wonderful piece of work and you've got to think of a way in which to make cinema, cameras, and all the cumbersome stuff, express this lovely thing. It was great.

AM: The play that I did was called *Play*, his one excursion into film was called *Film*, and it tells you that he was a formalist long before he was obsessed with content. It's interesting that Neil's done this installation at the Museum of Modern Art [IMMA] with seven versions . . .

NJ: He does force you to rethink the medium because Julianne [Moore] had to do this—it only made sense if it was done on one long take so every angle we did had to encompass the entire performance. Mostly in a film, if you look at the bits you've got, the tiny bits, the entire film is a composite of those bits. In this case the bits I had were all of the same length, of the entire piece. It was interesting just to say let's put all these bits together and let people look at them at the same time. Beckett makes you think that way.

TS: Is that a paradoxical aspect of the project, that the concerns of the Beckett estate and the precision of Beckett's dialogue and stage directions gives you the opportunity to draw back right into the camera?

NJ: You stick yourself in a tiny confine and you have to work out not only how to photograph it but what the act of photographing it means. For me it was an opportunity to do something you'd never get the opportunity to do, to engage with ideas you'd never get the chance to engage with in commercial cinema, at all.

For me, and I'm obviously a fan of short films, I just find that people move on from that and part of the delight of this project is that people who'd never make a short film have gone back and made a short film and I hope to keep on making short films—it's a beautiful medium.

TS: And having made a film that's so short it's odd to have to publicize it so much! (Laughter all round).

Film Ireland: Will the experience inform what you do next?

DO: I think so, absolutely. It has made me think seriously about the kind of films I want to make and the form of films both short and long. I found the whole thing quite revitalizing in a way.

AM: One of the things I think is really good about this project is that one of the most contentious areas of movie-making is the possessory credit— "A Neil Jordan Film," "A Damien O'Donnell Film," "An Anthony Minghella Film." What's interesting here is that it's a Samuel Beckett Season, a cycle of Samuel Beckett films, and our contribution is muted and rightly so. The other odd phenomenon is that it's very strange if you're a filmmaker because you very rarely meet other filmmakers. You meet actors, you meet editors, you meet all kinds of other people, production designers, but directors are very rarely in the same place or working together on the same project so this has been fantastic and really nourishing—to be in Toronto with Damien and Conor McPherson and Kieron J. Walsh—just talking about being a filmmaker. Talking about our reactions to working in this particular world and environment. It reminds us that were all trying to say something using this form, that everybody loves Beckett, that everybody loves film.

TS: Does the normal industrial way of working militate against what Anthony's just spoken about?

NJ: Yeah, of course. For one thing you work in a medium where the audience just gets younger and younger and as you get older and older (laughter) you don't still want to speak to seventeen-year-old males. What I found liberating about this was the ideas were impenetrable but liberating in a strange way because you never encounter these ideas. I have to go back to watching some of those obscure Bergman movies like

In the Life of the Marionettes, the weird ones, where the guy was battling with ideas of performance and reality.

AM: One of the things about Beckett is that he was writing very much in a period where people working in literature became terribly conscious about their words whereas if you were working in a different discipline, like music or painting, you were able to create—you were involved in abstract language. In literature you were having to coopt the stuff of everyday life, people are talking and using language all the time. So he became so sensitized to not getting caught in the trap of idiom that he forced himself to go into another language to work. When he goes into theatre he's like someone who's never been in a theatre before, he reimagines what the theatre could be about, how it might work. I feel that it forces you to, as Neil was saying when you go into the arena of cinema, to reconsider the fact that you've got a camera, you've got an actor, you're making sound. Everything somehow is refreshed through his eyes and I think that has happened with this entire series. It's not only about being important and impenetrable and difficult, it's also about simply revitalizing everybody.

NJ: It's also about making different kinds of movies.

DO: Nineteen people got to make a Samuel Beckett film, everyone should have a go at it, I think. Every filmmaker should go out and make a Samuel Beckett film.

NJ: I think Joel Schumacher should go out there, and do them all . . .

DO: Definitely . . . (much laughter)

To Catch a Thief

Paddy Kehoe / 2003

From *RTÉ Guide*, February 21, 2003, 28–29. Reprinted by permission.

Upstairs in the Clarence Hotel, Neil Jordan is singing to himself and leafing nonchalantly through a magazine which has his face on the cover. It could mean either of two things: he's at ease with himself, or quite the opposite—he is trying to normalize what may be a slightly discomfiting prospect, an interview, begod.

I tell him I had just seen *The Good Thief* at a press showing "Oh, you just saw it?" he asks. "Oh dear." What's the "oh dear" about, I ask. "I dunno. Normally people have to digest things." His latest film is wonderful and mesmerizing and I tell him so. "Good isn't it?" he says, almost diffidently. "It was very hard to make because it's so much lighter than anything else I've done. And yet it wasn't really light because it was kind of amoral in some way." Soon he is in his stride, happy to tease over various aspects of his latest film, politely asking if he can smoke a cigarette.

The Good Thief was inspired by Jean-Pierre Melville's 1955 movie *Bob le Flambeur*. Like the original, Jordan sees his creation as a film noir which also moves towards the light and ends happily. "Normally I do the opposite, I start with more optimistic scenarios and go to blood and murder. In this case I started with a guy shooting up in a toilet of a club he shouldn't have been in anyway at his age. I then move him towards the kind of ease where he can wear a monkey suit in a Monte Carlo casino."

The guy in question is Bob Montagnet, brilliantly played by Nick Nolte as a self-destructive American holed up in Nice. Bob is a heroin addict and gambler who becomes embroiled in two heists. The first involves the robbery of a collection of priceless paintings kept in a secret vault, while the second concerns the robbery of the Riviera Casino safe.

In the fast-moving twists and turns of the action—you must be on your toes—Bob so engineers it that the second plot becomes his decoy for the first. Furthermore, the paintings hanging on the casino walls are generally assumed to be the originals, but Bob and his cohorts, know otherwise. The cohorts include Emir Kusturica as an eccentric security systems expert, young French-Moroccan actor Said Taghmaoui as Raoul, and Ralph Fiennes as a shady art dealer.

The French-Turkish actor Tcheky Karyo (*Nikita, The Patriot*) plays the detective on Bob's trail. The young Georgian actress Nutsa Kukhianidze is Anne, a seventeen-year-old prostitute who embarks ever so tentatively on a relationship with father figure Nick. Both actors play their parts with such intensity of feeling that all the time you sense a trail of disappointment in their back stories.

Jordan compares Bob and Anne to two lost souls, one too old to be in this edgy, sordid quarter of Nice, the other too young to be there. Anne misinterprets Bob's interest as sexual, but he has outgrown sex. "That was one of the reasons Nick was so interested in playing it, he wanted to play a person of failing powers, be it sexual or mental. Apart from giving her a place to stay for a while, all he can give her is a few lessons in survival. And it turns into a gambling lesson, which is a metaphor for survival in the world where chance and luck can put you in a dreadful place, but actually if you negotiate it with enough grace you can get through it."

The scene where Bob goes cold turkey is high melodrama, as he handcuffs himself to his bed to lie in a lather of sweat. "I think Nick's been through that kind of thing. I don't know his personal history, but he has battled with addictions in the past." Jordan considers Nick to be a very interesting actor because he allows himself to be vulnerable, even frail. "Most actors don't want to be seen that way."

How much did he actually direct Nolte? "If you've done your homework and you've got the actors right, as a director there's often very little to do, you often stay out of the way. But sometimes actors can go the wrong way. For example this was a really heavily written movie, the dialogue was very specific and the rhythms of it were very specific.

"At one stage Nick and Nutsa wanted to improvise a scene, but I had to tell them that they could do that, but the results wouldn't be very good, they probably wouldn't think as the characters think." They subsequently did two scenes, an improvised one which Jordan insists didn't work at all and a scripted one which passed. Presumably, there was some healthy tension in the air at that point, but it has to be said that the cast work as a taut ensemble, thick as thieves throughout.

"They were enjoying it so much they used to turn up every day, even when they weren't involved in scenes," Jordan recalls. "You get extraordinarily close relationships on movies, it's like a family." Interestingly, Nolte still sends him scripts and the director doesn't rule out working with him again.

Jordan admits that the most difficult thing about *The Good Thief* was to make a heist movie that was dependent on characters "to keep the plot of the robbery underneath the concerns of the central characters."

The result is a movie which has echoes of the morality tale that was *Mona Lisa*, with Nolte out to save the innocence of a young girl, much like Hoskins in that movie. In Melville's film, Bob simply plans a robbery which goes wrong. On the night of the crime he is meant to front as a gambler, but Lady Luck is on his side and he wins all around him. In Jordan's movie, Nolte also gambles at the end, with similarly staggering wins, but Jordan himself came up with that idea of the Picassos and Van Goghs on the walls. Japanese corporations, he learned, do in fact display perfect copies in public while keeping the originals in temperature-controlled vaults, as in *The Good Thief*.

"The whole thing became like a play on the real and the fake, so in a way I'm doing a remake, I'm doing a fake of an original. In another way Melville's movie was a fake of an original because it was a remake of *The Asphalt Jungle*." Everything in the movie (originally titled *Double Down*) is doubled up—two heist gangs, two versions of the paintings, two robberies. Twin security guards are pivotal to the action played by twin brothers, Mark and Mike Polish from Idaho, recently seen in *Twin Falls, Idaho*.

Jordan's vision of a romantic, noirish city incorporates beautifully composed night-time vistas of the harbor at Nice. Strings of bulbs were strung along the streets of the city's old quarter, and he shot mostly at night, over a three-month, off-season shoot. (Director of photography on the shoot was Chris Menges who shot two of Jordan's previous films, his debut *Angel* and *Michael Collins*).

Made without a distributor about eighteen months ago, *The Good Thief* took a long time to get released. Jordan intends that this film should be seen as another example of a reinvigorated European cinema, punching back at a flagging Hollywood of bland safe bets and sequels. He himself was asked to make another *Interview with a Vampire*, his most commercially successful film, but he was not interested. Similarly, he believes there is a remake of *Mona Lisa* on the cards, which he won't be involved in.

In each of his thirteen films to date, Jordan's task has been to bring something new to the medium, and he believes he has failed where this does not occur. He admits that he failed in *High Spirits* but also, to some extent, in this 1999 film *In Dreams* which was based on a Bruce Robinson script, rewritten by the director himself. "I liked what I did with that, but I'm not sure that I liked the subject matter, child kidnapping and serial killing. It's very familiar territory. Maybe that's a failure in a way, the choice of that material. Often you fail within things and people don't notice your failures, you notice them yourself."

Ultimately, he would like to be more logical and learn to make "cold, decided choices." I wonder about this—the fact that he refuses to make his film about the Borgias for less than the $55 million he needs is indicative of some resolve. "I'm very intuitive, and not amenable to logic," Jordan says. "I've never planned anything, I've never planned a career or anything like that." Mercurial as ever, Jordan continues to make magic without a game plan.

The Screen Writer

Tara Brady / 2003

From *Hot Press*, March 12, 2003.

TB: Going by *Angel*, which slyly references *Le Samourai*, you seem to be a big Jean-Pierre Melville fan. Didn't that make it difficult remaking *Bob Le Flambeur*?

NJ: Yeah, I do like Melville. Definitely. It wasn't as daunting as you'd think though, because the original film was so tiny. Really small. There's almost nothing there. So I was asked to do this, and I agreed, or at least I agreed to try, and then suddenly they bought the rights and that was expensive. So then I just had to get on with it and I had to basically think of a way I could make something without trashing the Melville movie, and I came up with the idea of a double plot.

TB: Doubles and duplicates seem to be everywhere in your movie . . .

NJ: Yeah, the whole thing is in doubles. Basically, I decided that I was kind of making a fake, and the movie was about pictures that were fake, and a robbery that was fake, so everything just got doubled up, and then twins were thrown in there as well. It became a kind of game with the original film, so everything Melville did, I did twice.

TB: It's probably your most generic film to date—did you find that quite confining?

NJ: Yeah, I've never done anything like it before. It's very difficult to do that kind of stuff. It's very easy to be dark—you just follow the dark path. It's easy for me anyway. So the best thing about this movie for me is that it starts as a film noir, but it has a happy ending. Someone has said that it's probably the only film noir that has a happy ending, so that needed a kind of adroitness, a sleight of hand. So that was quite difficult to do.

TB: Nick Nolte puts in a virtuoso performance. How did you find working with him?

NJ: He was great. I had written this character, a recovering addict, using the program and language of twelve steps, but in an immoral way. Like when he walks into the Narcotics Anonymous meeting and then straight out the back door because it's just a ruse to fool the police. So, it was a very complicated character, and it's the kind of film where you could cast Bruce Willis or Harrison Ford, or any of these people, but I thought that if I could find the right actor, I would direct myself. So I met Nick in San Francisco. I saw him in a Sam Shepard play and I met him afterwards and thought—this is as close as you can get to the character. He has a history of addiction himself, and you'll never meet anyone less at home with the prevailing culture of Hollywood.

TB: He's always seemed to have a persona more like that of an ageing rock-star than a Hollywood leading man . . .

NJ: Yeah, Nick's had a life, hasn't he? But he's definitely one of the best actors in America, but because he doesn't do the Hollywood thing that much, he doesn't get nearly enough opportunities to strut his stuff really.

TB: And the rest of the cast is a real Euro-pudding mix. How did you assemble them all together?

NJ: Well, when you want a mix like that, you just go to Paris. Basically, they were all in Paris, except for the two Polish twins. I met Gerard Darmon (*Betty Blue*), Tcheky Karyo (*Nikita*, *GoldenEye*), Said Taghmaoui (*Three Kings*, *Hideous Kinky*)—and they all really wanted to be in a movie like this. And then Emir Kusturica (the Sarajevo-born director of *Black Cat, White Cat* and *Arizona Dream*), of course.

TB: Was he easier to work with as an actor, because he has a near-legendary bark as a director?

NJ: Has he, really? That's funny, I never knew that. He's a lovely guy, normally. He's a big huge Serbian bear, and he was appalled that I was doing reams of dialogue in single takes. The prospect of learning all those lines—he was not happy having to learn the whole lot. But he liked his character, because it's the kind of figure that shows up a lot in American movies—the tech-head—nerdy, wimpy guys with big glasses. So this was the big, huge Eastern European equivalent.

TB: And how did you discover newcomer Nutsa Kukhianidze?

NJ: Well, I was looking for a young kid, and around the Mediterranean, there are just thousands of kids from Albania or Georgia milling around. She had done one other movie before which I hadn't seen, called *Stolen Kisses*. She just had extraordinary poise. I was looking for that kind of gamine youthfulness, and you either have it or you don't. It can't be faked, and it's quite a devastating quality.

TB: Though he's not in this movie, the most established relationship you have with an actor is with Stephen Rea. What is it about that enables you to work so well together?

NJ: Well, I have written several parts specifically for him, like with *Angel* and *The Crying Game*. It's a relationship where we both started out together, and I have certain instincts that suit the actor very well. Or course, it helps that Steve is one of the best actors around, so it's been a very fruitful relationship for me. He has an intelligence, and a conscience as an actor, but there was nothing for him in this film. I didn't want him turning up as an East European gangster or to have to make him put on a French accent!

TB: He managed terribly well though with the English accent for *The End of the Affair*?

NJ: Yeah, that's true. That was a great experience. It was hard to get him into that role—a pompous Englishman—but once he did, it was brilliant. I was happy all round with that one. I was happy with the way the script turned out, and it was great working with Ralph Fiennes and Julianne Moore.

TB: You did seem to capture certain Graham Greene sensibilities perfectly with the screenplay—that very arch humor for example . . .

NJ: Yeah, there's a bitter, black laughter there. There's a savage humor attached to the way that the main character looks at stuff, but that wasn't that hard to do, because it was all in the book. The hardest aspect of doing that script was changing the ending, because I always felt that the ending of the book was a bit theological, and a lot of the critics—especially in Britain—didn't like what I did with the ending. But I realized that the problem there was that the book is so bloody short, they could all manage to read it before seeing the film! I wouldn't have had nearly so much criticism had it been a longer book.

TB: Even your films which are overly political—like *Michael Collins* or

The Crying Game—focus on the personal. Are you consciously apolitical when it comes to your art?

NJ: Well, I just like things to be complicated. I've never made a political movie like *Z* or *Hidden Agenda*, just because I think that the realities are more complicated than that. I suppose the movies that I've made about Ireland—like *Angel* or the ones you've mentioned—are about people who are stuck in the greys of morality. I just think that's more interesting, and I've never really seen things in black and white when it comes to Irish politics, which is why I prefer to examine things from the personal.

TB: Your next two films—based on the Borgia papacy and the *Odyssey*—seem a lot bigger than the personal though?

NJ: Well, you'd be surprised. The *Odyssey* movie I'm making is small. It's called *The Return* and it's literally just that—the last part of the journey. *Borgia* is a kind of *Godfather* thing. Now that is a big, huge production, but as yet I can't get enough money to do it. So, we'll see.

TB: Has that part of the job gotten easier over the years, or can financing still be a nightmare depending on the project?

NJ: Exactly. It very much depends on the project. I mean, when you're looking for $60 million—then they want a sure thing. They want a movie with big stars and that kind of thing. It's very difficult at the moment. Unbelievably so. There's a huge economic downturn everywhere, so Hollywood responds with endless sequels—*Terminator 3* and so on. So, it's a very bad time to be coming up with unusual projects that need serious investment. Then of course, in England there's been the collapse of Film Four and here things are quiet too, though I've read great things about *A Song for a Raggy Boy*—so it's not all bad news.

TB: When you look back on your first foray into the world of Hollywood, do you feel you could've kept control of *High Spirits* and *We're No Angels* better?

NJ: No. I think that the first time a director goes to Hollywood, it's very hard especially if, like me, you've made two or three European movies. I mean, I had made *Angel, The Company of Wolves,* and *Mona Lisa,* and there was never any question about who was the author of those films. No matter what—you work things out for yourself and you go with what's interesting for you. That's all part of becoming a filmmaker. Then you go to Hollywood, and it's shocking. It was certainly shocking for me.

People were actually trying to stop me from making the movie. It was really bizarre.

TB: It makes you wonder why they bother hiring directors in the first place . . .

NJ: Exactly. I remember on *High Spirits*, I walked on set one day and everything was blindingly bright. And it was like—oh, it won't be so bright when we film it—and then I saw the rushes. It was just too fucking bright, but everyone else is reasoning—oh it's a comedy, it has to be bright. It was unbelievable. What a stupid practice—producers trying to direct. It makes no sense.

TB: Was it easier when you returned there to make *Interview with a Vampire?*

NJ: Yeah, it was. Well, I suppose I was older, so when I was asked to do it, I was able to say—I don't want this to happen. But I think a big problem—especially with big special effects pictures—is that maybe only 40 percent of them end up being directed by a director. Everything else is added in post-production. So they choose young directors, from advertising and so on. The movies are made by committee, basically.

I mean, recently, I was being shown bits of the *Harry Potter* movie, in the special effects house, and it was a shot of Harry on top of a huge sculpture waving a sword, and there was all this stuff going on, but all the director did was stand the kid in front of a screen and filmed him waving a sword and then said "Now do it again." That was it. That's a director's job now apparently.

TB: The only really special effects–based movie like that which you've done is *The Company of Wolves*. Is it a genre you've ever wanted to return to?

NJ: Well, in a way, you're always involved in special effects. You use them all the time. But in terms of fantasy-based movies—I would quite like to get back there sometime. I loved *Lord of the Rings*. It's the first time that you can really see the gamut of possibilities, of what can be achieved using digital effects. It's the same story. When you put a director with a vision in control of this stuff, they can come up with marvels. I mean, there are good and bad things about Hollywood, and one of the good things is that every now and then they can make a decision like that and have the resources to back it up. It keeps you going, you know?

TB: Yeah, because I've read that you considered returning to writing novels prior to the success of *The Crying Game* . . .

NJ: Yeah, but I probably wouldn't have written more novels than I have. I'm just so used to working in film. It's easier. It's more immediate. I work better in that context. When you've been working on screenplays for ages, like I have, then writing prose becomes tortuous.

TB: Is that because of your background in visuals, with most of your family being painters?

NJ: No. I think it's just because film is what I started out doing, and it's too late to go back now!

Songs of Innocence

Lir Mac Cárthaigh / 2006

From *Film Ireland* 108 (January 2006): 12–15. Reprinted by permission of the author.

Lir Mac Cárthaigh: *Breakfast on Pluto*, from the source novel to the cast to the financing, is very much an Irish project.
Neil Jordan: Totally an Irish project, almost totally. In terms of financing it's Pathe, and it's what Alan Moloney could put together.

LMC: Was it deliberate; making a very Irish film?
NJ: No, not at all. I had a deal with DreamWorks; I kept buying books that they didn't want to do, and one of them was *Breakfast on Pluto*. They gave me a very comfortable deal, and I managed to pay Pat McCabe for a first draft of the script. But it's not their kind of material, so we ended up doing it independently—that's what you have to do with most things.

LMC: If you want to do them the way you want to do them?
NJ: If you want to do them at all, actually. I mean you'd say "of course I'll compromise if you'll do it," but they don't even want to do it! Basically, Pat had written a draft, then I began to write different drafts. Both myself and Pat wanted to depart from the novel, to use the novel as a springboard, really.

Because to a certain extent he thought he hadn't finished the book—seriously! And the movie's quite different from the book: we were both anxious to finish it in some way. The first thing he did was bring the father back in—the priest—he had a meeting towards the end, and that was quite a departure. And then I began to take over the script myself, and rewrite and rewrite. It was a long process because I was doing different things. I'd tested Cillian when we had arrived at a script that was interesting—I really wanted to see could anyone play the part! (Lir chuckles.)

No, seriously, because it is a big deal. I mean if somebody had played that part with the kind of camp you get in *La Cage aux folles*, or even in *Priscilla, Queen of the Desert*, it wouldn't have worked at all. Cillian gave this amazing performance, so I then knew that somebody could do the role. But I was doing other things, I was finishing a novel, *Shade*, and I think I was making a movie, *The Good Thief*, and I kind of put it off for a bit. Cillian kept coming back saying "you have to do it, you have to do it." The script was quite wild and quite provocative. So I sent it round to various studios, and various independent studios in America, and we didn't get a great response. I kept revising the script, and eventually we reached a point where I was really happy with it. I had a meeting with Cillian and Alan where all three of us talked about it, and Alan said, "Well, how much is it going to cost?" and I said, "Probably about $12 million," and he said, "Look, give me three weeks or four weeks to put it together," and he did. Then we just went into making it, really. So it was one of those fortuitous things, you know?

LMC: In terms of the "Kitten" part, the character is in almost every scene . . .

NJ: Yeah; well, that's what made me want to do the movie. Because, frankly, it's dealing with a lot of subjects I've dealt with before, you know, terrorism, the kind of repression of small-town society, sexual issues, and all that sort of stuff. But the dynamic of that character was so beautiful, the clarity and the humor and the grace of the character was just . . . I just love the character. That's why I wanted to do it in the end.

LMC: Kitten's world is molded by sentimental love songs and movies, but you've managed to create that world in the film in such a way that it's not cheesy, or pastichey . . .

NJ: Absolutely, but it was my memories of the period. I was twenty in 1970; the book happens, between 1970 and 1974, and the movie happens in that period. It was just really a matter of recreating everything I remembered, the clothes, the sense of glamour in the world, the feeling of being in an environment where the colors were either green and grey or dark brown, and this character introduces lemony yellow and pink. I was actually thrilling to do in that way because I was kind of recreating things that I did remember very, very well.

LMC: The London section is a fantastic recreation of a Soho that's gone now.

NJ: (Sadly) It doesn't exist anymore, no. That wasn't in the book, the peepshow section. When I was doing *Mona Lisa* we were wandering around Soho and looking at all the dip joints, and we found this place—it was a co-operative run by a bunch of girls who otherwise would have been prostitutes. So they were in charge of their own environment; there were no sleazy pimps involved, there were no men around . . . it was a horrible environment, you know, it was a peepshow thing—the men would go in and look and jerk off and all that sort of stuff—but the girls themselves were totally secure. And they kind of created this little erotic wonderland. So I put him [Kitten] in there, and I recreated that; it was quite specific, you know.

LMC: There are some great female roles in the film, and you have some great people to play them, Ruth Negga, Eva Birthistle. . . . Do you feel there are enough strong roles written for women?

NJ: Well. I've found over the last ten years making films here . . . take *Michael Collins*: Okay, I know everybody gave out about me casting Julia Roberts—maybe they were right, maybe they were wrong—but anyway, but the point was that there weren't as strong a group of young female actors then as there were young male actors. The ones who were really great—say even when I came to *The Butcher Boy*—were the older ones like Rosaleen Linehan, Ruth McCabe, Anna Manahan, people like that. But when I came to do this, lo and behold, there were three or four really, really good equivalents of the male starry types. So things have changed, and I'm really glad of that, actually. It's been a male game for so long, you know? I mean, there were other people I could have considered for both of those roles, but Eva and Ruth are great actresses. Also, it was great to see the *glamour*, really, the glamour gives a physical kind of bounce to it.

LMC: For a film that features such a strong evocation of a particular period, was it difficult to orchestrate the various departments: wardrobe, make-up, art department, and so on?

NJ: It was quite difficult. It was a bit like making an independent movie. I suppose I was doing very large things with very small resources, and really plugging into the way in which independent movies are made here. I put an enormous amount of pressure on the system, and they probably hadn't experienced that much pressure for a while. It was quite tough, I have to say. But Eimer is a great costume designer, Declan Quinn is a very good cameraman, you know. So we were all trying to push the whole thing to a visual level where it hadn't been before. I mean, it's quite easy to make Irish movies and get the dynamics of the social realist or the documentary aspect of it going, but to get a sense of strong visual statement you need a lot of preparation and you need to explain things very carefully to people. So it was quite hard, but it was worth it really. I thought Eimer, particularly, did sensational work.

LMC: As an Irish film, it takes the received notions of what an "Irish film" is, and, through Kitten's approach to the world, turns them on their head. Was that something you intended?

NJ: I was very conscious of that, I was very conscious of photographing environments that have been photographed so many times before—even by myself. But I wanted something to be really deeply pleasurable about the images, and I wanted the film to have a redemptive pleasure to it. I know what you mean, because I was conscious of that while I was making it; I was conscious that every little piece of set design, every little piece of art direction, could actually be one of these really depressing Irish movies where the father dies of cancer and the mother kills herself . . . I don't know, whatever. But it actually wasn't that story because the entire sequence of events was redeemed by the central character and by her imagination as well. Because it's really a story that should have been a tragedy, but the central character insisted on turning it into a comedy—in the broadest sense of the term—I don't mean a laugh a minute, but in the broad span I think its comedic, redemptive.

LMC: There's a huge amount of music in the film, and a very wide range; obviously, music is very important in creating Kitten's world.

NJ: Absolutely, of course. Well, I had Pat there, and Gavin Friday—he suggested a lot of tunes. There were some things written into the film: there was "Breakfast on Pluto," which I couldn't use really; it was too clunky to express the bounce of the character, there wasn't enough glamour to the tune. He referred to "Honey" and "Children of the Revolution," so I used those; and then it was actually a matter of listening to everything I could find from the seventies, and just finding what fitted. I suppose the music needed a certain bubblegum quality to work. I mean, I listened to a lot of David Bowie, but it just didn't fit and I don't know why. And I would have thought it would be perfect, because he's androgynous, he was using make-up and all that, but I think the songs were too epic, in a strange way. Then I started playing Harry Nilsson against it, and for some reason this guy just fitted the film. It was also a matter of expense, there was a John Lennon song I would have loved to have used, which I couldn't use because there was too much money; there was a piece of Pink Floyd we were going to use. . . . So I basically had to just trawl and trawl to see what fitted the film.

Music operates in a really strange way; logically David Bowie's "London Boys" would suit the film, because it's about London rent boys or whatever, but when you play it against the film it just doesn't work at all. So it was a matter of finding the emotional texture that suited the character. We ended up with a lot of those Harry Nilsson tunes, even a tune by Slade—I never thought I'd put a tune by Slade into a movie! I owe a great debt to Van Morrison actually, because he allowed me to use two of his iconic songs, and he really facilitated us in pushing that through. So thank you, Van!

LMC: There are two well-known musicians acting in the film: Gavin Friday and Bryan Ferry.
NJ: Bryan, yeah. We didn't use any Roxy Music, either! There you go, it's weird, isn't it? But it was great to get Bryan in the film, because he's always sung like an actor, hasn't he? But he's never acted. There were so many English actors we could have cast in that role, but to cast Bryan was great because you just don't expect to see him in a movie—and you go, "Is that Bryan?!"

LMC: How did you find out he could act?
NJ: I didn't, I just took a chance. I talked to him about it; he seemed interested. I did a little reading with him, but I didn't do an audition, really.

LMC: Gavin Friday is fantastic as Billy Hatchet, another really great character . . .
NJ: That was great, wasn't it? It's weird, I mean, there's no Billy Hatchet in the book, as you know. Nor is there a magician in the book. Gavin is great. Gavin was particularly nervous about acting, because he's not really done it. Again, I did a little test with a video camera, and he was electric.

LMC: How did Bertie come to be a magician?
NJ: Bertie in the novel was—what was he? He used to play the organ, or something—he was a really depressing character. I don't know, I just wanted to write this character who didn't know who he was. I mean the thing that's in common between Bertie in the novel and Bertie in the movie: they are attracted to this kid in a way that they don't want to

admit fully to themselves, but they know exactly what the attraction is. So it was just a matter of exploring this. I kind of had to make up that character, really; he was almost like a failed actor who had turned to strange magic tricks to keep him in show business—you know that kind of way?

LMC: It's magic that's very stagy on one level, but it's very visceral at the same time.

NJ: Well, there's a bit of Tommy Cooper in there, isn't there. I kind of designed those magic tricks for Stephen, because poor Stephen was learning to pull rabbits out of a hat, and all of that sort of corny stuff. So I said, "Let's make up something that's specific to the character," so I invented that card that went on forever, and the idea of the Grand Guignol stuff—a bit more like a horror movie version of a magician. But the main thing about Bertie was that he was a hypnotist, so he can speak to the central character through hypnotism.

LMC: And another new accent for Stephen Rea!

NJ: Yeah, he was very specific about that. He kind of made him one of these failed middle-class English gents, you know?

LMC: Obviously the priest character is in the book, but he's very different from the film's—in fact the whole third act is quite different; did that come from Pat, or you, or was it both of you?

NJ: What happened was Pat introduced Fr. Liam back at the end; when they came back to Ireland there was a reconciliation with the father, which was really interesting, but it wasn't that emotional. Then I began to write those peepshow scenes, and then I thought I'd bring Fr. Liam into the peepshow. Then I wrote the scene where he goes to see his mother, where he dresses up as his version of Margaret Thatcher. So then it became really rich: the father doesn't really want to reveal himself to the boy, but he knows the boy wants to see his mother. So the father will come to this confessional thing—and it's kind of a mirror of the confessional at the start—and the father will tell the son what he wants to know: where his mother is. And perhaps also to tell the son that his idea that he was born out of an act of rape is wrong, that there was some kind of relationship there. Then at the end the son will realize that he wasn't looking for his mother, he was looking for his father. And then it became really rich, we just arrived at it really, it was where the story wanted to go.

LMC: Your films are gradually getting released on DVD, and you've recorded commentaries for some of them; how important is your back catalogue to you, and what kind of control do you have over the films?
NJ: None at all, I don't own any of them—I wouldn't mind it! I'd like to recut some things. . . . I mean, I had to do the DVD for *The Company of Wolves*, which I loved doing, actually, but I really would like to recut some of it. Some of the effects are too lumbering . . . I mean just basic stuff. But apart from that it was lovely to see it again, you know. The fact that DVD is there is amazing, because it makes your films part of a continuum. Before that they just vanished. But I've never been able to own any of the negatives, or anything like that, so I don't fully control them. In fact somebody's trying to remake *Mona Lisa* at the moment: Larry Clarke. It's really bizarre, but I can't stop it.

LMC: *The Miracle* is a film I'd love to see on DVD . . .
NJ: I must get that out on DVD, Jesus. So few people saw that movie it might be hard to get someone to release it on DVD—unless I do it myself!

• • •

Lir Mac Cárthaigh: This is your first time working with Neil as a director; are you an admirer of his?
Cillian Murphy: Ah yeah, I mean growing up in Ireland I think you'd have to be. But I think he's a world director first and foremost; his movies are loved by everyone all over the world, and even though he deals with Irish themes, he's also dealt with themes as far removed from Irish topics as you can get. There isn't a great visual history in Irish cinema, you know what I mean? Great storytelling, but . . . I think he has the visual flair. I think his films always look beautiful, and they're always interesting, and so all of those things appealed to me, years and years before I had a chance to even meet him!

LMC: What drew you to the role of Kitten?
CM: Well, *The Butcher Boy* had a tremendous effect on me—the book and the film. I read *Breakfast on Pluto* when it came out, and I fell in love with that character as well. It's one of those roles of a lifetime; I'm very careful not to use that phrase too lightly, but I think it applies in this context. I did a screen test for Neil when he was thinking of doing it about four years ago, maybe longer. We both felt there was something there, but I

don't think he had the money or the inclination to go back to those topics that soon. Then Alan Moloney, who produced *Intermission* with Neil, came to us and said, "What about this *Breakfast on Pluto* script?" We were out one night in Dublin somewhere and he said, "Look, give me three weeks and I'll have the money for you." We sort of drunkenly said, "Go on," and he did it, you know?! He deserves a lot of credit for getting this thing going.

LMC: The film as a whole sort of rests on your shoulders; your character appears in almost every scene. Was that a frightening prospect or was it something that excited you?
CM: I think if you look at the thing and go, "Yeah, I can do this," you're starting from a weak position. It was terrifying, the prospect of it, because it's sort of the ultimate informative role, but that's what actors thrive on isn't it? Well they should, anyway! But when you've a director like Neil, as well, you feel in very safe hands. But if you don't feel sort of scared or trepidatious about it it's not worth it for me, really.

LMC: Neil's talked a lot about innocence, in terms of Kitten's character, but she's also very fearless and wise. Was it a difficult balance to achieve?
CM: Yeah, it's very, very interesting because she's very dynamic, with all of the conflicting strengths and weaknesses that she has. Someone asked us if the film is about the loss of innocence, and Neil said it's about the maintenance of innocence, you know, which I think is a smart way of looking at it. But I think that she's very, very intelligent and knows exactly what's going on; she feigns innocence, and feigns ignorance of the troubles and what side is what. But it's a defense mechanism ultimately, isn't it?

LMC: As the film progresses, your costume and make-up get more extreme. Did this make it easier or more difficult to act?
CM: I kind of knew very early on that I could do the looking pretty, looking beautiful stuff; it was to back that up with the soul of the character, that was the challenge. We had brilliant hair and make-up on this job; Lynn Johnston did the make-up, and she was just incredible. But it was a joy, I loved doing all of that—that's what we do, we put on clothes and we put on funny voices. You get into looking pretty and beautiful very easily. The only thing I did that was sore was shaving the legs, and chaffing, but you know nothing that was unbearable. There were a lot of hours in make-up; you have to commit to it 100 percent, so I did.

LMC: The rest of the cast is a real roll-call of Irish acting. You've worked with most of them before, but was there anyone you particularly enjoyed doing scenes with?

CM: I've a particular soft spot for Brendan Gleeson; the problem with doing the stuff with him was trying to not laugh! But I did my first ever part in a film with him, the barman in *Sweety Barrett*, and I just remember he was so gracious and generous back then, and has continued to be all the way up. I always go to him for advice and stuff you know. And he had that character John-Joe down from the start, right from when we walked into rehearsals. The whole thing from the look, the accent, everything, as did Stephen Rea's character, and Liam Neeson—I guess they have the shorthand with Neil, they know what he's going to want, and they know they have a freedom to go a bit mad. I also found working with Ian Hart was amazing, like in that scene in the police cell he didn't lay a finger on me, and it was a very, very brutal scene.

LMC: Obviously, the Irish public is well aware of your range, but do you worry that you'll be typecast internationally as a villain, based on the more extreme roles you play in films like *Batman Begins* and *Red Eye*?

CM: Yeah, I mean that's probably a fair point; I do enjoy characters under pressure, and I do generally enjoy the darker side of things, although Kitten is the complete opposite in that regard. In terms of *Red Eye* and *Batman*, I did get a lot of that in the American press, you know, "Hollywood's latest bad guy," but it was just a fluke of distribution. I shot *Pluto* in between the two of them. And of course most of the movie-going public there wouldn't have seen the earlier films. Having said that, I've just finished Ken Loach's film about the troubles in West Cork . . .

LMC: *The Wind That Shakes the Barley?*

CM: Yeah, and the flying columns and stuff. And then I'm doing Danny Boyle's movie, and I'm certainly not the bad guy in that. Having said that, they're dealing with pretty heavy conflicts, both of them. I guess that it's not a deliberate thing, it's just that in the scripts that I've read the ones that appeal to me are the darker ones. That's not to say that Woody Allen movies don't, or anything like that, but my movies, and the great sort of works of art I find in fiction and film anyway, the ones that investigate the dark side of the psyche I find more appealing. I'd love to do a good Woody Allen movie, or a very smart comedy, and I think that when these films come out—the Loach one and the Boyle one—that hopefully they'll show a slightly different side of me.

Neil Jordan in the New Millennium: 1999–2011

Carole Zucker / 2011

Interview conducted March/April 2011. Previously unpublished.

Carole Zucker: Can you talk about how *In Dreams* came about?

Neil Jordan: What happened was Steven Spielberg sent me that script, and they had just set up DreamWorks. I'd done a movie with David Geffen, and they were very anxious that I do a film for them, and they sent me a script by Bruce Robinson which was called *Blue Vision*, and it was about somebody sharing dreams with a killer. They asked me to consider making it and I said: "Well, why don't I just have a go at the script and see what I come up with." Because there were problems with the screenplay. Basically, I wrote a script, and they got very, very excited about it, and very rapidly put it into production. That's the way it happened.

CZ: Because I remember reading Robinson's script when I was at your home doing research, and it seems to be quite different to what you wrote.

NJ: Well not entirely different, not entirely. I mean it was one of those conventional scare thrillers in a way. When I got my hands on the script, I looked at things that were the background. I made it very phantasma-goric—the whole idea of them sharing the same dreams and the same experience, I brought to the forefront. And I got quite excited by the Grand Guignol possibilities of it all, let's put it that way. It was one of those films where when we finished the movie, there were quite a few problems with it. Because I suppose the realistic aspect of the plot, the last third of it, didn't turn out to be very convincing. And it was one of those issues where, I suppose, one does a rewrite and a rewrite and a rewrite but one doesn't solve some of the problems with the basic concepts. But I mean I love . . . I really like the movie.

CZ: It's one of my favorite films.
NJ: Well I mean it's hard to love, it's hard to love.

CZ: I want to go into it more, because I think it's one of your best films, because there are so many real tour-de-force scenes in it, and it's incredibly beautiful as well. It deals with underlying things that I find in all of your work, like myth and ritual, and the structure and meaning of fairy tales, and the particular view that you have of the family, something that casts the viability of the family unit into doubt, violence and psychic and physical damage . . .
NJ: Well now the real thing—if you want to know the truth—that attracted me to the whole thing was the image of that buried town at the very start of the script. I developed the story a bit more about the character that Robert Downey played . . .

CZ: Vivian . . .
NJ: Vivian, yeah, and I placed him in that drowned town and made the whole idea of a drowned town and 1950s America be center to the story. I suppose what I did when I began to do it, was to work on all the dreamlike levels. All the dream elements of the script, I brought to the forefront, and the realistic ones I pushed to the background, so it became phantasmagoric.

CZ: It's interesting that in most horror films what you have is a long section at the beginning that establishes the normality of the world, and *In Dreams* that lasts for about five minutes.
NJ: Well yeah but that's all you need really because the images of that town are so arresting. The awful thing about horror movies and about serial killer movies is, and this is what I find a little bit disappointing in the movie, in the whole concept of the script, Bruce's and my work, is that you always end up with some explanation for the central character: dementia, and it's always something to do with childhood and childhood abuse, and the kid who's locked in a box or put in a coffin by a demented father, something like that. That becomes cheap Freudianism, and it's always a little bit disappointing. I would love if a monster were just monstrous because say, somebody robbed their sweets when they were kids. Does it always have to be a demented parent who locks them in a box?

CZ: For me it's not just a serial killer film, like all of your films, *In Dreams* deals in some way with the creative process, and in this case it's Claire's drawing—she's an illustrator, there's Bendrix in *The End of the Affair* who is a writer, and Bob in *The Good Thief* who recreates his identity at the film's end, as well as playing the fabulist storyteller during the course of the film. You always create identities that are in transformation, in some way.

NJ: The real thing that attracted me to *In Dreams* was the fact that she actually was dreaming about somebody else's life. There is this famous ghost story of the woman who has this one consistent dream of a house with a picket fence and she keeps having this same dream. And as she goes through the town, she walks down the street to the picket fence, and she opens the door into the house, and she observes peoples' conversations in the house, and they don't know she's there. For some reason the phantom, the woman who keeps having this dream at one stage actually ends up in this town, and she walks up to the house with the picket fence, and knocks on the door, and the two women who have been in her dreams answer the door, and she says to the women, "There's something strange about this house," and they say "Yeah, it's haunted." And she says, "Well who is it haunted by?" and they say, "Well you should know, it's haunted by you." But the idea of the haunting being absolutely nothing to do with the individual at all, some kind of accident—you cross over into some dream or psychic plane, that's what it feels like to me.

CZ: The idea about the permeability of consciousness and the idea of crossing boundaries that used to be secure is, for me, the most frightening feature of horror films. You find that with stories like *Dr. Jekyll and Mr. Hyde* and then you have all the remakes of *Invasion of the Body Snatchers*, the whole idea of penetration, and it's especially frightening when it's an invasion not just of the body but of the mind. In a way it leaves the character played by Annette Bening, Claire, in a very dehumanized and fragmented state that separates her from the rest of the community.

NJ: Yeah, yeah . . . but the reason I did the movie were for all those reasons, but I can't claim the film is an entire success . . . really it was a commission, it was something I was asked to direct, somebody else's product. Somebody handed me the script, and I did make it my own. What was really interesting about it was that if you take the central character of Claire, everybody dies, her husband dies, her dog dies, the daughter's dead, so we were stuck in the end. The only thing is to have her die, so it ends up being a very black film for a studio to make, but people took, and the critics took severe objection to that, they really did.

CZ: But how does that make you feel, is it something that you can shrug off?

NJ: Well not really. Very often, the great temptation of Hollywood movies, of Hollywood, is they offer me something and I say, "It's almost good, it's not great," and they say, "But that's why we want you, you're going to make it your own, you're going to make it this thing." And then you start working on the film, you start making it, you're trying to make it your own, they say, "Hang on, this is not what we want, we want a nuts and bolts horror movie here." So it's the temptation, the offer always comes with the sting in its tail, and sometimes the sting in the tail harms the entire thing in a way. It's a tough one for someone like me to take a generic Hollywood movie, really. When Jodie Foster asked me to do *The Brave One*, it was almost similar in a way except it was a much more realistic story. But then again, what you often find with Hollywood movies is that the scripts go through that system, and often never come to a conclusion. The endings are very rarely satisfying, and I found that the case in both films, it was very, very difficult to resolve the ending. It's very, very difficult to come up with an ending that the characters themselves seem to want, because I suppose there's too many fingers in the pie, too many story-writing or executive opinions.

CZ: When I read the script, I noticed that the film ended in water, with Claire touching her daughter. Then Claire asks, "Where are we going?" and the daughter says, "Home." The ending as it is now, was not in the final shooting script.

NJ: We had to shoot a few endings to that film. I mean when we finished the movie, people, the executives at DreamWorks, liked the film but the ending wasn't satisfactory, so we thought about one ending, and another and another, and, and in the end I wrote this ending where Claire actually had died, and that seems logically the only place to go. But I can't pretend it was hugely satisfying. But at least it was logical.

CZ: You don't find that the ending where she returns as a revenant satisfying? Because to me it seems like a form of justice.

NJ: Oh yeah, where she returns and haunts him in the jail cell, yes, it did make sense. But it was arrived at after a lot of conversation and tossing ideas around. It was the only place the story could go in some strange way.

CZ: I want to talk about working with Annette Bening, because she's one of my favorite actors, and I understand that she does a lot of preparation for her roles.

NJ: Annette was very, very prepared, she thought out all the psychological ramifications for the character. It's a very difficult role for her to play: she'd lost her daughter, she's going crazy, she loses her husband, she loses her dog. (Laughs.) But what was great about Annette was that, actually, when we needed to go to those psychological places where her mental world reflects the world of Robert Downey Jr., she was able to go into those irrational places with all the rationality that she brings to her preparation as an actor. And that is superb. Really superb.

CZ: It seems that she throws herself completely into everything she does.
NJ: Totally, yeah, Annette made that part her own, indeed.

CZ: There's that wonderful Snow White scene, which is quite brilliant.
NJ: I mean there are several things I brought to the script, one was the elaboration of that whole child's play, in the forest, the other was the expanding of the idea of a drowned town in general, and the third thing was the making the fact that they share each others' dreams part of the story. Those are three things that I brought to the script that Steven Spielberg had commissioned.

CZ: Yes.
NJ: And I wrote a play to happen right in the middle of the story. It was all to do with the apple, wasn't it? Snow White, and all that . . . like a version of *A Midsummer Night's Dream* that would be presented to an audience of parents. But, I went through a lot of work to make the play itself reflect what was going on in the broader story, or to have the essence of the broader story somewhere within the play.

CZ: Once the play is over and Claire wanders through the crowd and looks for her daughter, and she comes upon all of these little girls dressed in gossamer wings, then everything is thrown into complete chaos and hysteria.
NJ: Yeah, it becomes totally nightmarish. And the other kids don't care, and they're playing evil little fairies and nasty stuff like that, and then

she finds the wings, and . . . it's like every parent's nightmare, really, isn't it?

CZ: The rebellion against the house is a very gothic element. The scene where Claire wildly throws the apples into the sink, the apples that inhabit her dreams, and the repetition of the song "Don't Sit Under the Apple Tree," and the computer-generated apples on the Apple computer . . . the house in a way rises up against Claire when it spews the apples out of the garburator . . . it's so intense and really horrifying. She has this artistic practice that's part of her repertoire as a designer—she redecorates the house in red paint with words scrawled on the walls, and dripping paint like some crazed graffiti. It's this internal and external devastation, the ravaged home becomes an externalization of what's going on inside of her. And then, this is replicated when Claire goes to the ruined hotel to find her husband dead. She's wearing a red chiffon dress that's like the gossamer wings of the children in the Snow White scene, it's quite dream-like and exquisite.
NJ: Yeah . . . well, thank you! (Laughs)

CZ: The other part that's intriguing is that Claire adopts Vivian's broken identity, and becomes his double.
NJ: It was very simple in a way. She has the conviction that somebody is out there who's doing these monstrous things, yet nobody believes her, that she has this connection, and she's able to see what this monstrous person is doing. She alienates herself from every rational force around her, from her husband, from the cop, from the psychiatrist, from the whole familial middle-class unit and she ends up in a place where the only person that can understand her is this monster. That's what I found interesting about the story, really, was that she ends up understanding this monster and he ends up understanding her, and in a strange way, they're the only two people who can understand each other. So he's done the worst possible thing to her but she ends up in a place that is so irrational that the only person that she can talk to is him. That's what I found interesting and that's why I wanted to make the movie.

CZ: I understand what you're saying and it has a lot to do with the gothic, where there's no redemption possible, and the world is seen as a place of fragmentation and defenselessness—especially for women. It's intriguing that you've been called a misogynist by various people.
NJ: I have?

CZ: Yes, and I don't understand that because Claire is a very active character, who pursues her tormentor and goes to very dangerous places . . .
NJ: Who said that?

CZ: I think it was Marina Burke, an Irish interviewer talking to you about *The Crying Game.*
NJ: Oh yeah, a lot of Irish people objected to *The Crying Game* because, all the men were feminized and all the women were masculine. It was a period when that kind of conversation here was a bit nuts. That's a specific Irish perspective on certain things that . . . but I mean, come on, *In Dreams* is about the punishment of a woman, isn't it?

CZ: But she's still someone who's willing to go to the end of the end.
NJ: Oh yeah, of course, she's the only actor in her own destiny, but I mean, the spectacle of the film is this woman being torn apart, really.

CZ: And watching her in this unbearable suffering in the rubber room—I think there are very few scenes of incarceration that are as painful to watch as that. She's in a quasi-anesthetized stupor, and she has these visions of her husband being slain, and she's impotent with rage. When Claire screams "The bastard's in my brain and now he's murdering my husband!" of course that's taken to be a sign of her madness. There's always a very heightened sensitivity and sense of empathy in your films because, even while Claire is locked away in this horrible place, she still has an understanding of Vivian, and says "Maybe he's lonely."
NJ: Yeah well, he's the only one who can understand her in the end. That's what attracted me to the story.

CZ: Can you talk about your collaboration with the editor, Tony Lawson. You've been working with him for a long time. Can you talk about how you work together?
NJ: Oh, well Tony's a great editor. And, he's, he's almost like the librarian of one's thoughts in a way. I mean I've worked with him for so long that if I shoot things and I show them to him I can trust him to deliver me a judgment on whether the ambition is being achieved in what I'm shooting or not, do you understand what I mean? And sometimes I send him scripts in advance of shooting, and at the moment I'm doing *The Borgias,* and Tony is a supervising editor on that. I've written nine episodes of *The Borgia* chronicles, and there were three other directors—that was the first time I ever had to watch directors direct work that I've written, and

it was a very complicated place to be artistically. And I've worked with Tony for so long that even on a project like that I can trust his voice and his eye as the supervising editor, for the whole series. We just ended up working together, you'd have to ask him why. I mean he cut *Barry Lyndon* with Stanley Kubrick, but Stanley at the time would claim he does all the editing himself . . .

CZ: You had some correspondence with Kubrick, didn't you?
NJ: It was on *In Dreams* actually. I knew Stanley Kubrick yeah, we used to speak on the phone, and I've been out to dinner with him several times, and been out to his house, yeah. But when I was doing *In Dreams*, the young girl that I cast initially as Rebecca, was the young actress that had been in *Eyes Wide Shut*. And Stanley had apparently finished his movie and, the girl's agent and parents said she had no obligation to Stanley whatsoever, but I think he had some re-shoots in mind, so he didn't want me to use her, so we got into quite a few back and forth conversations about that.

CZ: And on that film you worked with Leslie Shatz on the sound design, and he's, I think, one of the best in the business.
NJ: Well he did the sound design on the movie and he also dubbed it. He was his own dubbing editor. So yeah, it means he's got a complex engagement with the sound track that he did. It's so long ago . . .

CZ: It's very present to me because I've written about it, so I've thought about it a lot, and it's a film I really adore.
NJ: Well that's what horror movies should be. In a strange way they should be derided by the community at large, and they should be found out, and they should have their small aficionados. One of the best horror movies ever made is (George Franju's) *Eyes Without a Face.*

CZ: Yes, it's very beautiful.
NJ: Extraordinary.

CZ: The scene when the birds are released is so poetic and atmospheric.
NJ: Mmm, yeah amazing.

CZ: I want to go on to *The End of the Affair* because that's something very different. Is that more present to you, do you think?
NJ: I remember it better. I'll tell you why, because actually I wrote the

whole thing. So, I had read the book when I was a kid and I re-read it when I started making movies and I thought it would make a wonderful film and I asked Jeff Berg, my agent, could he find out who had the rights. He found out the rights were owned by Sony at Columbia—and John Calley then took over Columbia, and he's a brilliant executive, one of the last great executives really, and he liked the book as much as I did. So I commissioned a friend of mine, John Banville, to write a screenplay on it. And, John made it contemporary and it didn't quite work.

CZ: I found that so strange, the treatment he wrote with Bendrix as a corrupt police officer, and Henry as a Colombian drug lord . . .
NJ: You read it? But that was just one of those cases, where somebody goes off on the wrong direction. So I spoke to John Calley about it and John said, "Look, you have a very clear idea about what you want to do with this book yourself, so why don't you write it?" I basically thought there's a great opportunity in this novel to show the same set of events from two or three different points of view, and that's the way I approached the whole thing, really.

CZ: But what attracted you to Graham Greene in particular?
NJ: Oh I love Graham Greene. I mean Greene is an extraordinary figure. I mean, for one thing, he's written one of the best English films ever made, *The Third Man*. Even some of the bad versions of his novels are good, and I just love his work. I like the fact that he worked in fiction and, to a certain extent, worked in cinema at the same time. He's an amazing figure and I think actually *The End of the Affair* is probably one of his best books. It's the book of his that will probably survive in the canon. And, the main problem I had with *The End of the Affair*—one always has a problem adapting other peoples' material—but, I always felt that the last third of the novel, Greene had almost given up his narrative responsibilities, given it all to God in a strange way. And the minute Bendrix has read Sarah's journal, he tries to contact her, and she won't speak to him, and then the husband comes and says, "A terrible thing has happened, Bendrix, Sarah's dead." Then he has all this whole succession of miracles, and he had a character who is a proselytizing atheist, who is a very difficult character to understand from a contemporary viewpoint. So I had to do a lot of work on that, and I put the mark on the face of the young boy, the detective's son, and I extended the relationship between Sarah and Bendrix after he'd read her diary, and critics who took exception to the film have always taken exception to that specific fact.

CZ: That you changed what's called Book Five in the Greene novel . . .
NJ: I didn't change the ending—I changed the penultimate ending. But something had to be done to the basic structure of the story to make it work as a movie, do you understand what I mean?

CZ: Yes, sure. You said that it was like making a film in a foreign language.
NJ: Well for me, it's just because of the Britishness of it all. And, I mean Greene is a very specifically British writer, he's a very unusual thing, he's a Catholic British writer. Or maybe that's not that unusual, there are a few of them—there's Evelyn Waugh and Gerard Manley Hopkins. Yeah, but he has all the English virtues of understatement, and also this raging, almost Irish guilt going on at the same time, so it's a very interesting combination. But the reason I found it was almost like making a film in a foreign language was because I was using English, which is my language, but this specific upper-middle to upper-class version of the language, during the war. It was almost like trying to recreate a foreign world in a strange way, I found, trying to recreate another culture entirely.

CZ: Because you have said the Irish have a totally different attitude toward language and expression . . .
NJ: Well, we don't tend to finish our sentences, we don't use clauses and sub-clauses. Anyway, I wouldn't say it's a particular virtue on either side, it's completely different.

CZ: And you've also said you found the level of irony in Greene impenetrable, and that you approached the book with a scalpel and cut away everything that was unnecessary.
NJ: Yeah, well I tried to. I mean I love the level of irony in Greene, but all his irony collapses in the face of God. In that book he brought a deus ex machina towards the end, which is terribly satisfying, but is slightly unjustified by the realistic nature of the events.

CZ: There is a level at which an awesome mystery happens, that is deeply spiritual. And you talked about falling away from Catholicism and how it left a hole in your life.
NJ: Did I say all of that? Jesus Christ . . . I used to be an altar boy.

CZ: Oh really?
NJ: Oh yeah, oh yeah . . . because I'm doing this *Borgias* series at the moment, and I was on the net, reading what people were writing about

it, and somebody accused me of being an atheist, and I was very upset. There's no way I'm an atheist, I'm just a bad Catholic really. The Irish version of bad Catholic. It was wonderful to explore that in that movie—because basically it's the story of a man consumed with jealousy, but in the end, when he's jealous of Henry, it's fine—the husband that's with her all the time—he's jealous of this imagined lover, it's perfectly fine, but when he finds the imagined lover is actually some divine, infinite thing, there's a wonderful irony in that isn't there. Because he's jealous of something that he refused to acknowledge.

CZ: It seems like there's that constant play in your work between sensuality and cold empiricism. That's the argument that Sarah and Bendrix have in *The End of the Affair* when she says, "Can you love someone that you can't see?" and he says, "That's not my kind of love."
NJ: Hmm, well it's a wonderful Saint Augustine thing, really, isn't it. It's all of that English Catholicism, between the wars. (Laughs)

CZ: I see a relationship in your work to Lars von Trier and this whole idea of the "wrath of God" because God does seem particularly energetic in *The End of the Affair* in the destruction of love, or making it impossible. And that's also something that comes up all the time in your films, this idea of impossible love.
NJ: Yeah, well inappropriate would probably be more like it.

CZ: Uh huh.
NJ: But everything comes out of your childhood I think. It comes out of where you grow up, where you went to school, what you were taught before the age of eight or nine. I don't think you ever escape it, really. And I grew up in the north side of Dublin, and went to Catholic school, and was taught by Christian brothers and priests and didn't have any problem with it really at all, but it was a fascinating complex of things that you're given in your childhood.

CZ: It's the first time you show love-making in your work.
NJ: Oh I've never shot sex scenes before, no. It's terribly embarrassing, really.

CZ: For the actors or for you?
NJ: For everybody. And in a way, they're a contradiction, because, any erotic act is so bloody subjective, you never want to see, you never should

see it in long-shot, really. Anyway, but that was the nature of that story, so we had to do that.

CZ: You have said that it's always intrigued you that violence has become more dominant in American cinema rather than sexuality, which belongs to European cinema.

NJ: Yeah, well having made *The End of the Affair* and directing a few sex scenes, I understand why. (Laughs) Because violence, believe me, is much easier. Tony Lawson said to me when I was shooting these sex scenes, "People have two responses in the cinema to sex scenes, it's either embarrassment or laughter," sometimes both. What I loved about *The End of the Affair* was the fact that all the desire was concentrated on isolated things like her shoes, and her clothes. You want to be very, very specific about all those things, and in the end the eroticism of the movie has far more to do with memory than actuality, the whole film is something about somebody remembering. The whole story is told from the point of view of memory, and different kinds of memory.

CZ: You move from extremes of tenderness to coldness to raging passion. To me, it is your most complex film adaptation because of the temporal changes. You've talked about the idea of pivot points and how difficult that was to organize because there are sixteen changes of time in the film.

NJ: Yeah, it was a really interesting central problem because I had to photograph the same series of events, always from two different points of view, so I had to design and orchestrate them so they could be seen from two different points of view. And they all came to climax in that bomb blast which is seen from three different points of view—his point of view, her point of view, and near the end when Bendrix is reading the story, from some God-like point of view. So it was a fascinating thing to do, and it's something that's right at the heart of cinema, isn't it, point of view, how we see things, and what we see, when we see things, and how they can be seen otherwise to other people.

CZ: Did you want to signal the point of view of Sarah as different through camera movement?

NJ: Oh absolutely. And the point of view of the detective, Parkis. With this prosaic note-gathering, train-spotting behavior. It's his own point of view in turn. And that he collects ashtrays from great divorces.

CZ: That's one of my favorite lines in that film, "If ashtrays could speak..."

NJ: Mmm, so funny.

CZ: One of the areas I particularly engage in, in the book I wrote about your work, is film acting. Because it's those small details that are the most significant. There's the scene on the train between Henry and Bendrix, when he asks Bendrix to be there when Sarah dies, and there's a moment when Bendrix grasps Henry's sleeve, which is quite moving. Do you feel that acting for screen is inherently different to any other kind of performance?

NJ: Well you see I've never worked in the theatre.

CZ: Didn't you do something in Dublin, a few years ago?

NJ: I did it once, I wrote a play, and I directed it myself. I'm not comfortable in the theatre at all, and it's precisely because of that, it's because the acting that you can get on the screen can have an immediacy and a realism to it, and it can be like an event—it is an event, actually—that's happening in real time. It is happening before your eyes and you're photographing it with the camera. The kind of performance that happens on the stage, it's a different thing to me, and I've never been really comfortable with it. But, that scene between Bendrix and Henry was quite beautiful really, because they were, they were both so shy with one another, in a way, and yet they needed each other so much. It was something that in contemporary context, people would see a homoerotic kind of element to it. But because it was set in this clipped, unironic kind of world, of real politeness, and both actors managed to play it in that very simple way, I thought it was lovely. I felt what they did in that scene was gorgeous.

CZ: And after Sarah's death, when Henry runs out of the room, he and Bendrix embrace, and he says, "I can't live in a world without Sarah," and weeps openly. Because he's so contained through the whole film, that has a very explosive quality, much more than if he had been very expressive throughout.

NJ: Well, that's the whole irony of the story being told was that they end up together. It's very bizarre, but it's also very understandable in some way.

CZ: I think that you learn that Henry's very human, that he has these deep feelings for this woman, that are suddenly fully expressed. And the scene afterwards, when Bendrix is serving him cookies, which is quite beautifully shot with the space carved up in a strange way—and Henry says, "I'm glad it was you." That's very touching, and very honest. He's so vulnerable and childlike.

NJ: Well Bendrix has worked out who he hates, and he realizes it's not Henry. (Laughs)

CZ: Let's move on to *The Good Thief.* What attracted you to Melville's film, because the film you made is so completely different in tone, and doesn't really dwell on the heist mechanics as Melville's film does.

NJ: What attracted me to Melville's film . . . it's very hard to say. Stephen Woolley liked it a lot, he said, "Will you look at this movie? It would make a great remake," and I watched it, and I thought there's a lovely story there. I love Melville's work, but I don't think *Bob le Flambeur* is among the really huge masterpieces like *Le Samouri* and *The Red Circle*. Stephen tracked it down, and it was Warner Bros. who own the rights to it. And I said, "Look, let me begin to write, see what I can do with the story, see if anything comes up." And as I began to write the story and come up with this character Bob, and the whole thing of the fake paintings and the real paintings, and the possibility of making the story of the Melville movie, a sort of blind or a front for an actual robbery that was going on, and I thought, "Oh, this is really interesting." Because I can come up with a scenario and a screenplay that actually uses the original movie inside it, and then I can make a movie that is about the act of imitation and fakery, and all of that. That's what attracted me to it in the end—it became all about fakes and fakery, fake robberies and real robberies. Then I thought it was worth making. If I hadn't worked with that kind of concept, I wouldn't have even thought of making it. The only thing that worried me was making it in the south of France with people speaking English, which I always felt was a pity.

CZ: You have an almost uncanny ability to immerse yourself in a great variety of worlds, and what I found really extraordinary about that particular film was that you were able to write dialogue for characters who are so exotic, and who live in such a different world to your world. Is that something that intrigues you about filmmaking?

NJ: No, no, you just get obsessed—well I just get obsessed—with the story and the world of the story, and particularly with the way people speak in the world of the story. And in that screenplay, they spoke in a certain way, and there's nothing I could do about it. Either the characters find their own mode of speech and they come alive, or they don't. It's the same with this *Borgias* stuff I'm doing now, all the characters speak in a certain way. Every time I write these characters they speak in a certain way, and it's a deeply ironic Renaissance version of the quietus talk. But they do speak in a certain way, and similarly on *The Good Thief*, Bob particularly ended up speaking in a certain way, and everybody imitated his speech patterns because they regarded him as this hero. In *The End of the Affair*, they spoke in English but it's a totally different world of English. And what happens with me is when I do a film I get obsessed with all those details and all those little things, but they're very hard to explain to anybody else. Like *The Butcher Boy* is a movie that's based on Pat Mc-Cabe's book, obviously, but once I finished the screenplay, every person in that film spoke in a really specific way, and sadly, it was a way that was hard for American audiences to understand, but it was very important to me that the speech was there, and manifest.

CZ: I understand what you're saying, and I think there's a musicality to the rhythms of speech that you pick. Perhaps it's your training as a musician . . . and that you like music so much.

NJ: It's also if you like the way people express themselves, and you let those people talk. You have to know how people talk really, to make them live.

CZ: You've worked with Elliot Goldenthal a lot; how much does he contribute to the use of source music?

NJ: The use of source music in *The Good Thief*?

CZ: Tracks like "Parisien du Nord."

NJ: Oh, right . . . it was Cheb Mami and all those guys. But that was the world of French music at the time, that was the world of immigrants, and I found it extraordinarily beautiful, all those Moroccan North African French rhythms—that was their version of hip-hop at the time. And I wanted to use it, because some of the characters were Arabic.

CZ: There's a great pre-credit shot with the camera panning, and swirling around the buildings and while that music is playing.

NJ: That's Cheb Mami there. He has a particularly beautiful voice, that guy. Then we used the Leonard Cohen, and we used a bit of . . .

CZ: Johnny Holiday.

NJ: Yes, and we used a bit of bloody "Je t'aime," didn't we as well? It's a different way of putting together a soundtrack. And Elliot came up with a whole series of different sounds that he'd worked on in New York, and he had a conception that he wanted to make his score out of these almost industrial rhythmic sounds that he was collecting. Some of that worked, and some of it didn't, then we had to get into conventional scoring as well. Yeah it was lovely. But in terms of *The Good Thief*—there was an element of play to the whole thing, and everything's about gesture and play and appearance.

CZ: Can you talk about working with Nick Nolte? He's also one of my favorite actors.

NJ: Well Nick's amazing, actually.

CZ: I've heard he comes onto every set with a stack of notebooks.

NJ: He comes onto every set with a lot of things. (Laughs) Yeah, Nick goes through the script, and he does all sorts of free association, he writes out histories for different characters, and sometimes he can misunderstand things. Like, I had a reference to Mimi in the script, from . . .

CZ: *La Boheme.*

NJ: *La Boheme*, yes. Nick thought it was a real character in Bob's past life, and came up with this entire history for me. (Laughs) I said, "No, no, Nick, it's an opera, he remembers the opera," and he went, "Oooh okay." He had a whole notebook written about this character, who had died.

CZ: But if it makes it more real to him, it doesn't really matter in the end, right?

NJ: No it doesn't.

CZ: There's this pervasive sense underlying the film about emotional bruising and a frailty in Nolte's character that I find very beautiful.

NJ: Well what I found lovely was the nonsexual relationship between him and Nutsa Kukhianidze. Nutsa, the girl who played Anne—between Nick and her, because it's quite a difficult thing to do. The awful situation you get in Woody Allen movies where a seventy-year-old man is falling in love with a nubile twenty-two-year-old girl is generally repulsive, but Nick managed to construct a relationship with this terribly beautiful young actress who had never done a proper film before. And it was chaste, and I thought it was lovely. He was more like a guardian, a paternal guide.

CZ: Well he's sort of past it, isn't he . . .
NJ: He's totally past it, yeah. Maybe he understood that.

CZ: Did you think of *The Good Thief* as an examination of masculinity?
NJ: Yeah, yeah, we're talking about an old bull, someone who can hardly stand up anymore. This legendary figure who just has one last blast at rediscovering their youth, and what they were really good at. That's what it's about—that over-the-hill masculinity, really.

CZ: There's also an incredible pacing of the narrative through montage, and moving camera.
NJ: I know, it feels that way in the movie but it's very difficult to achieve, actually. Chris Menges was the cinematographer, and he is quite the genius, Chris. But some of those effects, some of those shots took an incredibly long time to achieve. I mean on the one hand we had the nervy druggy, energy of the street photography. And on the other hand we had these suave lamp-lit interiors of the casino. So there were two aesthetics going on there.

CZ: There's a great shot when they go into Le Club Dice. It's one long camera movement in which the colors change as they walk through each environment, and there's a different activity going on in each room.
NJ: Well the opening is that nervy handheld, lurid, nightmarish thing. But the whole atmosphere of the casino, this languor and opulence and wealth, is quite different. Anyway, one strives for these things and then can't fully articulate them.

CZ: Okay, I wanted to move on to Beckett.
NJ: Oh, to *Not I?* Yeah sure. That whole Beckett project was a very interesting one. This guy Michael Colgan (one of the producers) basically asked me, "Which of Beckett's plays would you love to do?" and I looked at *Not I* and I thought, this is about a mouth, which is fascinating. And if you read the text of *Not I*, it's very difficult to understand what it means, it's about being born, it's about screaming in the middle of something called life, and then there's some strange vision that happens. But it's very difficult to know what the logical explanation is, and what the text is itself. What I found fascinating was the idea of a mouth, just making

a film of somebody's mouth, the idea, the thought of speech, because speech is the only thing, in the end, that allows us to leave a mark of what the experience of being in the world is. So, I just thought it was fascinating. I took the text as read and asked Julianne (Moore) to do it several times, many, many times. And Beckett himself had done a version of his own play for the BBC with Billie Whitelaw, and he just used one camera, and it was absolutely hypnotic. And I used five cameras, and I edited them very, very heavily. But from my point of view, just photographing a mouth for ten or so minutes was fascinating.

CZ: But in the actual play, there is an auditor who stands by the side wearing a hood, and listening, and the stage direction is "in helpless compassion."

NJ: Well yeah, that auditor didn't exist in the film that Beckett made, they cut it out, and in some productions of the play the auditor does not have to be there. So Beckett allowed the auditor to be there or not be there.

CZ: So Beckett's estate didn't bother you . . .

NJ: He seemed not to have made up his mind about that character. The only thing I wanted to do at the start of it was to show that it was a performance. And I also wanted to show the restrictions that Beckett demands and placed upon the actors. To get that light on this mouth, your head has to be absolutely still, so, whoever performs it on stage has to have their head in a device, that is almost like it's a torture device from medieval times. I wanted to show Julianne sitting down in that chair, getting into that position, and I wanted to show the physical conditions that Beckett has set up to do the piece. So it was just that shot, and then it was shot at five different angles on the mouth.

CZ: For me, Mouth didn't have an identity. . . .

NJ: Well no, it becomes a hypnotic thing. And this is why Beckett is so clever—if you look at a mouth for that long, I mean normally we don't look at anything for that long, we look at things for two minutes, twenty seconds, but if you look at a mouth for that long, it comes to look like different things. It looks like a cave, it looks like a vagina, it looks like Marilyn Monroe's lips . . . it creates its own associations. But it definitely looks like a birth canal, it looks like a cave, it looks like somewhere where you'd be born out of, somewhere where you might die.

CZ: It looks as if it's devoured the whole body—I was thinking of Francis Bacon when I saw it.
NJ: Mm, perhaps, yeah.

CZ: You said at one point that Beckett is trying to diminish the human presence, and hogtie the actor through physical and linguistic restraints.
NJ: Well yeah that's what he does, I mean for God's sake, he puts people in jars, he buries them up to their head in sand. (Laughs) I think he's got a perverse attitude towards the human frame, doesn't he? He wants to somehow, eliminate it so we can think of the bare facts of speech and thought and being on a stage, and being in any corner of the earth. It's an extraordinary thing that Beckett did, absolutely extraordinary.

CZ: But did you find it oppressive to have those constraints on you?
NJ: No, not at all. It's great.

CZ: So you don't find it anti-human at all? The idea of stripping away all these things and suppressing human agency?
NJ: Yeah, but I mean he strips and he subjects the human frame and the actor's frame and the actor's body and the physicality of the actor, but in order to illuminate something about the human condition. That's what he does, and that's why it's fascinating, but it's also like a form of torture.

CZ: I found that he creates a world in which the possibility of purposeful human action is very remote and that the only condition of being alive is to suffer.
NJ: Yes, well yeah there's not a lot of hope in Beckett, not at all. But in a strange way, there's an enormous amount of spirituality in him. There's an enormous amount of yearning. There's a mystical strain to him—I'm sure he'd hate even the use of that term—but there is something akin to that.

CZ: Beckett says, "Christianity is a mythology with which I am perfectly familiar," which I thought was an interesting statement.
NJ: I understand that. Look, the reason that I did *Not I*, and the reason why I delighted in doing *Not I*, was because it brought up none of those questions. To make a little movie about that piece that he wrote, I didn't have to be a Beckett obsessive, I didn't have to have an opinion on the past body of his work, I didn't have to enter this mythology of Sam and all that kind of stuff. All I had to do was look at this tiny little piece that

he had written, seven pages long, and think about it. I thought it was great. I was just trying to do service to that specific text, you understand what I mean?

CZ: Okay, let's go on to *The Brave One*. There's a passage from Colm Toíbín's most recent book of short stories that I thought was very appropriate to the situation of the main character in *The Brave One*. It's about Lady Gregory and her former lover: "She was lonely without Blunt, but she was lonelier at the idea that the world went on as though she had not loved him. Time would pass and their actions and feelings would seem like a shadow of actions and feelings, but less than a shadow in fact, because cast by something that now had no real substance," from *The Empty Family* (with the kind permission of the author).
NJ: (no response)

CZ: Okay. So, can you talk a bit about the evolution of that project?
NJ: It's very simple. Jodie Foster sent me the script, and I read it, and there was something very vulgar and compelling about the basic drive of the script. And, I just liked the unholy dynamic of it. I went over and met her, and then met the writer, a woman called Cynthia Mort, and decided to do it, and see what I could make of it. But I really did it to see Jodie in that role, to see what she was like in the part; I wanted to go on the journey with her, because she's such an amazing actress. And I thought it was an amazing part for her. What we never did in that movie, was to work out the ending. That so often happens with Hollywood projects, there's incredibly good elements in things that Hollywood sends to people like me, but the endings are unresolved or disappointing in some way.

CZ: There's the idea of impossible love again, I think, between Erica and the Terrence Howard character, Mercer.
NJ: Oh yeah, I do love that about it, and that's one of the things that drew me to the project. These two characters who know each other so well, there's so much distance between them, and there has to be so much distance between them. So I thought that was fascinating. But, basically, Cynthia Mort had a script and the impetus behind it was a remake of *Death Wish* by Michael Winner. I mean, *Death Wish* is not one of the best movies ever made. It's one of these guilty secrets, isn't it? But it's actually quite good in a way, quite shocking, how irredemptive it is, and how politically incorrect it is, in some strange way. And the idea of

putting a woman in that Charles Bronson role is not a bad one, really. Anyway, the film was what it was, and I loved making it.

CZ: One of the things I found very interesting about that film was the moral ambiguity of it. I was thinking about *Psycho*, and there's a way in which after Norman Bates has dispatched Marion Crane, that you can say "the dirty slut deserved to die." And there's a similar feeling about the punks that are killed on the subway, that calls for the judgment of the audience for or against that idea.

NJ: I know, I understand that. The one interesting thing about the screenplay that Cynthia wrote, actually, was the fact that she commented upon what she was doing as she did it.

CZ: Can you explain?

NJ: Well, she was this radio host, she recorded her musings and her thoughts. She talked about what she was doing, and the changes that were going through her, so that's what was fascinating. That's one of the reasons that I did it as well.

CZ: I was also thinking about the idea of memento mori. Erica misses this memorial service for David, and when she wakes up, he's already buried, and his mother has to break the news to her. I thought somehow that was significant, that she had missed the ritual to commemorate him. And then there's a scene in which Erica gives her crucifix—a gift from her boyfriend—to the girl in the hospital, Chloe, who she has saved.

NJ: Of course. She wasn't allowed grief, she wasn't given the opportunity to grieve. But, basically there was a raw power to what Cynthia Mort had written, and the screenplay was almost like a prequel to one of these superhero avenger type of movies. There was that element to it that I liked as well.

CZ: Okay, so let's move on to *Ondine*, then. Obviously it's related to Celtic myth and folklore.

NJ: Yes.

CZ: And you had said Ireland is a world that teaches you the value of fables, and you talked about Yeats and Beckett and Joyce as being the three people who influenced you the most.

NJ: Well, the reason I talked about Yeats with regard to *Ondine* is because Yeats collected fairy tales. Early on in his career he had a book called *The Irish Fairy and Folk Tales of Ireland*. And, I thought, it is an endemic part of the Irish imagination, that seems to have fallen into disarray or disuse recently. He published that collection when he was about nineteen or twenty. One of these fairy tales he collected was called the *Lady of Gollerus*, and it was about a fisherman who pulls a woman from the sea, he marries her, and she goes back to the sea, eventually.

CZ: You said, "I work on stories that illuminate the soul rather than the brain."

NJ: Well, the reason I like fairy tales is, because, actually, they're a bit non-rational. They don't deal in psychology, they don't deal in psychological motivation. Of course they're unrealistic, but they also strike very deep. And there is something universal in them because the same types of story crop up all over the world. When I began to look at *Ondine*, I said okay, the Irish version of that is the selkie, and the one that everybody knows is the Hans Christian Anderson fairy tale, *The Little Mermaid*. There is a French version of it, which is actually called *Ondine*. (N.B. There is a medieval version of the story in France called *Mélusine* by Jean d'Arras in the thirteenth century.) And, I believe there's a Filipino version of it too. So it's one of these universal connections, and I began to write this little fantasy that I thought would be lovely, and charming, and it would turn into this movie script, and I made it. I was aware when I was making that film . . . the thing that really frightened me about it was that I build up an apparent fairy tale, and then I tell the audience that it's actually real. So I disenchant the audience at the end, and I often wondered, would a movie survive that? Or would the audience get annoyed?

CZ: Do you mean because there's a realistic explanation for Ondine's character?

NJ: Yes, there's a realistic explanation in the end. And I do think a lot of people that when the realistic explanation presents itself, they were disappointed because they were so captivated by the possibility of her actually being from the water, and actually being a mermaid, of being a selkie. But anyway, that's the nature of the story I wrote, and, that's what it was.

CZ: I was thinking about the human bonds that storytelling creates, and

I think it's very much part of your ethos as a filmmaker, to establish that bond between a film and the audience.

NJ: Yeah.

CZ: And Syracuse starts by telling a story to his daughter rather than reading it, which I thought that was interesting. And it's very Dickensian, it was a good time and a bad time, it's like *A Tale of Two Cities*—the best of times and the worst of times. And Annie is also a storyteller with a tale about the seaweed knickers and scallop bra.

NJ: Yeah, well that was the construction of the screenplay. I mean he pulls the girl out of the water, he doesn't know where she's from, he tells his daughter a story about it, his daughter decides okay, she must be this or that or the other, and she begins to research selkies, the daughter tells him about selkies, and he comes to believe in selkies. So they impose this story on Ondine who's happy to accept this. So the movie was about storytelling as much as about anything else. And that's what I wanted it to be about. That's also why it had to have this realistic ending, in the end, because he had to find out that the story was just a fabrication.

CZ: Yeah, because it does have so many fairy tale elements in it—the mother (Dervla Kirwan) as the wicked witch; the villain (whose entry was very much like something from *Night of the Hunter*), the idea of a magical donor, which would be Annie's electric wheelchair and the other magical donation is the kidney found to restore Annie's health. It's like the wands in *Star Wars*—something that is given to a character that gives them an extraordinary power and helps them along their path. Something like the red cloak in *Company of Wolves*.

NJ: Well, it's a fairy tale after all, isn't it? And in all fairy tales there's something terrible and something wonderful that happen at the same time, doesn't it? A wish comes true, and with the wish coming true somebody dies.

CZ: I was just wondering about the use of the Sigur Ros music. Because they sing in a made up language, right?

NJ: Yeah, I was in the odd position, because they have a made-up language for most of their songs, and we used the only one that they've written in English. Basically, I needed a song to be part of the revelation, and at the time I was listening to a lot of Sigur Ros, and I thought I'd use it. And, their music is quite beautiful. But it was lovely to make that movie, it was almost like living underneath the sea for two months. Quite a delightful thing to make.

CZ: And you used Christopher Doyle as a cinematographer—his work is very extraordinary.

NJ: Yeah, well Christopher needs that engagement of the camera with the landscape for that whole film to work. And Christopher's a very special animal, he really is, totally Australian.

CZ: Let's go right to *The Borgias*, because I know that's what's been preoccupying you. You've been wanting to do this project for a long time. Can you talk about how the project developed, because it was stalled for a while, and I remember it had a different cast.

NJ: Oh yeah, when I was doing it as a movie I was speaking to Anthony Hopkins initially. And I went through a lot of different actors, but I could never get it going. It was one of those projects that, when there's a possibility of it being made, a lot of different actors were interested, but I could just never get the money for it.

CZ: But you did actually go to Italy I remember, doing pre-production and location scouting . . .

NJ: Yeah I was in pre-production at one point. We were just at the point of building sets. I was going to make it with Viggo Mortensen, he was committed to it. He was going to play Cesare, and he asked to see the script, and then he went off to make another film

CZ: Do you feel that doing a series that is going to go to be an international broadcast affected your process at all?

NJ: No, it didn't, not at all. The only thing that affected it was the hour-long nature of series television. Basically, it's the format of cable shows, and the span of the series and the span of the characterizations, and the development of plotting. You don't have a feeling of doing justice to the broadness of the story, really. And I took the opportunity when it was suggested that we do it as a cable show, to find anything that had been written about it.

CZ: And you did all of the writing?

NJ: I did it all, yeah.

CZ: When you were writing about it, did you think of it as being a contemporary commentary, or do you feel that history tends to repeat itself endlessly in the same way?

NJ: Oh yeah, contemporary parallels . . . well, from the time I wrote it to now, there have been three presidents. To me the whole series is about power. And the interplay of power and religion, that's what I wanted to examine, that's what attracted me to it, the reason I made it. Machiavelli's *The Prince* really hooked me into it. The point of view I want to take in my whole series is what people do to get power, what it does to them once they have gotten it, and how they have to disguise their efforts to get it. And the way they disguise it is generally in morality and religion, and that's what I wanted the whole series to be about, and that's why I wanted to make the movie in the first place.

CZ: Pinturicchio is a character in the series, and a lot of the film in terms of how the characters look, their stances, their postures, their clothing seems to be based on Renaissance paintings and frescoes. Is that something that you would investigate yourself, or are there particular paintings that struck you when you were on trips to Italy?

NJ: Pinturicchio's painting? You mean in the Borgias' apartment?

CZ: Yeah.

NJ: No, I mean Pinturicchio means "little painter," yeah, he was the least of the great figures at the time, when you had Raphael and Leonardo and Michelangelo and all the rest. I mean the one thing the Borgias did not have was great taste. I just used it as a joke in the series, that they chose the cheapest of all the painters available, really. His works are there just to be seen in the Borgias' apartment. He was their official house painter in a way, wasn't he? The way Hans Holbein was the painter of Henry VIII. Holbein was a great painter, Pinturicchio was a not-so-great painter. What the Borgias did not do was become great patrons of the arts.

CZ: They weren't?

NJ: No. Not at all. They're not known for that, anyway, maybe other people would disagree with me. Rodrigo Borgia became Pope Alexander VI, and the one who succeeded him was a guy called Cardinal della Rovere who became Pope Julius II, and he is the guy who commissioned Michelangelo to do the Sistine Chapel, he's the guy who remade Saint-Peter's, he hired Raphael, Michelangelo . . . and that architect . . .

CZ: Antonio da Sangallo?

NJ: Yeah, yeah, he became the great patron of the arts, the Borgias did not. They were too busy killing people.

CZ: From what I've read, Alexander is considered one of the worst Popes historically.

NJ: Apparently so, yeah.

CZ: I was struck by the scene where the Pope is crowned, because there's this look on Jeremy Irons's face of real unhappiness and almost misery. He seems so isolated, and he confides to Cesare later about the loneliness of his position, with "only the silence of God as your witness."

NJ: Yeah.

CZ: And I thought that was key to the whole thing, in some way.

NJ: Yeah, I wanted the character to definitely be a believer, as most people were then. And I wanted him to be overawed suddenly by the thing he had grasped. I wanted him to face this, to have this terrible sense of aloneness, which is painful, because there's nobody else he can talk to except this imagined God who doesn't talk to him really, you understand what I mean?

CZ: Yes.

NJ: And I'm sure the president of the United States must be a lonely seat to occupy. At least they have ex-presidents to talk to, whereas you only become Pope when your predecessor is dead. You can't talk to another Pope and say, "What's it like being Pope?"

CZ: I thought it had a lot of echoes with *The End of the Affair*, actually.

NJ: Perhaps, yeah.

CZ: In the episodes that I watched there was a subtext of surveillance and watching and witnessing where the whole court is privy to every activity that people were engaged in. There seems to be no privacy at all.

NJ: No, but there wouldn't be then, would there? Particularly at a place like the Vatican. You'd be constantly feeling observed. And your performance would be constantly under scrutiny. I just imagined it as the most paranoid place in the universe. But then again, if you choose any center of power like that, like the Vatican, like the Kremlin under Stalin and maybe even Rasputin, the White House under the Kennedys, I'm sure they would have been these centers of extreme paranoia. My hope is that people will get engaged in that state of mind, and see it not as an ancient, medieval thing but as a perennial thing.

CZ: There's the issue of the public sphere versus the private self—you have the domestic life with Joanne Whalley's character and the family, and then with Cesare and Lucrezia . . . I don't know how that evolves in the series. The way that it's presented in the first two episodes, their relationship doesn't seem very sibling-like.
NJ: No, they seem obsessed with each other.

CZ: She says, "When can I marry?" and he says, "Never if I can help it."
NJ: Yeah, I mean that will be a theme, that will become a theme as it is develops. Cesare did kill one of her husbands, the only one that she liked. I don't know whether historically they ever had sex.

CZ: She's quite a fascinating character—there's evidence that there was both fraternal and paternal incest. I don't know if you went there . . .
NJ: Not yet, no. Not in the first year.

CZ: There's also quite a very perverse relationship between Cesare and Michelotto, the assassin. The sequence when the assassin says, "Whip me, my lord. Harder," . . . and then, della Rovere squeezes lemon onto Michelotto's wounds, and the assassin says, "These wounds will last for a lifetime," and della Rovere says that "They are proof of your loyalty"—it was quite strange.
NJ: That's the way I developed the character. I wanted the series to be based as much on cruelty as on everything else.

CZ: Okay, and there seems to be this relay of desire and punishment and lust.
NJ: Well that's the theme, isn't it? For sure sex must have been much more fun in those days, because it was so forbidden, and so bound up with spiritual yearning. Those Catholics had the great thing of confession didn't they, the great institution. They could confess, they can sin as much as they want and confess the next day and be washed clean. I mean, that's one of the reasons the subject interested me so much is because of the Catholic Church. When I grew up in Ireland as a Catholic, that specific mindset I find absolutely fascinating. And, the way, one can

have a world full of such guilt, and then such possibility of redemption at the same time.

CZ: Yeah. I also found an underlying theme in *The Borgias* concerning appetite—I think that's what you're getting at—it's not only foods that are stuffed with messages, but the appetite for sex and power, and all those excesses and preparation for the Pope's installation, and the purchase of the papacy with "endearments." Is that something you return to?

NJ: Well, it was endemic to the subject matter. I mean I wanted the thing to be full of ironies. So the first, the greatest irony of them all being that Rodrigo buys the papacy, and the minute he gets it, he's terrified of what he's gotten, and what he's gotten into. In the first nine episodes that I've written, none of these characters have yet become the monsters that they are reputed to have been by history. Cesare is not yet the figure that Machiavelli wrote about, Lucrezia Borgia is not this monster . . . when they started they were ordinary people. And particularly Cesare, we see him as an attractive, fascinating brother, an incredibly able person, without a conscience, really. And I wanted to see him develop into this amoral monster. But I don't want to present him as that at the start; I want the audience to see him become that. In the second season, he'll kill his brother.

CZ: The bastard son, the one who is in the military.

NJ: Yes, he does kill him. I mean he wants his brother's job, doesn't he. And the only way he can get it in the end is by killing his brother, he can never prove to his father that he deserves it, so in the end he kills his brother, and his father just throws his hands up, and says, "Take it."

CZ: And, are you in the process of making *The Graveyard Book*, by Neil Gaiman or starting to think about that?

NJ: Well I've written a script, they're trying to raise money. They're finding it very difficult, they haven't entirely succeeded, so I'll see what happens. Yeah, I'm going to do another season of *The Borgias* next year, they've commissioned it, and I'm going to make the movie as well.

CZ: At one point you were attached to *Skippy Dies* by Paul Murray, right?

NJ: I bought the rights to it, yeah. It's a lovely book, isn't it? A delightful book. Well, I'll just have to get around to it at some stage. I haven't begun to write the script yet, but I will soon. I'd love to make it a film.

Additional Resources

Books

Giles, Jane. *The Crying Game.* London: British Film Institute, 1997.

Jordan, Neil. *Dream of a Beast.* London: Chatto and Windus, 1983.

———. *High Spirits.* London: Faber and Faber, 1989.

———. *Michael Collins: Screenplay and Film Diary.* New York: Plume Books, 1996.

———. *A Neil Jordan Reader.* New York: Vintage, 1993.

———. *Night in Tunisia.* London: Bloomsbury, 1980.

———. *The Past.* New York: George Braziller, 1980.

———. *Shade: A Novel.* London: Bloomsbury, 2004.

———. *Sunrise with Sea Monster.* London: Bloomsbury, 1995.

Jordan, Neil, and David Leland. *Mona Lisa.* London: Faber and Faber, 1986.

Pramaggiore, Maria. *Contemporary Film Directors: Neil Jordan.* Urbana & Chicago: University of Illinois Press, 2008.

Rockett, Kevin, and Emer Rockett. *Neil Jordan: Exploring Boundaries.* Dublin: The Liffey Press, 2003.

Zucker, Carole. *The Cinema of Neil Jordan: Dark Carnival.* London: Wallflower Press, 2008.

Articles and Interviews

Abramowitz, Rachel. "Young Blood." *Premiere* 8, no. 3 (November 1994): 66–72, 116.

Barra, Allen. "Here Comes Mr. Jordan." *American Films* 15, no. 4 (January 1990): 36–41, 55.

Beebe, John. "He Must Have Wept When He Made You: The Homoerotic Pathos in the Movie Version of *Interview with the Vampire.*" In *The Anne Rice Reader*, edited by Katherine M. Ramsland, 196–211. New York: Ballantine Books, 1997.

Bew, Paul. "Collins Wrong on Essential Points." *The Sunday Independent,* September 29, 1996, 8.

Booth, Philip. *"In Dreams*; Get Real, Please." *Sarasota Herald Tribune,* January 15, 1995, 15.

Boozer Jr., Jack. "Bending Phallic Patriarchy in *The Crying Game." Journal of Popular Film and Television* 22, no. 4 (Winter 1995): 172–179.

Brett, Anwar. "Director's Chair: Neil Jordan." *Film Review,* February 2006, 76–80.

Chumo, Peter. "*The Crying Game,* Hitchcockian Romance, and the Quest for Identity." *Literature Film Quarterly* 23, no. 4 (October 1995): 247–53.

Clancy, Luke. "Ireland's Eyes" (interview with Neil Jordan). *Magill,* February 1990, 37–41.

Crowdus, Gary. "The Screenwriting of Irish History: Neil Jordan's *Michael Collins." Cineaste* 22, no. 4 (1997): 14–19.

Cullingford, Elizabeth Butler. "The Reception of *Michael Collins." Irish Literary Supplement* 16, no. 1 (Spring 1997): 17–19.

———. "Virgins and Mothers: Sinéad O'Connor, Neil Jordan, and *The Butcher Boy." Yale Journal of Criticism* 15, no. 1 (Spring 2002): 185–210.

Dodd, Philip. "Ghosts from a Civil War." *Sight and Sound* 6, no. 12 (December 1996): 30–32.

Donovan, Katie. "Capturing the Big Fellow on Film." *Irish Times,* February 7, 1995, 10–12.

Dretzka, Gary. "Eire Jordan: Irish Filmmaker Neil Jordan's *Affair* to Remember." *Fade In* 5, no. 4 (March 1, 2000): 84–86.

Dwyer, Michael. "10 Days That Shook the Irish Film Industry." *In Dublin,* April 8, 1982, 24–28.

———. "Dynamic, Thrilling, Epic Cinema." *Irish Times,* November 8, 1996, 12.

———. "Neil Jordan in Conversation with Michael Dwyer at the Galway Film Fleadh, Sunday, July 13, 1997." *The Fleadh Papers* 2, Galway: A *Film West* Publication (1997).

Edge, Sarah. "'Women Are Trouble, Did You Know That Fergus?' Neil Jordan's *The Crying Game." Feminist Review* 50 (Summer 1995): 173–86.

Farley, Fidelma, "Neil Jordan." In *Fifty Contemporary Filmmakers,* edited by Yvonne Tasker, 186–94. London: Routledge, 2002.

Ferrante, Anthony C. "Robert Downey Jr.'s More Disturbed Than Usual in Director Neil Jordan's Psychothriller." *Fangoria* 180 (March 1999): 26–29, 82.

Fuller, Graham. "A Sensual Nightmare." *City Limits,* August 28–September 4, 1986, 12–15.

Gibbons, Luke. "Demisting the Screen: Neil Jordan's *Michael Collins*." *Irish Literary Supplement* 16, no. 1 (Spring 1997): 16-17.

Glicksman, Marlaine. "Neil Jordan's Angel Heart: Irish Eyes." *Film Comment* 26, no. 1 (January 1990): 9-11, 68-71.

Gray, M. "Review of *In Dreams*." *Film Ireland* 70 (April/May 1999): 36-37.

Grist, Leighton. "'It's Only a Piece of Meat': Gender Ambiguity, Sexuality, and Politics in *The Crying Game* and *M. Butterfly*." *Cinema Journal* 42, no. 4 (Summer 2003): 3-28.

Handler, Kristin. "Sexing *The Crying Game*." *Film Quarterly* 47, no. 3 (Spring 1994): 31-42.

Hill, John. "Crossing the Water: Hybridity and Ethics in *The Crying Game*." *Textual Practice* 12, no. 1 (Spring 1998): 89-100.

Hoggard, Liz. "*The Good Thief*." *Irish Independent*, February 21, 2002, 1-2.

Hopper, Keith. "'Cat Calls from the Cheap Seats': The Third Meaning of Neil Jordan's *Michael Collins*." *Irish Review* 21 (Autumn/Winter 1997): 1-28.

———. "Hairy on the Inside: Re-visiting Neil Jordan's *The Company of Wolves*." *Canadian Journal of Irish Studies* 29, no. 2 (Fall 2003): 17-26.

Jaehne, Karen. "Neil Jordan on *The Butcher Boy*." *Film Scouts Interviews*. Accessed on May 30, 2011. http://www.filmscouts.com/scripts/inter view.cfm?File=nea-jor.

James, Joy. "Black *Femmes Fatales* and Sexual Abuse in Progressive 'White' Cinema: Neil Jordan's *Mona Lisa* and *The Crying Game*." *Camera Obscura* 12, no. 3 36 (September 1995): 33-47.

Jones, Alan. "*The Company of Wolves*." *Cinefantastique* 15, no. 1 (January 1985): 4-7.

———. "*High Spirits*." *Cinefantastique* 19, nos. 1-2 (January 1989): 16-20.

Jordan, Neil. "Beauty and the Beasts." *Time Out* (September 13-19, 1984): 18-21.

———. Foreword to *Travels in Greeneland: The Cinema of Graham Greene*, by Quentin Falk. London: Quartet Books, 2000.

———. "Neil Jordan's Guilty Pleasures." *Film Comment* 28, no. 6 (November 1992): 36.

Katz, Susan Bullington. "The View from Here: A Conversation with . . . Neil Jordan." *Journal of the Writers Guild of America* 2, no. 4 (April 1998): 36-42.

Kearney, Richard. "Avenging Angel: An Analysis of Neil Jordan's First Irish Feature Film." *Studies* 71, no. 283 (Autumn 1982): 296-303.

King, Claire Sisco. "The Man Inside: Trauma, Gender, and the Nation in

The Brave One." *Critical Studies in Media Communication* 27, no. 2 (June 2010): 111–30.

Landy, Marcia. "The International Cast of Irish Cinema: The Case of *Michael Collins.*" *Boundary 2* 27, no. 2 (Summer 2000): 21–44.

Lappas, Catherine. "'Seeing Is Believing, but Touching Is the Truth': Female Spectatorship and Sexuality in *The Company of Wolves.*" *Women's Studies* 25, no. 2 (January 1996): 115–35.

Lee, Nathan. "*Breakfast on Pluto.*" *Film Comment* 41, no. 6 (November 2005): 72–73.

Lockett, Christopher. "Terror and Rebirth: 'Cathleen ni Houlihan,' from Yeats to *The Crying Game.*" *Literature Film Quarterly* 33, no. 4 (2005): 290–305.

Lugowski, David. "Genre Conventions and Visual Style in *The Crying Game.*" *Cineaste* 20, no. 1 (July 1993): 31–33.

Lurie, Susan. "Performativity in Disguise: Ideology and the Denaturalization of Identity in Theory and *The Crying Game.*" *Velvet Light Trap* 43 (Spring 1999): 51–62.

Lyall, Sarah. "Filming the Drama Between the Novelist's Lines." *New York Times*, June 6, 1999, AR13.

Macnab, Geoffrey. "Such Sweet Sickness." *Sight and Sound* 16, no. 1 (January 2006): 20–23.

McIlroy, Brian. "Interview with Neil Jordan." In *World Cinema 4*, 108–18. Wiltshire: Flicks, 1986.

———. "Neil Jordan and the Anglo-Irish Gothic." In *Horror International*, edited by Steven Jay Schneider and Tony Williams, 128–40. Detroit: Wayne State University Press, 2005.

McLoone, Martin. "The Abused Child of History: Neil Jordan's *The Butcher Boy.*" *Cineaste* 23, no. 4 (1998): 32–36.

Mooney, Joshua. "Neil Jordan Bites the Big One." *Movieline* 6, no. 3 (November 1994): 64–69.

Murphey, Kathleen. "A Study in Scarlet." *Film Comment* 35, no. 2 (March/April 1999): 12–15.

O'Hehir, Andrew. "The Dying Game." *Salon.com*, January 15, 1999. http://www.salon.com/entertainment/movies/reviews/1999/01/15reviewa.html.

O'Rawe, Desmond. "At Home with Horror: Neil Jordan's Gothic Variations." *Irish Studies Review* 11, no. 2 (August 2003): 189–98.

Pizzelo, Stephen. "*Interview with the Vampire* Taps New Vein." *American Cinematographer*, January 1995, 43–52.

Pramaggiore, Maria. "The Celtic Blue Note: Jazz in Neil Jordan's *Night in Tunisia, Angel* and *The Miracle*." *Screen* 39, no. 3 (Autumn 1998): 272–88.

Rodenberg, Hans-Peter. "Bridging the Abyss: Neil Jordan, Irishman in Hollywood." *Journal for the Study of British Culture* 5, no. 2 (1998): 155–70.

Smith, Webster. "Observations on the *Mona Lisa* Landscape." *Art Bulletin* 67, no. 2 (June 1985): 183–99.

Smyth, Gerry. "*The Crying Game*: Postcolonial or Postmodern?" *Paragraph* 20, no. 2 (July 1997): 154–73.

Taubin, Amy. "Screenings: *The Brave One*." *Film Comment* 43, no. 5 (September/October 2007): 70–71.

Toíbín, Colm. "The *In Dublin* Interview: Neil Jordan Talks to Colm Toíbín." *In Dublin* 152 (April 29, 1982): 14–19.

White, Armand. "The Camera I: Chris Menges Interviewed by Armond White." *Film Comment*, March 1988, 48–50.

Wynne, Catherine. "Crossing the Border: Post-Colonial Carnival in Neil Jordan's *The Crying Game*." In *Moving Pictures, Migrating Identities*, edited by Eva Rueschmann, 139–58. Jackson: University Press of Mississippi, 2003.

Yates, Candida. "Masculine Jealousy and the Struggle for Possession in *The End of the Affair*." *Journal for Cultural Research* 10, no. 3 (July 2006): 219–35.

Zilliax, Amy. "'The Scorpion and the Frog': Agency and Identity in Neil Jordan's *The Crying Game*." *Camera Obscura* 12, no. 2 35 (May 1995): 24–51.

Žižek, Slavoj. "From Courtly Love to *The Crying Game*." *New Left Review* 202 (November/December 1993): 95–108.

Zucker, Carole. "*The Brave One*: 'There's Plenty of Ways to Die.'" *Cineaction* 75 (Winter 2008): 62–69.

———. "*In Dreams* and the Gothic: The Moment of Collapse." *Cineaction* 28, no. 1 (Winter 2001): 58–66.

———. "An Interview with Stephen Rea." *Canadian Journal of Irish Studies* 26, no. 1 (Spring 2000): 86–98.

———. "The Poetics of Point of View: Neil Jordan's *The Butcher Boy*." *Literature Film Quarterly* 31, no. 3 (2003): 203–8.

———. "'Sweetest Tongue Has Sharpest Tooth': The Dangers of Dreaming in Neil Jordan's *The Company of Wolves*." *Literature Film Quarterly* 28, no. 1 (2000): 66–71.

Index

www.ingramcontent.com/pod-product-compliance
Lightning Source LLC
Chambersburg PA
CBHW020401100426
42812CB00001B/154